DENNIS BARON

Grammar
and
Gender

YALE UNIVERSITY PRESS
NEW HAVEN AND LONDON

Designed by Sally Harris
and set in Monticello type by Graphic Composition, Inc.
Printed in the United States of America by
Vail-Ballou Press, Binghamton, New York.

Library of Congress Cataloging-in-Publication Data

Baron, Dennis E.
Grammar and gender.
Bibliography: p.
Includes index.
1. English language—Sex differences.   2. English
language—Reform.   3. English language—Gender.
4. Sexism in language.   5. Women—Language.   I. Title
PE1074.75.B37   1986   420′.1′9   85–14614
ISBNs 0–300–03526–8 (alk. paper)
0–300–03883–6 (pbk.)

The paper in this book meets the guidelines for
permanence and durability of the Committee on
Production Guidelines for Book Longevity
of the Council on Library Resources.

10   9   8   7   6   5   4   3   2

for Rachel Elizabeth Baron

CONTENTS

A preliminary version of part of the discussion of *Ms.* in chapter nine originally appeared as "Is It [mɪs] or [mɪz]?" in *Verbatim, The Language Quarterly* 11 (Autumn 1984): 10, and is reprinted with permission. Some of the material on the epicene pronoun in chapter 10 was originally published as "The Epicene Pronoun: The Word That Failed," in *American Speech* 56 (1981): 83–97, and is reprinted with permission of the University of Alabama Press.

My work on *Grammar and Gender* was made possible in large part through released time provided by the Research Board of the University of Illinois and by an appointment to the University's Center for Advanced Study. I would like to thank Richard W. Bailey for his valuable criticism of my manuscript during the many stages of its preparation. John Algeo, Frederic G. Cassidy, Margaret Dickie, Mary Ritchie Key, Barbara Herrnstein Smith, and Paula Treichler all offered their comments and support, and Ellen Graham of the Yale University Press was both an encouraging and a demanding editor. I would also like to thank Nancy R. Woodington and Elizabeth Casey of the Yale University Press for their expert editorial assistance. My wife, Iryce, saved me time and again from infelicities of style that could prove explosive in a work on the sensitive topic of feminism, antifeminism, and language. I have attempted to follow the advice of my friends and colleagues wherever I could, and I reserve for myself alone the blame for any errors of fact or interpretation that remain.

CHAPTER 1

The Mark of Eve

Grammar was made for man,
not man for grammar.
Maurice Weseen

Linguists are fond of remarking in introductory lectures that language is one of the fundamental traits distinguishing human beings from the lower orders of life on earth. Despite recent challenges from primate researchers, most people agree that, along with such traits as opposable thumbs, bipedal locomotion, and the use of tools, the ability to use language is an adaptive characteristic that has helped mankind to climb the evolutionary ladder.

Whether it has helped womankind is another matter altogether, for, as the title of this chapter suggests, there is a common though mistaken notion that, as women derive from men in the biblical story of creation, women's words, or anything linguistically associated with women, can be seen as derivative of, and by implication inferior to, the masculine equivalent. Just as women have been blamed for the expulsion from Paradise and praised for providing the opportunity for mankind's redemption, many writers on language have regarded women's language as a subset of man's, to be praised or condemned, ridiculed, ignored or, at best, studied as a curiosity.

In their attempt to achieve sexual dominance, men sought to limit the range of women's activities to the domestic spheres of housekeeping and child rearing. The onerous restrictions placed by men upon women's social experience have been rationalized (by men, and sometimes even by women) in terms of the protection that is necessary for the supposedly weaker sex. Men have also tried to limit the range of women's linguistic activity to home and hearth. This too is rationalized in terms of protection, not just for women, whose use of language is often perceived as weaker than that of men, but for language as well, since despite their supposed linguistic infirmities, women are also cast in the role of preservers of linguistic tradition. For example, Cicero finds the redeeming quality of conservatism in the speech of his mother-in-law. Listening to her, he is reminded of the language of Plautus, an older and presumably a purer form of Latin that was already becoming extinct. Cicero explains that women retain the linguistic patterns they learn as children because they are not permitted the same range of activities as men. Unlike men, women must stay at home, and consequently their limited experience does not expose them to the corrupting influence of other people's language.

Women have long been considered by some to be the guardians of the English language. Like Cicero, Thomas De Quincey ([1840–41] 1897) feels that women "cling to the ancient purity of diction," though at a price. They must either confine themselves to the domestic sphere or, if they enter the world of men, they must deny themselves both home and family: "The educated women of Great Britain—above all, the interesting class of women unmarried upon scruples of sexual honor—and also (as in Constantinople of old) the nurseries of Great Britain,—are the true and best repositories of the old mother idiom" (146). James Fenimore Cooper repeats in *The American Democrat* (1838) the commonplace notion that the nursery is the birthplace of our language habits and that women, whose dominion in the nursery goes unquestioned, "are the natural agents in maintaining the refinement of a people." Unfortunately Cooper feels that, contrary to the general rule that women speak better English, American women "have a less agreeable utterance than the men" and therefore represent a danger to the linguistic development of future generations (118).

As we will see, women's language is frequently the object both of faint praise and outright damnation. More often than not, however, the masculine in language, whether in word choice or in grammatical form, is assumed to be the norm, while the feminine is ignored or barely noticed. This reflects a distorted world view in which women function as the second sex and language simply holds a mirror up to nature. Thus Thomas Wilson, discussing faults in composition and the correct ordering of words in sentences, complains in his *Arte of Rhetorique* ([1553] 1962) that the natural order is violated when women precede men in sentence structure.

According to Wilson, order in language should be both logical and natural. For example, to those who would write "Helpe me of with my bootes and my spurres," Wilson cautions, "Geue him leaue firste to plucke of youre spurres, ere he meddle wyth your bootes, or els your man is like to haue a madde pluckinge." Although he recognizes a second kind of order, one in which the most weighty discussion is saved for last, Wilson favors the order in which "the worthier is preferred, and set before. As a man is sette before a woman" (234). Placing the female before the male is for Wilson an obvious example of hysteron proteron:

> Some will set the carte before the horse, as thus. My mother and my father are both at home, euen as thoughe the good man of the house ware no breaches, or that the graye Mare were the better Horse. And what thoughe it often so happeneth (God wotte the more pitye) yet in speakinge at the leaste, let vs kepe a natural order, and set the man before the woman for maners sake. [189]

The notion that the masculine gender is the most worthy is a common one in discussions of language. In *Hermes,* an influential grammatical treatise published in 1751, James Harris observes that "the supreme Being . . . is in all languages Masculine, in as much as the masculine Sex is the superior and more excellent" ([1751] 1765, 50). And Goold Brown, the nineteenth-century Quaker grammarian, repeats in his massive *Grammar of English Grammars* ([1851] 1880) the traditional assertion that in all languages, the masculine gender, like the sex it represents, is considered the most important (255). Even in present-day English, with the exception of the common formula *ladies and gentlemen,* the masculine precedes the feminine when a pair of gender-marked nouns occurs, for example, *boys and girls, men and women, lords and ladies, husbands and wives.*

The practice of treating the masculine as the linguistic norm has been called by Dale Spender, in *Man Made Language* (1980), "one of the most pervasive and pernicious rules that has been encoded" (3). Spender and other feminist language commentators complain that women must use a language that they regard as both man-made and male-controlled, and that it is men who have created and who enforce the stereotypes of women's speech. According to Spender, the masculine usurpation of language control is nowhere better illustrated than in the Genesis account of the creation of Eve from Adam's rib:

3

"This gross distortion of the male 'giving birth' to the female is an archetypal example of false naming by males" (166). This is not to say that women do not use language creatively. Rather, feminists maintain that because women in the past were excluded from higher education and positions of social, political, and economic power, their linguistic contributions could not influence the development of Standard English. As Spender puts it, "Women, no doubt, have generated as many meanings as men, but these have not survived" (53).

The question of the relative contributions of the two sexes to the development of the English language, standard or otherwise, is surely much more complex than either the feminist or antifeminist positions allow. Even if women were denied access to certain areas of cultural control—and it is clear that such denial, when we can prove that it did exist, was neither total nor permanent—the assumption that language is entirely made and controlled by men ignores the undeniable influence of women in language acquisition, in conversation, and in literature. But it is equally clear, as we will see, that ideas about men and women strongly influenced ideas about language and that early commentators on the English language, most of them men, accepted the story of Eve's derivation from Adam and imposed this mythological pattern upon linguistic phenomena, where feminine forms are almost universally derived from masculine ones.

These derived feminine forms are also generally marked ones: a suffix or some other morphological feature sets the feminine apart from the generic, which usually doubles as the masculine, for example, *man, woman,* or *author, authoress.* The feeling that such a distinguishing mark of Eve is linguistically necessary is so strong that remnants of the rib are sometimes found where they do not in fact exist. The *s* in *she,* for example, is occasionally treated as a prefix of sorts attached to the masculine *he,* a theory which falsifies the history of these unrelated pronouns. Similarly, the word *female* is popularly derived from *male.* The erroneous belief that these two words must be related caused *femelle,* the form borrowed by English from the French, to be altered so that the semantic relationship between the words is made orthographically transparent. Actually *female* derives from the Latin *femella,* a diminutive of *femina,* 'woman.' It is completely unrelated to *male,* which comes to us via Old French from Latin *masculus,* a diminutive of *mas,* 'male, masculine.'

4

Ironically, this mark of Eve makes the linguistically feminine visible only so that it may be rendered invisible once more. In the eighteenth and nineteenth centuries the feminine was formally subsumed under the generic masculine by virtue of a law of English syntax. In 1850 an act of Parliament translated the generic masculine into an even more formal law. In addition, campaigns have been waged over the past two hundred years to eliminate feminine marking for English nouns like _giantess, lady doctor,_ and _chairwoman._ Proposals for common-gender pronouns like _thon_ or _heer_ to eliminate the generic masculine _he_ may reverse the disproportionate emphasis in English on males, but they do little to make women more visible. Since the Middle Ages books on etiquette and the education of women have advised the daughters of Eve to avoid the trap of language that led to Adam's fall: women are counseled to use few words or, if possible, to remain silent.

PARADISE LOST

For some centuries, then, linguists and other commentators on language have allowed their opinions of women to color their views of women's language and the many connections between grammar and gender. Even the term _woman_ has been incorrectly derived from "woe to man" through folk etymology. Though not all these commentators trace the fall of man to the words of Eve, many if not most would accept the mistaken notion that woman's language, if not entirely fallen from grace, is secondary and derivative, inferior to man's, and an inappropriate model for imitation by either women or men.

We will begin our account with a look at a number of exercises in pseudohistorical linguistics which compare the creation of the English personal pronouns with the Genesis account of the creation of man and woman. Commentators have proposed a variety of intricate and unsubstantiated explanations in their attempts to derive the feminine pronoun from the masculine, or woman's language from man's, in much the same way that Eve is supposed to derive from one of Adam's ribs. Some of these accounts are based on the shaky assumption that English was spoken in the Garden of Eden, while others reflect equally suspicious theorizing about the original meaning of words. We will also examine the false etymologies, or incorrect derivations, of a number of words with masculine (*lad, bridegroom, father, brother*) and feminine (*woman, wife, mother, daughter*) referents: words for women are more likely than words for men to call up notions of physiology or social—particularly domestic—function in the minds of the invariably male etymologists.

The not always subtle antifeminism of the major English etymologists and lexicographers is only one aspect of the sexism that underlies commentaries on the English language. In our examination of the general notions of maleness and femaleness in language we find, for example, that the feminine gender in Indo-European languages is often perceived to derive from the masculine and that it is a mark of praise to call a language like English a masculine tongue, while French and Italian are condemned—by English commentators—as feminine, or even effeminate. Just as languages are stereotyped as male and female, women are often perceived as speaking distinct varieties of particular languages, the so-called women's dialects. In extreme cases, women are thought to speak an alien tongue, a language altogether different from that of men. Commentators on English seem obsessed with the notion that women's language is not men's. They often recommend that so-called women's speech—distinctive pronunciations, word choices, or performance styles—be avoided. For example, women are said by some critics to talk too much or too loudly, to gossip, lie, or concern themselves with trivialities, to pronounce words incorrectly or with too much precision, to use too many euphemisms, to be too raucous or too polite.

PARADISE RENAMED

Not everyone is content to accept such a harsh view of the linguistic position of women. Many language critics, hopeful of restoring the English language to some approximation of its supposed Edenic purity, have proposed reforms of usage and vocabulary that would eliminate at least from our speech if not from our society the sexual bias that they regard as pervasive. The reformers have focused on two controversial features of our language: the use of gender-specific nouns to mark women as different, unusual, or inferior, and the use of the generic masculine to render women silent and invisible. To redress the gender imbalance that exists in English, some reformers propose the creation of new sex-neutral or sex-specific terminology. Discarding old words and embracing new ones has become the key to entering the new, renamed linguistic paradise. Even the new computer technology has been enlisted in this effort to change our patterns of word choice: software is now available that can search for gender-specific words such as *mailman* and *chairman* and replace them with the sex-neutral *mail carrier* and *chairperson* (Winograd 1984, 136). But the reforms proposed have generated opposition as well as support, and the reformers have already discovered that, just as it is difficult to effect changes in the social structure, it is also difficult to control language, which seems to have a life and a will of its own.

Gender reformers do not always accentuate neutrality. While a good number of them advocate the creation of a new sex-neutral pronoun, one well-meaning grammarian called for the creation of additional sex-specific pronouns for the first and second person and for the plurals. In addition, feminists have coined words like *herstory* to emphasize the role of women in our society and their frequent exclusion from our language. Supporters as well as opponents of the title *Ms.,* whose initial popularity lay not in the hotbeds of radical feminism but in the socially conservative but linguistically innovative business community, will be interested to learn that as early as 1912 language reformers urged the expansion of the masculine paradigm to include a term corresponding to *Miss* in order to indicate an unmarried male and another corresponding to *Mrs.* to indicate a married one. In another effort at gender-balancing, a group of sex-specific words appeared briefly when, in the second half of the nineteenth century, women began to graduate from colleges and universities in significant numbers. A few institutions, some of them newly founded "female seminaries," concerned with advancing the careers of their women graduates and sensitive to the semantic impropriety of calling a woman a bachelor or a master, coined new degree names so that women would not be unfairly burdened with masculine titles. Women were actually granted degrees as Mistresses or Maids of Arts and Vestals of Philosophy.

In the area of employment classification, when one sex enters an occupation traditionally dominated by the other, new sex-specific terms may arise, for example, *man-midwife, congresswoman,* and *male nurse.* Such terms are often temporary. When men assumed the primary responsibility for delivering babies, they rejected the native English *man-midwife,* the French borrowing *accoucheur,* which was favored by Walt Whitman, and the Latin feminine noun *obstetrix,* literally 'she who stands in the way,' and chose instead to create a sex-neutral term, *obstetrician* (coined around 1828), which became, by association, masculine, and is only now becoming neutral once again as women choose this medical specialty. Often when women entered male-dominated professions, both during wartime and as a result of the generally increased range of women's opportunities, sex-specific job labels were attached to them. Many of these were later dropped; we do not hear much about *doctresses* or even *lady lawyers* any more, and no one would suggest such terms as official job designations. But quite a few sex-specific job titles remain. Many of these are compounds of *man,* for example, foreman and lineman; others are compounds using *boy* or *girl.* Recognizing that such titles tend to stereotype employees and lock people into certain jobs while excluding them from others, recent efforts, mostly on the part of the United States government, have resulted in the adoption of sex- and age-neutral employment classifications. We will examine the official list of such classifications, promulgated, ironically enough, by that division of the U.S. Department of Labor known as the Manpower Administration (its title has since been changed), and we will also look at a variety of other gender-related word coinages that have been suggested by private individuals either to combat or to sustain the supposed sex-bias of the English language.

It is doubtful that any one semantic gap in any language has ever received the attention that reformers over the years have lavished on our lack of a common-gender pronoun in English. We will conclude our study of sex-related vocabulary reform with a look at the history of the more than eighty pronouns that have been coined to fill this void. The first calls for the development of a new pronoun arose out of a concern not for the unfair exclusion of women from many English sentences but for stylistic accuracy: the use of the generic masculine *he, his,* and *him* in reference to indefinites like *someone* or *everybody* was seen to violate the grammatical requirement that a pronoun agree with its antecedent in *gender* as well as number. Another solution to the problem of pronoun agreement recommends not the adoption of a new neutral form but the acknowledgment of the plural pronoun *they,* often used with a singular indefinite antecedent, as a legitimate Standard English singular. Defenders of the generic masculine have had their say as well. A number of current usage guides, unwilling to accept either *they* or *he,* recommend rephrasing to avoid the problem situation, though this practice, if widely adopted, would have the additional effect of reducing the frequency of English indefinites, which happen to be some of the most sex-neutral words in our language. Clearly, if there is a way to regain linguistic paradise, it will not be through the pronoun system. One question is often ignored by those reformers who would rid our vocabulary of gender-specific terms: is it wise, let alone possible, to excise from our word hoard all those words which are unfair, biased, ugly, outdated, impertinent, and impure? It is one thing to hold up the vision of a new Eden before us, but quite another to expect us to leave our linguistic weapons at the door.

A note of caution should be voiced at this point. The catalogue of opinions about women and language is both copious and negative, and much of what follows can be characterized as a history of shame. Although it cannot be stressed too strongly that such opinions are based on a combination of myth and misogyny rather than on linguistic fact and that many of them are so absurd as to be laughable, their compilation in this volume presents what can be viewed as a depressing litany of insults.

It is also an unpleasant fact that many women have either assented to or actively perpetuated the negative descriptions of their use of language. Cheris Kramarae (1975) has shown that nineteenth- and twentieth-century American etiquette books, many of them written by women, take a dim view of women's speech. A few women writers have gone as far as antifeminist men in characterizing women's English as powerless, tentative, irritating, and trivial. In *Language and Woman's Place* (1975), the linguist Robin Lakoff portrays the speech of women as domestic and subservient, full of color terms and passive constructions. While her book was influential, subsequent research has shown that many of Lakoff's claims are not supported by the evidence.

Profeminist contentions about language can be as far-fetched as antifeminist ones. For example, Julia Penelope Stanley and Cynthia McGowan (1979) insist that British society was originally a matriar-

chy that was overthrown in the tenth century by a combination of
Scandinavian invaders and "the persistent encroachment of the Christian patriarchs on the old beliefs." Stanley and McGowan further
maintain that the borrowing of the word *husband* into Late Old English from Old Norse is evidence that "the notion of males living with
wimmin [*sic*] must have still been relatively recent" (499). However,
it is clear that before the borrowing of *husband,* Old English *wer*
meant both 'man' and 'spouse,' just as *wif* meant either 'woman' or
'spouse' (see below, chapter eight). Of course the extreme positions
taken by both men and women are balanced to some extent by the
more objective, descriptive work of contemporary linguists such as
Mary Ritchie Key (1975), Cheris Kramarae (1975, 1981), and Philip
Smith (1985), to name only a few who have contributed to research
in the area of language and sex.

The purpose of *Grammar and Gender* is not to damn women's use
of language. Nor will we demonstrate that women use language better
than men, or that women's and men's language is either the same or
different. Rather we will examine how attitudes toward men and
women have become attitudes toward language, attempting to place
in historical perspective the current debate over sex and language; and
we will show not simply how gender-related reforms of language have
failed in the past but how views of grammar and gender have been
distorted in the past. The English language has always recognized the
presence and activities of women and men, and there is no doubt that
it will continue to do so. It has responded and will continue to respond
to historical developments like the women's movement and the drive
toward equal treatment of the sexes. Perhaps this by no means complete history of attitudes toward women's words may help in some
small way to reverse the strong bias against them—a bias that is
shared by women as well as men—and encourage further study of the
complex history of grammar and gender.

CHAPTER 2

Eve's Rib

Our Philosophy is made Philologie.
Seneca, translated by John Webster

Two episodes in the story of Genesis have had a profound influence on English accounts of the origin and development of language: the creation of Eve and the building of the tower at Babel. Despite the relatively enlightened views of such writers as the Scottish philologist James Burnet, Lord Monboddo, who favored a human rather than a divine source for language, a surprising number of eighteenth- and even nineteenth-century commentators base their theories of language diversity and change on the confusion of tongues accompanying the destruction of the Babel tower. Still others have found in the account of human creation that occurs in the Book of Genesis a definite parallel between the origin of the sexes and the origin of the English language, and their erroneous descriptions of male and female language are often colored by the Old Testament view that woman was made from a man's rib, and is therefore dependent on, subordinate, and even inferior to him. For example, in the English translation of Augustin Calmet's *Dictionarium . . . Sacrae Scripturae* (1729), the *Great Dictionary of the Holy Bible* (1812), the creation of Eve is described etymologically: "And of the rib, (or piece from his side) thus taken from man, he made a woman (womb-man, Saxon), or, *man-ess*" and Adam, completing his task of naming God's creatures, confirms the translator's opinion that *man* is not a gender-neutral term, and that *woman* is created through an act of suffixation: "She shall be called *man-ess,* because she was taken out of man" (s.v. "Adam").

In one instance, nonetheless, the genesis of Adam and Eve is reversed. According to the *Life of Saint Pachome,* Saint Theodore of Tabenna (died ca. 368) was once called upon to answer a philosopher

11

who had come to his monastery to test the monks who were cloistered there. To the question, "What man was never born but died?" Theodore simply responded, "Adam," and the philosopher went away satisfied that the monks knew their natural history. Thirteen hundred years later the Barnabite monk Florentin Schilling felt compelled to gloss Theodore's answer. In a sermon, Schilling explained that Adam was the only man to die without having first been born, because he was formed from one of Eve's ribs (Bayle 1697, s.v. "Adam").

Perhaps Schilling made an honest slip of the tongue, or perhaps, as his Protestant contemporaries charged, he was merely an ignorant relic of the old order. It is even possible that Schilling put forth his radical misreading of Genesis on purpose. In any case, he provided us with a new and ambiguous metaphor to describe the relations between the sexes. Eve's rib is more than the feminine equivalent of Adam's rib, from which Eve is said to be formed. It is also—as Schilling's fortunate error illustrates—the rib which Eve herself uses in forming the human species. In this latter sense, *Eve's* rib reflects a theory of creation, both human and linguistic, that is the antithesis of the version found in Genesis, where Adam not only acknowledges that Eve has been formed from his body but names her as well: "And the man said: 'This is now bone of my bones and flesh of my flesh; she shall be called Woman, because she was taken out of Man'" (Gen. 2:23).

In the pages that follow we shall see that the double conception of "Eve's rib," woman seen both as creator (sometimes *creatrix*) and object of creation, permeates the discussions of grammar and gender that appear in works about the English language—dictionaries, grammars, etymologies, and general linguistic treatises—from the Renaissance to the present. Commentators on the English language perceive women's words in two ways. They either derive them from men's words in a manner that parallels the birth of Eve from Adam, in which case Eve's rib represents the linguistic mark by which the feminine in language is created from and made dependent on the masculine. Or in a more feminist spirit, and one that reflects a natural world in which women rather than men give birth, the rib of Eve stands for women's linguistic creativity, the force by which women generate a language neither born from nor subservient to that of men. Of course neither view of language is exclusively correct. Women and men are interdependent creators in language as they are in life. However, these

conflicting perceptions of Eve's rib both reflect and inform our stereotyped notions of the differences between the language of women
and men.

AN EDEN IN WALES

Renaissance discussions of language were generally Bible-centered,
but by the eighteenth century many scholars, influenced by the writings of Rousseau and by accounts of what were then considered to be
the primitive languages of the world, had abandoned the idea that
language was divine in origin. For example, in his six-volume study
Of the Origin and Progress of Language ([1773] 1967), Monboddo
rejects the notion of language as a gift of the gods. Instead he suggests
that the Old Testament story in which Adam receives from a divine
source the ability to name the animals in Eden is probably a parable
rather than a literal version of how human language came into being.
Citing reports of feral children, who survived alone in the wild without developing any language of their own, and studies of those who
are born deaf and must be taught the most rudimentary of language
sounds, Monboddo further concludes that language is not innate: human beings do have a natural *capacity* for speech, but language itself
must be acquired, and with some difficulty, at that. Furthermore,
Monboddo is convinced from the evidence of comparative linguistics
that the origin of speech is multiple rather than single, and that the
invention of language must be preceded in every instance by the establishment of some form of social organization. In other words,
Adam could not possibly have spoken before the creation of Eve.

Not all eighteenth-century language scholars shared Monboddo's
passion for the scientific explanation of linguistic phenomena. Many
let their views of the Bible influence their views about grammar and
gender. Not only did they attempt to reconstruct the lost original language of the Garden of Eden, or to prove that the first language was
really Hebrew, Greek, Celtic, Swedish, Dutch, Persian, Basque, or
even English, they assumed that, because Eve was created out of
Adam, her language was literally created from one of his linguistic
ribs.

For example, the Welsh philologist Rowland Jones, Monboddo's
contemporary, clung to the belief that the key to language lay in the

Old Testament; he set out to prove that Celtic was the language of the Garden of Eden, and consequently the source of all the other languages of the earth. Jones was convinced that English was the one modern language that had strayed the least from the Edenic ancestor that he sought to reconstruct, and he therefore based some of his derivations of English words on the Genesis account of the creation of Adam and Eve.

In *The Origin of Language and Nations* ([1764] 1972), Jones asserts that the name *Adam* comes not from Hebrew but from a supposedly Celtic *had-am* or *ad-am,* 'the seed of the earth,' while *Eve* is little more than a linguistic reminder of the masculine origin of the first woman. According to Jones *E-ve* actually means 'him,' because, as Genesis confirms, "she was taken out of him." Although Jones traces Latin *mulier,* 'woman,' to pseudo-Celtic *ma-il-wr,* 'the great race of man,' the English word *woman* represents for him a more direct reflection of the Genesis story: he derives it from *w-o-man,* 'an animal from man.' Jones reinforces this assumption by deriving *virgin* from *vir-* or *wr-* plus *ag,* which he defines as 'from man,' and *wife,* we are told, is simply a possessive form, *w-y-fi,* that is supposed to mean 'my animal.'

Jones is preoccupied with the phonetic and visual symbolism of our English letters and words. In *Hieroglyfic* ([1768] 1972), his attempt to write a grammar of the prelapsarian universal language which he postulates as the direct ancestor of Modern English, Jones claims that the letters of the alphabet are real or emblematic "personators" of ideas and things, as well as pictographic representations of the parts of the human body. He seems particularly interested in language as both a phonic and a pictorial reflection of human sexual characteristics. Like many early language commentators, Jones feels that women should be seen and not heard. Referring to the phonetic value of the letters, he regards the consonants *c, p,* and *t* as feminine because they are "silent" (that is, unvoiced). In addition these letters reflect two other feminine stereotypes: according to Jones they can represent either soft or passive substances. The voiced equivalents of these sounds, *g, b,* and *d,* are described by Jones as loud, active, and rough, characteristics which he regards as distinctly masculine. Although all of the English vowels are voiced, Jones manages to find gender distinctions among them as well. For him the vowel *a* represents earth and masculinity, "and things hard, rough, or interjectory," while *e* stands for "the element of water and any feminine, soft, or passive parts of things" (16).

Jones anticipates today's generative grammarians in a very literal sense: the alphabetic letters visually represent for him the human organs of generation. Thus he claims that *e* depicts the clitoris, *v* the vagina, and *g* the testicles. Lower case *f* shows "the penis in action"; while *p*, which suggests flaccidity to Jones, and which he describes as a phonetically feminine consonant, is a vision of "the penis not in action," as well as "animal and other dead parts" (13). The letter *o* demonstrates human sexuality in its most active form: it is the pictorial representation of the male and female joined together in the act of procreation.

Returning to Genesis in an intricate and idiosyncratic account of the development of the English personal pronouns, Jones traces the six different pronominal forms to the creation of the first six humans. Jones pictures Adam, the first man, as the letter *i*, which is also the number *1*. He waxes poetic in his description of the first letter: "The first personal pronoun . . . signifies man as an indefinite line placed alone or by himself in the centre of things" (31). The letter *u*, which is the second letter to arise, marks the creation of Eve from Adam, which Jones calls man's extension into "the male and female spring." It represents two *i*'s—the first two people joined together. Because Adam, a male, is the literal first person, Jones classifies the first person singular pronoun as grammatically and physiologically masculine. Similarly Eve, who was created as the second human being, also becomes the grammatical second person, and she is called by Adam *the + u*, or *thou*, which to Jones signifies both male and female joined, and the number *two*. Maintaining some consistency in his assignment of gender, Jones regards the second person pronoun as grammatically feminine because the second person to be created was a woman.

Adam's son (Jones gives no names to the subsequent characters in his genesis), the third human in order of creation, becomes the grammatical third person, and is called by Adam *he*, which is also the number *three*. When Adam's son has a son, he becomes the fourth human on earth (Jones momentarily skips Adam's daughter-in-law, who by rights should precede her own child), and the first family, consisting of Adam, Eve, the first son, and the son's son, become the

15

fourth person in Jones's grammatical paradigm, or what we would call in a more conventional grammar the first person plural, represented by the pronoun _we._ Jones makes no attempt to connect _we_ etymologically to the number four.

Eve and the first son's wife, who is counted fifth rather than fourth in Jones's complex patrimony, form the fifth person, or in traditional grammatical nomenclature the second person plural (which like the second person singular is grammatically feminine), represented by the pronoun _ye._ Next comes the first son's grandson, who is the sixth person, and he, together with all the rest already created and those still to come, or as Jones has it, _mankind_ in general, form the sixth grammatical person, or the third person plural, and are represented by the pronoun _they_ (47).

In his account of the third person singular pronoun that results from this second, or linguistic, Genesis, Jones considers only the origin of the masculine _he._ But he also recognizes the existence of a third person singular _feminine_ pronoun, _she;_ although there is no attempt to work it into his genetic paradigm, Jones does place _she_ on the low end of the masculine/feminine grammatical hierarchy. In his far-fetched derivation, _s_ is a letter that can be added to words to signify the feminine gender—Jones does not say so explicitly, but he must be referring to the suffix _-ess_ in such words as _duchess_—and this is just what Jones sees happening in the third person singular. The feminizing _s,_ which also represents for Jones the Edenic serpent and the evils brought into the world by woman, is prefixed to _he,_ which Jones now derives not from the number three but from Celtic _hi,_ 'high,' and which he translates as "the higher acting man." This act of prefixing is also an act of subordination. Just as the addition of _-ess_ in present-day English carries with it connotations of inferiority—compare, for example, such pairs as _governor_ and _governess_—so the addition of the feminizing, serpentine _s_ to the masculine _he_ creates the feminine pronoun _she,_ which according to Jones means "the lesser, lower, or female man" (73).

ENGLAND: THIS OTHER EDEN

L. D. Nelme, a contemporary of Jones and Monboddo, felt that Anglo-Saxon, not Celtic, was the language closest in resemblance to the universal language existing before the destruction of the tower of Babel. Nelme was convinced that by the process of "decomposition" our modern words could be traced back to the monosyllables of that first language. Furthermore, he found that there are thirteen primitive letters, all variations on the line and the circle, whose symbolism forms the building blocks of linguistic meaning. In his *Essay Towards an Investigation of the Origin and Elements of Language and Letters* ([1772] 1972), Nelme argues, for example, that the letter *c* "is the *symbol* of a receptacle, or a *ca-pacious* body: thence *ca-t,* an open-mouthed creature" (8).

Although he does not read sexual symbolism into the letters of the English alphabet, Nelme finds in the derivation of the English word *sex* itself a direct reference to the creation of Adam and Eve. He claims that in the original universal language, the word *sac* means 'speech,' and the "Sacsons," or Saxons, who both populated the British Isles and stocked its vocabulary, are really "the sons of hidden, *sec*-ret, *sac*-red speech" (37). But Nelme also finds that *sac* is closely related to *sec,* or 'cutting off,' and this explains for him why the Saxons called their swords *seces.* In addition, Nelme argues that *sec* is the basis of the English word *sex,* and he uses this connection to show how the English language can be used to confirm the Genesis version of the creation: "The word *sex,* whereby we distinguish the human species, expresses the cutting off or dividing the woman from the man; and confirms the Mosaic account, of her being taken out *from* him" (39).

Nelme's derivation of the English *man* is also influenced by the derivation of Eve from Adam. According to Nelme, *man* is a compound of *ma* (which means 'more' in Saxon and 'might' in Hebrew, a language that Nelme frequently treats as an offspring of Saxon) plus *-n,* 'one.' Nelme translates *ma* as 'the great one,' and the association for him is undeniably masculine. He notes that in Hebrew, *em* is used for the masculine plural, while the feminine plural is *en,* "whereby is intimated, that *man,* the masculine, was of a compound nature; the woman was taken from him" (128). Nelme apparently bases his claim on the notion that the *e* in both the masculine and feminine forms represents an original English third person singular pronoun that somehow made its way into Hebrew (127). *-Em* is thus composed of the pronoun *e* plus the masculine consonant, *m.* To form the feminine *-en,* the root vowel *e* is taken from the masculine *em*—much in the way Adam's rib was removed and used to form Eve—and combined with the suffix -*n,* which Nelme defines as 'one.' The feminine is thus by implication and derivation the second sex.

THE AMERICAN EVE

Nowhere is the parallel between human and linguistic creation stated more clearly than in a brief, anonymous article entitled "Pronouns" that appeared in 1875 in the *American Bibliopolist.* Although the author begins by noting that theories of the origin of language are generally "so amusing as hardly to seem the result of serious thought," he (we can safely assume the author's gender) goes on to present us with a theory of the origin of the third person pronouns. He assures us that pronouns are seldom found in the earlier, more primitive stages of language, and that their invention must therefore be regarded as "a triumph of civilization." Furthermore, he asserts that "English can hardly have been the language in which Adam and Eve held converse." But he then turns around and declares it only natural to assume that, just as woman was created from man in the Genesis story, the masculine pronoun *he,* whose initial use had to be to name the first man, might have "first found utterance through the lips of a woman." The writer here posits that Adam and Eve were alone in the Garden of Eden; that Eve would certainly refer to Adam—either in direct but obsequious address or perhaps in some unrecorded part of her conversation with the serpent—in the third person; and that when Eve spoke she used English pronouns as a matter of course.

The writer goes on to say that words have symbolic meaning beyond their ordinary representation: "They are the medium of the inner life between man and man." And pronouns, being expressive of emotion and personality, convey this transcendental semantics to an even greater extent than other words. Thus, like Rowland Jones, the writer claims that the pronoun of the first person is represented by a word, upper case *I,* that is equivalent to the number one and that *thou,* the second person pronoun, stands for 'two.'

But it is in the third person singular pronouns that the author finds the most significance. Stressing the conservative nature both of women and the pronoun system, he maintains that pronouns, "especially the feminine singular," do not readily change. He is apparently

18

unaware of two facts of language history available to his contemporaries, that *I,* whose capitalization is relatively recent, derives from Old English *ic;* or that the Modern English feminine singular *she* is a new word replacing Old English *heo,* which lacks the *s* so important to the argument that follows. Nevertheless, the writer goes on to suggest that our present third person feminine singular pronoun, like woman herself, was created in the earthly paradise through the use of an alphabetic rib: *she* is formed by adding "a line symbolic of grace and beauty," the letter *s,* which is described by the writer—who signs himself S. S. S.—as "the most perfectly curved letter of the alphabet," and which he sees in all modesty as a fitting symbol to convey the idea.

In this writer's genesis of language, the pronouns are created in an order and a fashion that mirror human creation—first the male, then the female, the male used to form the female. Just as *she* is regarded by S. S. S. as *he* with a prefixed *s,* the oblique forms of the paradigm, genitive and accusative *her,* consist of that same masculine *he* "with the addition of the letter which originally distinguished her from man," that letter being *r,* which clearly stands for *rib* in the mind of S. S. S.

There is one more way in which grammar mirrors nature, or scripture, for the writer. S. S. S. notes that unlike the masculine paradigm, which requires the distinct possessive and objective forms *his* and *him,* the two oblique cases of the feminine pronoun have no possessive, but are represented by a single object form, *her.* The reason for this is clear to him: women themselves are not possessive, or acquisitive, but are rather like property, to be acquired by men. Taking grammatical categories as emblematic of human behavior, S. S. S. claims that, as woman's nature "was not supposed to stoop to avarice, and she was more to be sought than one to seek, possessive and objective were the same for her" (165).

It is likely that S. S. S. intended his essay to be little more than a benign comment on language and the sexes. He no doubt felt that the compliments he was paying to women and their pronouns more than justified the liberties he took with philology—if in fact he saw himself as taking any liberties at all, for his tone suggests that many of his linguistic claims are serious. And he would probably be appalled at the suggestion that his linguistic sex stereotyping, which sees woman first as direct object of the grammatical hunt and then as thing possessed, can be offensive to both sexes, or that such stereotyping can have a negative effect on the reality which he presumed was passively reflected in the paradigm. Yet his characterization of women and their speech is typical not only of language treatises dating from the middle ages, the Renaissance, the Enlightenment, and the nineteenth century, but of much that is written about the English language today as well.

AN ANDROGYNOUS PRONOUN

Of course most accounts of the English pronoun system do not presuppose the creation of Eve from Adam in Genesis. While none goes so far as Florentin Schilling, who argued that Adam was created from a rib of Eve, a few language commentators, who may or may not have been influenced by the Midrashic accounts of an androgynous Adam who was subsequently split to form the first human couple, derive our pronouns from a bisexual rather than a masculine original. One of these was the eighteenth-century writer on usage, Robert Baker. Just as many of today's language critics regard their lack of formal linguistic training as an asset, Baker's credentials as an expert on the English language are negative ones: he boasts that he left school at the age of fifteen, knew some Latin and no Greek, and had never seen a copy of Samuel Johnson's influential *Dictionary of the English Language,* the first of whose many editions appeared in 1755. In his *Reflections on the English Language* ([1770] 1968), a guide to good usage, Baker claims that the masculine pronoun *he* was originally of epicene, or common, gender. Unmindful of Genesis, Baker theorizes that although there was no immediate need to create a separate neuter pronoun, *she* had to be invented before long to avoid ambiguity:

> There being a far greater Likeness between Males and Females, who are capable of the same Actions and liable to the same Accidents with each other, than between Males and Neuters, the Word *he* was much more frequently misunderstood, when spoken of a Male or of a Female, than when spoken of any Neuter Object; and consequently a feminine Pronoun became so much the more necessary. [10]

Like S. S. S., Baker knew little about the history of English. He is unaware, for example, that the Old English masculine *he* is similar to but clearly distinguished from both the feminine *heo* and the neuter *hit,* and that *she* is a much later addition to an already tripartite paradigm. Although Baker supposes the original pronoun to have been sex-neutral, he is not a crusader for equal linguistic rights for men and women. In fact, Baker uses his theory of pronominal origin to rationalize the traditional order of the genders, in which the masculine inevitably comes first chronologically and stylistically: "Supposing the Word *he* to have been originally masculine, feminine and neuter, *she* is the senior of *it.*"

Baker's predecessor Michael Maittaire (1712) accepts the sexual differentiation of the third person singular pronouns, though he pictures the common gender third person plural as a literal blend of the sexes. Thus he mistakenly analyzes the pronoun *their* into *t,* taken from the Old English article *ðe,* combined with pieces of the third person plural pronouns, "the mixture of the i and e from the Masculin hira and Feminin heora" (142). Etymologist John Horne Tooke supposes a monogenetic, sex-neutral origin for all the pronouns of the third person. In *The Diversions of Purley* ([1786], 1806), he incorrectly suggests that *it* derives from *hit,* 'the said,' past participle of the Old English verb *haetan,* 'to call,' and that it refers alike to masculine, feminine, and neuter, in both singular and plural number (2:46–47). Horne Tooke does not go so far as to propose *hit* as the source of all the personal pronouns, although John Fearn, in his *Anti-Tooke* (1824–27), while rejecting the derivation from *haetan,* asserts, like Baker, an epicene origin for the third person pronouns. Fearn accepts the argument of Alexander Murray in the latter's *History of the European Languages* (1823) that the personal pronouns are reduced forms of other words. Thus Murray claims that the first person pronoun comes from *hwag,* 'move with the hand, hold'; the second person from *thwag,* 'seize, take'; and the third person from *swag,* 'sway, manage with the hand, keep.' Fearn derives English *he* and *she* from the neuter *it,* which in turn comes from *swag, swagma,* or *sama,* meaning 'self' or 'the same.'

In still another interesting but misguided account of the origin of pronouns, William S. Cardell, founder and virtually the only active member of the short-lived American Academy of Language and Belles Lettres (1820–22), offers a comment on the origin of *her,* which he does not connect with the Old Testament or even explicitly with the masculine pronoun. In his _Philosophic Grammar of the English Language_ (1827), Cardell states that the first words to be used in human languages were not arbitrarily chosen sounds but significant reflections of "man and the functions which he characteristically performed." For example, Cardell derives _beast_, or in the more transparent orthography that he prefers, _be-est_, from the verb _to be_, defining the noun as "any thing which has life or being" (60).

Continuing in the same vein, Cardell finds that breathing is a basic human activity. Consequently, any group of people needing to create a new language would form some of its words as reflections of the act of breathing:

> The word, _noun_ and _verb_, for _breath_, and _to breathe_, would be in some degree imitative of that animal exercise, and equivalent to _he, hai, ho, hah, heh_, as written by different nations, or to the sound of our letter _h_ or _he_, the "mark of aspiration or strong breathing." In all languages in which letter writing can be traced, this word appears to be in common and important use, and, in all, to denote the same idea, whether called noun, pronoun, or verb. [58–59]

Cardell not only believes that words are expressions of transcendental reality, he is convinced that their ancient, original meanings have not shifted at all through the course of history. Instead, as is the case with the pronouns, their sphere of application has been limited. For example, Cardell defines _hen_ as "the Danish pronoun _she_. It is the _single female_ animal of any kind." In English, however, he finds that its use has been narrowed, so that it refers only to "the _she_ of birds in general" (60).

Cardell claims that the original significance of the masculine pronoun _he_ is "_breath, vitality, light, life, being; an animal; a being_ who _possesses_ and _exercises_ the _vital functions_, who _breathes_ and _lives_" (22). In Modern English, its range too has been narrowed, as has that of the feminine pronoun _her_, which Cardell derives from the masculine _he_, or 'breath,' plus _air_, despite the fact that Cardell regards air as something unknown to the framers of language:

> The primary meaning of the word _her_ is light. From the necessity of the case it included _air_, the existence of which, as a distinct substance, was unknown to early nations. . . . _Light_ and _life_, and _live_, are one word, as modified in the progress and refinement of language. To _light_, or _life_, or

liven, or *enliven,* one's self, was the verb; and the secondary or inferential use of the noun was the *possessor* of *light* and *life,* and the *enlivened being,* which is the exact meaning of *her.* [59]

Thus, according to Cardell, *he* means 'light, and life,' while *her* means 'possessor of light' and 'the enlivened one.' Cardell's etymology may represent an oblique reference to Genesis, in that the feminine pronoun is derived from the masculine just as Eve was brought forth from Adam. In calling *her* "the enlivened one" Cardell may also be referring to women's reproductive physiology, a tactic popular with etymologists, as we will see in the next chapter. But Cardell is silent on this matter. He does not discuss the relative merits of the genders, nor does he specifically connect the masculine to the feminine pronoun (he does not even speculate upon the etymology of *she*), which leaves us to guess at the significance of his etymology both for the relations between the pronouns and for those between the sexes.

Finally we have the derivation of *her* offered by lexicographer Charles Richardson (1836), who assumes that the original Old English pronoun *he* was a sex-neutral term. *Her* is derived by the addition of *er,* 'ere, or the front, the person coming before in time or space,' making *her* "the prime person or agent." Unfortunately, like Cardell, Richardson does not explain what he means by this suggestive comment, which is omitted from subsequent editions of his dictionary.

FEMININE MARKING IN ARTIFICIAL LANGUAGES

Despite their pretense at scientific objectivity, the creators of artificial languages tend to treat the linguistic feminine as an inferior or derivative form just as the commentators on natural language do, a form that may be said to bear the mark of Eve. Linguistic speculators often suggest that in the best of all possible worlds one universal language would replace or supplement the confusion of tongues that may or may not owe its origin to the incident at Babel. This *philosophical* language, cataloguing the natural world as well as the world of ideas, would be designed to meet all human communication needs. Since the seventeenth century, a number of universal languages have been proposed, and while the creators of these languages share a scientific rather than a scriptural approach, many of them treat the feminine in language or at least the feminine pronoun, either as linguistically marked in contrast to the unmarked masculine or as invisible.

Francis Lodowyck, in *A Common Writing* ([1646] 1969), does not provide for the feminine, even in the pronoun system, or rather, he simply assumes gender to be universally masculine. In Lodowyck's paradigm for the pronouns, *I* is represented by / , *thee* by / / , and *he* by / / / . In his *Universal Character* (1657), a scheme for a scientific alphabet, Cave Beck assigns numerical values to words and prefixes these numbered words with letters which stand for fixed particles of meaning. Gender is represented by such letters added to the numerical words. For example, *2477* (pronounced *tofosensen*) is the number of the word that stands for 'father.' The prefix *p* signifies 'noun substantive personal male,' while *pf* is the 'noun substantive personal female.' Accordingly, *p2477* means 'father' and *pf2477* represents 'mother' (cited by Knowlson 1981, 63). Since both forms share the marker *p,* the masculine marking is effectively removed, leaving the feminine marked by *f.*

In the Table of Particles of his treatise on philosophical language, the *Ars Signorum* ([1661] 1968), George Dalgarno also provides a particle to mark feminines, but none to indicate masculines or neuters. The masculine noun is treated as generic in Dalgarno's system, while the feminine is marked with the addition of *r,* for example, *pag* 'masculine,' *prag,* 'feminine'; *pagel,* 'father,' *pragel,* 'mother.' Other feminines are marked with the addition of the word for feminine, *prag;* thus *brother* is *steb vasa,* while *sister* is *stebprag vasa.*

In his *Essay Towards a Real Character and a Philosophical Language* (1668), John Wilkins favors a system of natural gender where sex, as a distinguishing characteristic, is marked by the addition of a suffix to a common, sex-neutral root rather than by the existence of words with separate roots (349). In Wilkins's *real character,* an alphabet designed to reflect meanings rather than sounds, the masculine affix is ', and the feminine ', each to be placed above the root. Thus ∠─᠌─┘ is to signify parent, while ∠─₃─┘ represents male parent and ∠─₅─┘ represents female parent. And in Wilkins's sample transcription of "The Lord's Prayer," *father* is rendered as sex-neutral *parent,* while in his version of the Creed, *son* appears as sex-neutral *offspring* or *child.* Wilkins even reverses the traditional association of *-a* with the feminine, giving the masculine particle the sound *ra,* and the feminine the sound *ro.*

However, the sex-neutrality of Wilkins's philosophical language is occasionally compromised: he frequently treats the feminine as a derivative of the masculine rather than a variant of the sex-neutral generic. Thus while *daughter* is labeled as belonging to the category child-female and *son* to the parallel child-male, the entry for *brother* in Wilkins's alphabetical dictionary directs the reader to the "Philosophical Language" subheading "relation economical I.4," while at *sister* we simply find the reference "brother (female)." *Man* is listed under the rubric "Kind W.V.5" while *woman* is found in the dictionary under "Man W.V.5 (female)." *He* is labeled as a pronoun; under *it* we are given a cross-reference to *he; she* is not to be found in the dictionary at all. In some cases, Wilkins expresses the female by means of a suffix which, "when attached to *Man*, will show *Woman*." Similarly the suffix will create *lioness* out of *lion, sister* out of *brother,* and *slut* out of *sloven* (318). At least one marked feminine has no masculine in Wilkins's system: *harlot* is represented in the glossary as *fornication + female.* There is no corresponding *fornication + male,* not even an entry for a sex-neutral *fornication.*

Nineteenth- and twentieth-century artificial languages also tend to mark feminines as derivatives of the masculine. The American Saxonist Elias Molee (1888) favors the use of masculine and feminine nominal suffixes, *-i* and *-a* respectively, affixed to a masculine root. Thus *broi* signifies 'brother,' while *broa* means 'sister'; similarly *fadi* is used for 'father,' *fada* for 'mother.' Esperanto, created by L. L. Zamenhoff (1859–1917), indicates both masculine and feminine nouns by means of a suffix, though the feminine is certainly based on the masculine and uses a form that is often associated in the romance languages with the diminutive: *la knabo,* 'the boy'; *la knabino,* 'the girl.' In Hom-Idyomo, an auxiliary language proposed by Cardenas (1923), the feminine may be indicated by a suffixed *-in* (*fratro,* 'brother'; *fratrino,* 'sister') or by a prefixed *fem-* (*kato,* 'cat'; *femkato,* 'female cat'). Helge Heimer's *Mondial* (1947) treats all nouns as masculine unless they specifically denote females, in which case gender is indicated by means of a suffixed *-a: dama,* 'lady,' *vaca,* 'cow,' *actora,* 'actress.' And in Noubar Agopoff's *Unilingua* (1967), nouns do not have grammatical gender, although natural gender may be expressed by the addition of a diacritical ˘ over the root vowel, to "moisten" or palatalize (*mouiller*) it in order to mark the feminine. Thus *dat* is '[boy]friend, or *ami,*' while *dăt* is '[girl]friend, or *amie.*' *Tid* in Unilingua is 'uncle,' *tĭd* is 'aunt'; and *tob* is 'man,' while *tŏb* is 'woman.' Finally, in Leslie Jones's *Eurolengo: The Language for Europe* (1972), we find that nouns do not have grammatical gender, although some "genuine feminine nouns add 'a'." Thus *le kusin* is 'male cousin,' and *le kusina* is 'female cousin.' In the pronoun system the same suffixing process pertains: *el* is 'he,' while the "genuine" or referential feminine *ela* is derived from the masculine, and stands for 'she.'

Although they do not employ the Edenic metaphor in their proposals—if anything the equation of scripture with language is anathema to them—even the creators of ideal communication systems have absorbed the notion that in language the female derives from the male. In their attempts to apply scientific principles to the construction of language, these philosophers of language ignore the evidence of the natural world, which generally requires both sexes to participate in reproducing the species, preferring instead to accept silently the patriarchal model of creation outlined in the Book of Genesis and mark the language of Eve as distinct from that of Adam.

We have seen how commentators on language have tried to connect the creation of language with the scriptural account of human creation. Stretching etymology even farther than usual and ignoring linguistic evidence with what often amounts to wild abandon, most of these writers have sought by their own versions of revealed truth to keep the first woman—and by implication, all women who come after her—in her linguistic place: silent, dependent, deferential, at best a latecomer to the world of words. While a few accounts trace English pronouns to an androgynous creation, Eve is still regarded by many as the archetypal *woman,* the person who brought woe to man, and it is Eve's ability to use language that is seen as the key factor in man's fall. Milton's Christ tells Adam in *Paradise Lost* that his doom is brought on essentially "because thou hast heark'n'd to the voice of thy Wife" (X:198). As we shall see in the chapters that follow, man has yet to come to terms with woman speaking.

CHAPTER 3

Etymologizing Man and Woman

Man is an etymologizing animal.
A. S. Palmer

Etymology is the area of linguistics that traces words back to their origins. When used correctly, it can establish relationships between words as different in form as English *hundred,* Latin *centum,* and Sanskrit *satem,* deriving them from a common Indo-European ancestor through a series of regular and predictable sound changes. Etymology can also illuminate the meanings of English words, telling us that *window* comes from a Norse compound that literally means 'wind-eye,' or that the *h* in *hangnail* is a recent addition to the original Old English *angnægl,* where *ang* means 'painful' (as in *anguish*) and has nothing at all to do with hanging. The eighteenth-century philologist Rowland Jones exhibits a naive faith in etymology when he claims, in *The Circles of Gomer* ([1771] 1970), that a knowledge of the derivation of words might be useful in preventing an unpleasant altercation between England and her American colonies. But not everyone conceived of etymology as a panacea. Its critics were only too happy to portray etymology as an enterprise which was frequently unscientific if not completely frivolous. The eighteenth-century logician Isaac Watts called it precarious and uncertain. The dialectologist Samuel Pegge ([1809] 1818) is more expansive: "Nothing in the world is more subject to the power of accident, of fancy, of caprice, of custom, and even of absurdity, than etymology" (272). Perhaps the most familiar attack on etymology is that attributed to Voltaire, who is said to have called it "a science where the vowels mean nothing, and the consonants very little at all."

The bad reputation of etymology is not entirely unjustified, particularly when we consider the etymologies that have been proposed for words which refer to women and men. It is true that early attempts to trace words to their beginnings were hampered by imprecise notions of linguistic genealogy. The idea of an Indo-European parent language as the ultimate source of English does not begin to affect our etymologies until the second half of the nineteenth century. Before that, the ancestors of English words were largely sought in the classical Greek or Hebrew, and occasionally in the German or the Celtic. But the incompleteness of the linguistic record is not often a barrier to etymologists. As A. S. Palmer ([1883] 1969) writes in his study of folk etymology, "Man is an etymologizing animal. He abhors the vacuum of an unmeaning word. If it seems lifeless, he reads a new soul into it, and often, like an unskilful necromancer, spirits the wrong soul into the wrong body" (xiv).

In their rush to fill "the vacuum of an unmeaning word," etymologists frequently reveal their sexual prejudices or stereotypes, forgetting for the moment that the derivation of *etymology* itself is 'the study of truth.' Even today, despite great advances that have been made in comparative and historical linguistics, etymology remains to some degree subjective and intuitive; in many instances, etymologists still do not agree on derivations. It is a rare scholar who admits that a word whose sources have been explained and reexplained over the centuries is actually of unknown origin, and a rarer one yet who acknowledges that etymologies may be influenced by the sexual prejudices of society.

THE ANCESTORS OF OUR WORDS

Despite the generally recognized inadequacies of etymology, the attraction of tracing a word back to its source was simply too great to be denied. Influenced by the popular notion, which goes back to the Greeks, that language is transparent, and that spelling and pronunciation are certain reflections of origin and meaning, many writers were easily convinced that words which looked or sounded alike actually were alike. Frequently, though, the apparent similarity of words led to folk etymologies that reinforced absurd notions already in place. In a sense Adam is the first folk etymologist, for in his naming of Eve—She shall be called woman because she was taken out of man— he incorrectly assumes that since Eve was formed from his rib, the Hebrew *ishhah,* 'woman,' derives in a similar fashion from *ish,* 'man,'

28

plus the feminine suffix -*ah*. In reality *ish* and *ishhah,* like English *male* and *female,* come from two distinct and unrelated roots (Gary Porton, personal communication). In another notorious example, the *Malleus Maleficarum* (1520), a treatise on witchcraft, argues that there are more female sorcerers than male because women have less faith. As proof, Latin *femina,* 'woman,' is incorrectly analyzed into *fè,* or *fides,* 'faith,' and *minus,* 'less' (cited in Palmer, xiv–xv).

The English language provided great opportunities for etymologizing man as well. John Cleland, better known today as the author of the less than sex-neutral *Fanny Hill* (1750), also displays a modicum of antifeminism in his attempts to trace the Celtic elements in the English vocabulary. In his *Specimen of an Etymological Vocabulary* (1768), Cleland makes the unsupportable claims that *wedding* is a corruption of *bedding* and that the Modern English word *queen,* as a name for the chess piece, is really a reworking of an earlier *quin,* 'head, king,' and has nothing to do with women, for whom the kind of power given to queens is unnatural.

Rowland Jones, who was of Welsh ancestry, made even more outrageous assertions in his efforts to prove Celtic the source of all the world's words. In *The Origin of Language and Nations* ([1764] 1972), Jones derives *daughter* from *id-w-ter,* 'she is the mother of men.' If this seems inverted, then Jones's derivation of *maid* is little more than paradoxical: he explains the word as *ma-id,* 'she is a mother.' Jones apparently esteems women, for he derives the English feminine personal pronoun *she* from *si-hi,* 'it is high,' while he traces the Latin feminine *illa* to a phrase which means 'a creature of high value.' But some of Jones's derivations reflect a different view of his sexual priorities. In discussing gender in Celtic, he indicates that women are lower than men in the chain of being: "The feminine gender [has] the particle *as* or *es* signifying less or lowest, and sometimes the diminutive particle *en* for a termination." For Jones, *lioness* literally means 'a lower lion.'

Some of Jones's derivations also reveal his ideas about sexual function or behavior. *Male,* he tells us, comes from *ma-al,* "the great upon or the great rider" (in *The Philosophy of Words* [1769], *male* is derived from the apparently incestuous *ma-el,* "upon the mother"), while *marry* is a derivative of the graphic *mi-ar-hi,* "me upon her," and *whore* derives from *who-ar,* "all upon her." As we saw in chapter two, Jones bases some of his derivations on the Genesis account of creation. In *The Philosophy of Words* Jones continues his wild speculation by tracing Greek *gyne* and Latin *uxor* to a pseudo-Celtic original which means "from man." *Woman* is derived as "a spring from man," and *wife* becomes "man's life, or himself," while *man* itself is said to mean "the great ionian, or my existence" (*Origin of Language,* 35).

Cleland and Jones are not the only writers whose etymologies reveal more about their attitudes toward women and men than they do about the words they purportedly explain. We have already seen how some accounts of the origins of pronouns reflect nonlinguistic sexual stereotyping. The explanations that have been proposed for other words with specific sex references tend to reflect such prejudice as well. Words are characterized as male or female insofar as they fit into a metaphoric system of sexual behavior. For example, Thomas Taylor echoes in the introduction to his translation of Plato's *Cratylus* (1793) the traditional notion that grammatical gender takes its etymology from the sex act: it is the nature of the female to be a receptacle, and of the male to enter into and mingle with her (see below, chapter six).

Specific comments on the etymology of individual words reflect even more clearly the assumptions of the deriver about sexual and social roles and about the physiology of men and women. For example, John Ruskin's discussion of the origin of *wife* has often been used to remind women of their proper place. It also exemplifies the extreme to which the more fanciful etymologies can lead us. Ruskin bases his argument both on his notion that native English words are more exact mirrors of their referents than the words of most other languages and on his notion that women naturally belong at home:

> What do you think the beautiful word 'wife' comes from? . . . It is the great word in which the English and Latin languages conquer the French and the Greek. I hope the French will some day get a word for it, yet, instead of their dreadful "femme." But what do you think it comes from? . . . The great good of Saxon words is, that they usually do mean something. Wife means "weaver." . . . You must either be house-Wives or house-Moths; remember that. In the deep sense you must either weave men's fortunes, and embroider them; or feed upon, and bring them to decay. [(1866) 1905, 336–37]

Ruskin's tone is elevated and idealistic. Like many who choose to speak of women in this way, he presumably intends no offense—even if offense may be taken—when he recommends, in the midst of this imaginary dialogue on mineralogy with students at a girls school—that women be weavers of the domestic fabric, rather than moths who destroy it.

Even the more scientifically disposed etymologists have difficulty maintaining objectivity when dealing with words that refer to women and men. The lexicographer Wilfred Funk, who offers a number of historically accurate comments on the fate of women at the hands of the English vocabulary, is eventually overcome by his own antifeminist prejudices. In *Word Origins and Their Romantic Stories* (1950), Funk observes quite rightly that "over the years many of the terms for the word *woman* have become degraded." Two of Funk's examples are *coquette,* which derives from *coq* and which, in its first metaphorical use, referred in a positive sense to men; and *wench,* which meant, in turn, 'child, of either sex,' 'working girl,' 'rustic female,' and finally 'lewd woman.' Funk ascribes such systematic pejoration to the linguistic power seized by males in the Garden of Eden:

> Until the most recent times, this world of ours has been a man's world and men have seen to it that the women would be blamed as the temptresses; and they made sure that the shame of Eve would be fixed upon all of her sisters in our very vocabularies! [248]

But apparently times have changed. Funk suggests that our world is no longer man's alone, and in some of his comments we can see that Funk has reacted to this redistribution of power by bonding with his fellow men in defense of their now-besieged vocabulary. For example, Funk narrowly defines *spouse* as 'wife,' despite the fact that in his illustrations of the word, the spouses referred to are, with only one exception, males (260). He also neglects to mention that since the thirteenth century, when the word first appears in English, it has been used to refer to marriage partners of either sex. Funk's uneven treatment of women and their words has its blunter side as well. He refers to Victorian women as "weak sisters" and, in deriving *gossip* from the earlier sex-neutral *God's sib,* 'god + kinsman, that is, godparent, godchild; close friend,' Funk explains the change in meaning by invoking the stereotype of women's supposed loquacity: "When women become close friends *gossip* is sure to follow" (255–56).

Wilfred Funk's negative attitude toward women's language is not

31

surprising in the light of the history of linguistic commentary. From the very first, women have been the objects of etymological fancy and prejudice. For example, Richard Verstegan, in his *Restitution of Decayed Intelligence* (1605), derives the word *lady* from what he presumes to be her peculiarly English domestic function. It is true that the Modern English words *lord* and *lady* owe their origins to domestic metaphor. The masculine term comes from Old English *hlaford,* ultimately *hlafweard,* literally 'caretaker of the loaf,' while *lady* comes from *hlafdige,* 'loaf-kneader,' but it would be difficult to imagine these as literal titles. Verstegan sees in the second syllable of *lady* not the root meaning 'knead,' but *dien,* 'to serve,' and he assumes that *lady* means the literal 'bread-server' (318). As further evidence for this incorrect explanation, Verstegan observes that English ladies still carve the roast and serve their dinner guests, a custom that he maintains is not followed in other countries.

Samuel Henshall, in *The Saxon and English Languages Reciprocally Illustrative of Each Other* (1798), takes a different but no less restrictive view of the origin of *lady.* Arguing that "our slow-speaking ancestors always annexed ideas, or common sense, to their words," Henshall impressionistically derives the English past tense marker *-ed* from a contraction of either *did* or *do.* He rejects the derivation of *lady* from 'bread-kneader,' preferring instead to take it from the verb *love* + *-ed,* 'love-did, i.e., the beloved.' John Horne Tooke also rejects the standard derivation of *lady,* arguing instead in the *Diversions of Purley* ([1786] 1806) that it comes from the supposed Old English adjective *hlafdiȝ,* 'lofty, exalted' (according to the *OED, lofty* does not occur until the sixteenth century). For Horne Tooke, ladies are not born but made, though they do not become ladies through their own efforts: he defines a lady as "one lifted to the rank of her husband or lord."

ETYMOLOGIZING *WOMAN*

The word *woman* comes from the Old English compound *wifmann,* literally 'female person,' but even today's linguists disagree over the original sense of the Indo-European ancestor of *wife.* Together *woman* and *wife* have received from the English etymologists an astonishing number of incorrect interpretations, most of them based on the presumed sexual or domestic function of women. Again Verstegan

(1605) is perhaps the earliest to offer a detailed analysis of *woman,* finding it a compound of *womb* and *man* that, because of its presumed transparency, is superior in structure to its Latin equivalent:

> The name of *Mulier* hath no dependance in sound with the name of *Homo,* as our name of woman hath with man. It should in deed be written *womb-man* for so is it of antiquitie and rightly, the b. for easynesse and redynesse of sound beeing in the pronountiation left out: and how apt a composed woord this is, is plainly seen. And as *Homo* in Latin doth signifie both man and woman, so in our toung the feminyne creature also hath as wee see, the name of man, but more aptly in that it is for due distinction composed with womb, shee beeing that kynde of man that is wombed, or hath the womb of conception, which the man of the male kynd hath not. [193–94]

John Minshew, in *The Guide into Tongues* (1625), reinforces Verstegan's derivation by alleging the parallel composition of Latin *femina,* which he incorrectly explains as *foetans homines,* 'one who bears a fetus.' The *womb-man* derivation was popular for several centuries and still survives in folk etymologies. It is repeated by Meric Casaubon (*De Quatuor Linguis Commentationis,* 1650), who regards the womb as woman's most important part, and by Stephen Skinner in his *Etymologicon Linguae Anglicanae* (1671). Nathan Bailey cites *womb-man* in the *Dictionarium Britannicum* (1736), although he prefers another popular derivation, *web-man,* 'weaving person,' said to reflect a woman's primary domestic occupation; and Noah Webster, whose family name derives from the Middle English term for female weaver, writes in *An American Dictionary of the English Language* (1828) that *woman* is "a compound of *womb* and *man.*"

Hensleigh Wedgewood is the most recent of the etymologists to argue strongly for *womb-man.* In his *Dictionary of English Etymology* (1872), Wedgewood rejects the competing notion of woman as weaver, claiming that "it was to be expected that the distinctive names of man and woman should be taken in the first instance from their physical construction. The woman would be viewed as the childbearing, and the word *wife* would be satisfactorily explained if it could be identified with *womb.*" Wedgewood does not explain what physical attribute *man* is supposed to represent, and his contemporary A. S. Palmer rightly pointed out that *womb* in Old English is primarily a synonym for *belly.* It can refer to the uterus where context supports that interpretation, for example, the translation of *fructus ventris* as 'fruit of the womb,' but otherwise, like the Latin *venter,* it is not particularly restricted to women.

William Somner, in the *Dictionarium Saxonico-Latino-Anglicanum* (1659), reflects a less popular tradition that derives *woman* from *wifmann,* interpreted not as 'female person' but as 'man-woman, or Amazon.' This etymology results from the misinterpretation of a line in King Alfred's Old English translation of the *Orosius, Wæs micel ege from þæm wifmonnum,* 'there was great terror from the women,' where *wifmonnum* means 'women' but refers in this instance to the terrifying Amazons.

One current folk etymology defines *wifmann* as the 'wife of man,' and has prompted a respelling of the word as *womyn* (plural, *wimyn, wimmen*) to avoid any suggestion that *woman* is subordinated to or derived from *man.* A number of writers, including Nathan Bailey, mention a popular Renaissance folk derivation of *woman,* 'woe to man.' The *Oxford English Dictionary* provides a citation from Thomas More, and Palmer adds a more recent one from Robert Southey (1847): "Look at the very name—*Woman,* evidently meaning either *man's woe*—or abbreviated from *woe to man,* because by woman was woe brought into the world" (447). Only S. Rowley (1605) comes to Eve's defense: "How ill did they define the name of women, adding so foule a preposition: To call it woe to man, tis woe from man" (cited in Tilley 1950, s.v.).

THE TANGLED WEB

Old English *wifmann* was often paired with *wæpmann,* literally 'weaponed person,' a word with sexual as well as military reference, in the general sense 'adult male.' Recognizing the compound status of *woman,* a number of etymologists, who attended to the consonants but felt that vowels were insignificant, formulated incorrect assumptions about the origins of *wife.* More often than not they ignored the primary meaning of the word, 'adult female person,' seeking its origins instead in the supposed duties of female spouses. Minshew (1625) derives *wife* from the Greek *Phoebe,* 'the moon, sister,' while Somner (1659) suggests that its ultimate source may be *Eve,* the first woman and wife. Skinner (1671) has no trouble seeing in *wife* not the mythological Phoebe but another Greek word that strikes him as more appropriate to the wifely function, *'oiphein,* 'to copulate,' though he does admit the possibility that *wife* may have come directly from a native English source, the verb *swive,* whose meaning is also 'to copulate.' Skinner fails to explain how the initial *s* of *swive* might have been lost, but even more damaging for his theory is the fact that *swive* does not develop its sexual connotations until well into the Middle English period. Its Old English meaning is simply 'to move, or sweep.'

Francis Junius, in his *Etymologicum Anglicanum* (1743), supports Skinner's derivation with a claim that Latin *mulier* comes directly from a Hebrew word meaning 'to copulate.' Some writers prefer to derive *mulier* from Latin *mollis,* 'pliant,' a reflection of yet another female stereotype of woman as weak, soft, or obedient, and Johann Georg Wachter, in his *Glossarium Germanicum* (1737), finds possible sources for the German cognate *Weib* in the Greek *phoizas,* 'prophesying or wise woman,' the Germanic *wyff,* 'weaver,' or the Celtic *wautela,* 'bearer of woe.'

The most popular explanation of *wife,* however, incorrectly relates it to Old English *wefan,* 'to weave.' We have already seen Ruskin's comment on wives as weavers, an idea which he probably took from one of the dictionaries of his day. While Samuel Johnson does not consider the etymology of either *woman* or *wife* in his *Dictionary of the English Language* (1755), other major lexicographers, including Nathan Bailey (1736), Charles Richardson (1836), and Joseph Emerson Worcester (1860)—Noah Webster's chief American competitor—derive *woman* from *weaver.* Johann Ihre, in his *Glossarium Suiogothicum* (1769), an etymological dictionary of Swedish, traces Germanic *wif* to *hwif,* not the act of weaving but its product, a shawl, hood, or veil worn by women. Samuel Henshall (1798) contrasts *wives* and *spinsters* as weavers and spinners in an explicit paradigm of the natural division of domestic tasks among our forebears, though unfortunately for his theory, the suffix *-ster* has nothing to do with stirring:

> Spinster is placed in opposition to Wife. Search for the distinction—
> wif—wives—weave, wove, weft, woof—spindle-stir, (i.e.) move—
> Spindster, modern Spinster—Hence we obtain information that the
> Matrons superintended the Loom, the Virgins the Spinning of the
> Wool. [59]

E. Cobham Brewer also connects spinners and wives. In his *Dictionary of Phrase and Fable* ([1894] 1898), Brewer treats *wife* as the past participle of *weave,* and he assumes that woman's defining function on earth is to prepare her wedding garments. Brewer finds that, contrary to the proverb, a woman's work does sometimes come to an end: "Woman is called the *distaff.* . . . While a girl was spinning her wedding clothes she was simply a spinster; but when this task was done, and she was married, she became a wife, or one who had already woven her allotted task" (s.v.). A. S. Palmer ([1883] 1969), who rejects most other folk etymologies, also accepts the unsubstantiated notion that weaving was a wife's "chief occupation in primitive times." But Palmer explains *wife* on a metaphorical level as well: she is "one who is joined or 'knit together'" with her husband (446). And lastly James Mitchell, in *Significant Etymology* (1908), finds in the contrast between *wifmann* and *wæpmann* yet another reflection of the sex-differentiated labor of medieval England: "The *wife-man* . . . remained at home to weave . . . as distinguished from the *weapman,* or him who goes out to use the weapons of war" (109).

In an unusual act of scholarly indecision, Joseph Emerson Worcester (1860) combines without explanation the two most common etymologies proposed for *woman,* taking its singular from 'womb-man' and its plural, *women,* from "wif- or woof-men, i.e., weavers." But the presence in Old English of two terms, *webbe* and *webba,* for male and female weaver, respectively, indicates that, at least in historical Old English times, weaving was an occupation that was shared by the sexes.

Ernest Weekley, in *An Etymological Dictionary of Modern English* (1921), sees yet another source for *wife,* "the veiled being, in allusion to marriage custom." This notion, although echoed in Eric Partridge's *Origins: A Short Etymological Dictionary of Modern English* (1959), is not a popular one. Etymologists have come to favor vibrating rather than weaving or covering with veils as the chief etymological source of *wife.* Isaac K. Funk's *Standard Dictionary of the English Language* (1893) derives the word from the root *wib,* 'tremble.' W. W. Skeat, in *An Etymological Dictionary of the English Language* (1910), traces it to an Indo-European root **weip,* the source of Old High German *weibon,* 'waver, be irresolute' and Latin *vibrare,* 'vibrate, quiver.' Partridge states, "Semantically, the Germanic word for a woman appar-

ently means either 'the vibrator' (IE) or 'the veiled one' (OGmc). . . .
The former notion is the more basic and, historically, the more probable" (1959, s.v. "vibrate").

The proponents of *woe-to-man* did not hesitate to prove their argument by pointing to the mythological trouble caused by women,
and the advocates of *womb-man* were quick to remark that women
were physiologically equipped with wombs. Similarly, those who favored *weaver* were certain that attending to cloth was what defined
Indo-European womanhood. While none of the advocates of 'vibrator'
go so far as to say that the derivation is attractive to them because
women are wavering, or irresolute, as cognates of this supposed root
suggest, or even that women are good at vibrating—although Partridge does find this last notion somehow "basic" to women—it seems
clear that they find the etymology semantically compelling.

Faced with a mass of inconclusive and often incorrect arguments,
and reluctant to decide among the possible sources for *wife,* the linguist Roger Wescott (1978) has offered a hypothetical Indo-European
form **wey-,* whose seven different meanings fit any number of explanations of *wife:* 'turn, twist' (producing *wife* as 'weaver, hip-swiveler,
or fickle person'); 'drip, flow' ('menstruator'); 'grow, sprout' ('gesta-
tor'); 'magic, sorcery' (*witch*); 'fault, defect' ('weaker sex'); 'strong,
vigorous' ('person of stamina'); and 'wither, wrinkle' ("one who [both
blooms and] ages rapidly"). It seems that man, the etymologizing
animal, cannot rest until he explains *woman* to his satisfaction. Only
C. T. Onions, in the *Oxford Dictionary of English Etymology* (1966),
and the staff of etymologists of the *American Heritage Dictionary*
(1969) have refrained from extravagant derivations based on unveri-
fiable stereotypes, and are content with the most neutral and objective
etymology, taking *wife* back only as far as a general Germanic term
meaning 'woman, i.e., female human being,' whose origin is otherwise
veiled and unknown.

ETYMOLOGIZING *MAN*

Man, which can mean both people in general and males in particular,
has not excited the imagination of the etymologists in the same way
as *woman.* Despite the probability that the generic meaning of the
word precedes the sex-specific sense, many etymologists see in *man*

an allusion to Adam, the first man, rather than Adam and Eve, the first couple. Thus Minshew (1625) traces *man* to either the Hebrew *mun,* 'imago, i.e. the image of God' (which is, by implication, Adam) or *mana,* 'to constitute, appoint, put in charge,' presumably because God placed Adam in charge of the earth. While we can only infer that Minshew pictures the first human male when he thinks of *man,* Wachter (1737), is clearly concerned with masculinity rather than general humanity in his definition of German *man* as *vir fortis,* 'strong male.' Noah Webster (1828) begins his own misguided discussion of *man* in generalities, but his conclusion reveals which man he is thinking of: "The primary sense is form, image, whence species, coinciding probably with Fr. *mine,* Eng. *mien* . . . look, aspect, countenance. . . . *Man* in its radical sense, agrees almost precisely with *Adam,* in the Shemitic languages."

A number of etymologists are attracted by Skinner's connection of *man* with Greek *menos,* 'spirit,' and Latin *mens,* 'mind.' For example, Richardson (1836) says, "the name [*man*] is, in the opinion of all etymologists, derived from the powers or faculties of body and of mind with which man has been furnished by Nature above all other animals," and he adds that Latin *vir* (which refers solely to males) is expressive of this same power. Richardson prefers to relate *man* to an Old English word, *maeg,* from *magan,* 'to be able or strong' (also the source of the Modern English modal auxiliary *may*). William S. Cardell, in his *Essay on Language* (1825), identifies *man* with the word *moon,* though unfortunately he does not supply a rationale for this interesting decision. And Wescott (1978), who finds seven distinct Indo-European meanings for *wife,* lists only three for *man:* **men-,* 'think,' **man-,* 'hand' (for *man* as 'manipulator'), and **mon-,* 'man, human being.' However, just as they are reluctant to speculate on the origins of *wife,* neither the *Oxford Dictionary of English Etymology* nor the *American Heritage Dictionary* traces *man* beyond a basic Germanic ancestor that means anything more than 'person.'

The etymologists concerned themselves with the domestic duties of husbands as well as wives. A husband was presumed to be a 'house-master' (Camden [1605] 1614); the literal *band* holding the family together (Tusser 1580, cited in Palmer, 184); a 'house-dweller' in opposition to a *land-buend,* or 'land-dweller' (Richardson 1836); a man *bound* to an overlord (Jamieson 1840–41); or simply a farmer

(Minshew 1625; Brewer [1894] 1898). In any case, the debate over *husband* ignores both *wives* and the existence in Old English of a feminine *husbonde*, 'house-mistress,' alongside the masculine *husbonda*, 'house-master,' centering instead on whether a man (that is, male person) was in charge of a household or was simply bound either to the land or to an overlord. Only Joseph Shipley (1945) feels compelled to remark, in a comment unworthy of a treatise on etymology, "*Wives,* attention! *Husband* is the master of the house."

SEPARATE AND UNEQUAL

A variety of other words referring to males and females have prompted unequal as well as implausible speculation from etymologists. As the following lists indicate, for the Modern English pairs *lad/lass* and *boy/girl,* whose origins remain uncertain, the masculine term has prompted neutral or positive suggestions from the etymologists, whereas the feminine term has often evoked negative stereotyping and exaggerated speculation.

Lad is derived variously from
  Hebrew *jalad,* 'boy.' Minshew (1625)
  lyte, 'little.' Skinner (1689)
  to lead, because boys are led by study to become men (no mention of education of girls). Hickes (1689)
  Old English *leoðe,* 'people.' Johnson (1755)
  Dutch *loot,* 'small branch or shoot.' Webster (1828)

Although present opinion suggests that *lad* and *lass* do not share a common source, most earlier commentators have built the feminine from a rib of the masculine.

Lass is traced to
  unattested *ladesse,* that is, *lad* + feminine suffix -*ess.* Bailey (1736), Partridge (1959)
  Icelandic *lǫskr,* 'weak.' Skeat (1910)
  Alas! Robert Southey (1847), who considers it a sigh, "breathed sorrowfully forth at the thought the girl, the lovely and innocent creature upon whom the beholder has fixed his meditative eye, would in time become a woman, a woe to man!" (*The Doctor* 7:77)

Boy is derived from

Greek *pais*, 'male child, servant' or Celtic *bach, beag*, 'child.' Junius (1743)

German *bube*, from *bubu*, a natural sound supposedly made by children asking for a drink. Wachter (1737)

a baby word, like *mama* and *papa*. Weekley (1921)

boi, a Frisian cognate meaning 'young gentleman,' though the term has never had this positive sense in English. *OED* and Partridge (1959)

Old French *embuier*, 'to fetter,' ultimately from Greek *bous*, 'ox,' whose hide was the source of fetters. Onions (1966)

Girl (originally a child of either sex, though by the sixteenth century its reference is entirely feminine) is derived from

Latin *garrula*, 'talkative.' Minshew (1625)

Greek *koré*, 'daughter, whore.' Casaubon (1650)

Italian *girella*, 'weathercock,' because of the supposed fickleness of women. Bailey (1736)

Icelandic *karlinna;* and Old English *ceorl* (source of *churl*), referring exclusively to males. Hickes (1689)

Low Latin *gerula* (from *gero*, 'to carry'), "a young woman employed in tending children and carrying them about." Webster (1828)

girdle, or *gir'le*, a belt worn by brides and removed by their husbands, or

gull, 'one easily cheated,' or

darling, from Old English *deorling*. Brewer (1898)

Old Norse *gaurr*, 'clumsy, stupid person,' associated with females because of the influence of the feminine name *Gill*. Weekley (1921)

Old English *gyrela*, *gyrele*, 'male or female virgin,' respectively. Onions (1966)

Commenting on the variety of proposals for *girl*, Joseph Shipley (1945) remarks inappropriately that the derivation from *garrula*, 'chatterbox,' is "surely appropriate enough!" and he concludes his list of the uncertain sources of this originally epicene word with the gratuitous comment, "A *girl* can keep any boy guessing."

WOMEN'S WORDS

Other words for women have produced incorrect and biased etymologies that reveal the sexual prejudices of the deriver rather than those embedded in the language. The commentators are often concerned with rationalizing the power that is assigned to women. *Dame,* generally traced through French to the Latin *domina,* 'mistress of a household,' is said by Minshew (1625) to come from a Hebrew word meaning 'tamer,' because a woman tames her family, while Junius (1743) reasons that the wife is not the tamer but the tamed, because, like an animal, she is subjected to the marital yoke.

Maid is also seen as expressive of feminine power. Although it is likely that the word applied originally to both sexes or was even limited to males, either the early etymologists do not know the original common-gender sense of the word or they dismiss it. Minshew derives *maid* from *macht,* 'might, power, virtue,' cautioning his readers that power here refers only to the limited sphere over which women hold sway, and not to the domain of men. Skeat (1910) is also attracted to the connection between *maid* and *might,* though like Minshew he finds it necessary to qualify the connection by noting that *might* is ordinarily an attribute of males. Other sources posited for *maid* concern marriage and virginity: Wachter (1737) derives the cognate German *magd* from *machen,* 'to join, unite,' because the purpose of maidens is to be united with husbands, and Junius derives Old English *maegden* from Greek *medo,* 'to be concerned for, mindful of,' not, he says, because virgins fear the loss of their honor but because fathers cannot be too careful to preserve the virginity of their daughters.

As the erroneous derivations of *girl* and *maid* reveal, the etymologists could idealize women as young and sexually inexperienced. However, as we saw in the various derivations of *woman* and *wife,* they were most imaginative when confronted with woman as a sexual being. Illicit female sexuality stimulated the etymologists even more: when it came to terms meaning 'prostitute,' they were more than willing to assign far-fetched, graphic, negative derivations to reflect their views of woman as an unclean sex object. While most of these words are now considered to be of unknown and possibly unknowable origin, earlier writers assumed them to be transparent enough to reflect

41

their derivation. For example, *doxy*, a word traced by Onions (1966) to sixteenth-century rogues' cant, is assumed by Skinner (1671) and Bailey (1736) to come from Dutch *docken,* 'to give, yield willingly, or quickly.' Masculine terms denoting immoral sexual conduct are rarely given the extended treatment provided feminine terms. *Pander* is generally traced to Pandarus, Troilus's friend, or to Latin *pignus,* 'pledge, payment,' while *pimp,* when discussed at all, is assumed to come from a French word referring either to a kind of eel or to the process of primping, or sprucing up. Only Skinner (1671) connects *pimp* directly with male sexuality, deriving it from Latin *penis.* The list below illustrates the incorrect derivations assigned to a number of words meaning 'prostitute.'

Harlot, a word that originally meant 'a man of no fixed occupation, vagabond, beggar, or rogue,' and later developed the sense 'entertainer' as well, referred only to men until the late fifteenth century. It is traced by Onions (1966) to medieval Latin *arlotus,* 'glutton,' and is first used to mean 'prostitute' in 1475, appearing frequently in Bible translations as a more polite rendering of *whore.* Popular though incorrect derivations trace *harlot* to

Arlette, Herleva, or *Herlothe,* the concubine who was the mother of William the Conqueror. Lambarde, ca. 1570, cited in *OED*

Arlotha. Skinner (1689) misreads Lambarde's reference, concluding that she was William's concubine rather than his mother, citing Italian *arlotta,* 'proud whore,' as additional evidence.

Whore + diminutive suffix *-let,* 'little whore.' Bailey (1736)

Welsh *herlawd,* 'stripling, lad' or *herlodes,* 'hoyden'; also source of Modern English *lewd;* either because lads crave *harlots* or *harlots* lads. Webster (1828)

Old High German *heri,* 'an army' (compare Modern German *Heer*) + *-lot,* 'loiterer,' that is, 'camp follower.' Skeat (1910); Shipley (1945) adds that "since the camp-followers were mainly women, the sex and meaning grew limited accordingly."

Punk, classified by Onions as of unknown origin, is derived from

OE *punʒ,* 'pouch, purse,' which, like Latin *scortum,* acquired the additional meaning "an old Bawd, as dry and wrinkled, with stradding over the fire, as an Horses hide, dried in the Sun, which, being continued there, draws up like a purse." Skinner (1689)

pyngan, 'to prick, puncture.' Horne Tooke (1806)

punk, 'dry wood fit only for burning,' or

puncta, that is, 'a girl frequently punctured.' Partridge (1959)

Strumpet, of unknown origin, is traced variously to

French *tromper,* 'to cheat,' or to

German *stront,* 'excrement' + English *pot,* because a strumpet is fit only for use as a chamberpot. Skinner (1689)

Greek *masropos,* or

Scottish *striopach,* both meaning 'pimp, procuress.' Junius (1743)

Stropo, an "old word" meaning 'pallet,' and

Latin *stuprum,* 'rape, immorality.' Johnson (1755)

Middle Dutch *strompe,* 'a stocking,' and

Norwegian *strumpen,* 'stumbling,' therefore 'one who trips or makes a false step.' Skeat (1910)

Dutch *strompen,* 'to stride, stalk,' since *strumpets* are stalkers of men. Partridge (1959)

Trull, also of unknown origin, is traced to

Greek *matrulle,* 'procuress.' Casaubon (1650)

Italian *trullo,* 'fart.' Bailey (1736)

Welsh *trul,* 'cylinder,' presumably a physiological reference. Junius (1743)

English *thyrl,* 'drill, perforate.' Horne Tooke (1806)

troll, 'to stroll,' presumably because that is how prostitutes attract their customers. Webster (1828)

Italian *trulla,* 'dirty woman.' Richardson (1836)

troule, 'sow or strumpet,' from French *troulier,* 'to wallow in the mud.' Wedgewood (1872)

Irish *truaillim,* 'I defile.' Palmer (1883)

droll, 'a merry companion,' the only positive source. Skeat (1910)

troll, 'giant or demon.' Partridge (1959)

Wench, like *harlot,* did not at first refer exclusively to women. It comes from *wenchel,* originally 'a child of either sex,' though it also has the meanings 'servant, slave, or whore.' Onions and the *OED* derive it ultimately from Old English *wancol,* 'unsteady, inconstant, wavering,' an association with youth, not femininity, and the *American Heritage Dictionary* sees its Indo-European root as **weng-*, 'bend, curve.' But Skeat (1910), who thinks of women as wavering and bendable, is not surprised by the shift in the reference of *wench* from sex-neutral to sex-specific: "As the word also implies 'weak' or 'tender,' it was naturally soon restricted to the weaker sex." Other etymologists also see in the source of *wench* a reference to men's perception of women:

German *Wensch,* 'wish, thing desired.' Minshew (1625)

Venus, or, quasi-seriously

wince, related to *whinny:* "Girls shrink from a touch the way unbroken steeds whinny and shy away when their grooms rub their chests and stomachs." Junius (1743)

Old English *wincian,* 'to wink,' "i. e. One that is *winked at;* and by implication, who may be had by a nod or a wink." Horne Tooke (1806)

German *wenig,* 'little.' Webster (1828)

German *Mensch,* 'man,' with the implicit justification that Eve was Adam's rib. Wedgewood (1872)

Whore, originally *hoor* (the modern spelling, with initial *wh-,* is unetymological), is today generally traced to Indo-European **ka-,* 'to like, desire,' with such cognates as *care, caress,* and *cherish.* Skeat argues that the word originally meant nothing worse than 'lover' and refrains from speculation about the development of a negative sense. Verstegan (1605) is the first of many writers to imagine in *hoor* the native English verb *to hire* because, as he put it, "such incontinent women do comonly let their bodyes to hyre" (335). Other writers generally trace the word to foreign sources:

Greek *koré,* 'girl,' or

'oaroi, 'venereal sport,' from *'oar,* 'wife.' Casaubon (1650)

Greek *xoiros,* 'sow; female genitalia.' Skinner (1671)

Greek *'oraia,* 'beautiful,' "because prostitutes are beautiful, or at least they seem to be when they are working." Junius (1743)

German *heuren,* 'to conduct business,' or

horo, 'excrement,' "because in ancient times whores were led through the streets, while young men threw dirt at them." Wachter (1737)

Hebrew *horh* or *hurh,* 'pregnant.' Ihre (1769)

Polish *kura,* 'hen,' seen as the source of *kurwa,* 'prostitute.' Wedge-
    wood (1872)

Old English *horh, horu,* 'filth,' or

haran, 'to pour out, urinate.' Palmer (1883)

MARRIAGE AND THE FAMILY

Students of the English language have generally brought the same
prejudices to bear on licit sex as they have on the illicit variety. Just
as English married women gradually lost their common-law rights,
usage critics and etymologists sought to strip them of their linguistic
rights. As early as 1567, William Lily, in his *Shorte Introduction of
Grammar,* tied marriage roles and linguistic functions, defining Latin
nubo as *viro trador,* "to be married to a man, For it is in the Womans
partes onely" (L iii verso). Although the original sense of Latin *nubo*
is 'to cover, veil' and refers to the veiling of the bride during the wedding ceremony, the word extended its association to the state of marriage as well as the act itself, and according to Lewis and Short its
field of reference in classical Latin poetry and postclassical prose included husbands as well as wives.

The English word *marry* comes to us through Old French from
Latin *maritare,* 'to marry,' and *maritus,* 'married, husband,' the source
of the Modern French word for husband, *mari.* Onions (1966) derives
marry from the hypothetical Indo-European forms **mer-, *mor-,*
which referred to either sex and which are represented in the historical
Indo-European languages by a variety of words meaning 'young man'
and 'young woman.' According to the *Middle English Dictionary,*
marry first appears in English around 1325, and the English word
has always applied equally to men and women. However, some commentators have insisted on an etymological bias toward the masculine.
Webster (1828), Skeat (1910), and Weekley (1921) all trace *marry*
to Latin *mas,* 'male'; Webster bolsters his position by offering as cognates both Finnish *mari* or *mord,* 'male,' and Arabic *mara,* 'to be
manly, masculine, brave.' Richardson (1836) goes even further, suggesting that the Latin *mar,* 'male,' derives from the same source as
English *man* and *maid,* the modal verb *may.* Richardson implies that
the male is the active element, the female the passive one, in this etymology: the infinitive, *mayen,* produces *man;* the past participle,

may-ed, gives *maid;* the agentive *may-er* produces Latin *mar* and eventually *mas,* 'male,' which is the source of English *masculine.* The *American Heritage Dictionary* recognizes that women have a place in the etymology of *marry,* though its derivation of the word from two Indo-European terms, **mari-,* 'young woman,' and **mari-to,* 'provided with a bride,' continues to reflect a male-centered view of marriage.

The notions that the bride is property conveyed to the bridegroom and that the husband is the active participant in marriage while the wife remains passive are reflected in Richard Grant White's comment in *Words and Their Uses* ([1870] 1891) on the proper use of the verb *to marry.* White argues that the word derives from the French *mari,* and he rejects any sentence which asserts that women marry men. For him, women cannot serve as subjects of the active verb *to marry* for etymological as well as practical reasons, and he therefore relegates them to a position of grammatical as well as social passivity:

> Properly speaking, a man is not married to a woman, or married with her; nor are a man and a woman married with each other. The woman is married to the man. It is her name that is lost in his, not his in hers; she becomes a member of his family, not he of hers; it is her life that is merged, or supposed to be merged, in his, not his in hers; she follows his fortunes, and takes his station, not he hers. And thus, manifestly, she has been attached to him by a legal bond, not he to her; except, indeed, as all attachment is necessarily mutual. But, nevertheless, we do not speak of tying a ship to a boat, but a boat to a ship. And so long, at least, as man is the larger, the stronger, the more individually important, as long as woman generally lives in her husband's house and bears his name,—still more should she not bear his name,—it is the woman who is married to the man. [140]

This tendency to see the man as semantic agent and the woman as semantic patient, when it comes to marriage, is reflected in contemporary linguistics as well. In *Indo-European Language and Society* ([1969] 1973), Emile Benveniste echoes White when he explains that there is no term for marriage in Indo-European because "the situation of the man and that of the woman have nothing in common." (Even if this were true, it would not explain the absence of the word, unless marriages did not in fact take place.) According to Benveniste, the Indo-Europeans had a patrilineal social organization whose terms for the relations between men and women reflect a basic disparity in their situations:

> In speaking of the man it is simply said . . . that he 'leads' (home) a woman whom another man has 'given' him (Lat. *uxorem ducere* and *nuptum dare*); in speaking of the woman, that she enters into the 'married state', receiving a function rather than accomplishing an act (Lat. *ire in matrimonium*). [193]

Benveniste claims that the masculine terms for marriage are verbal, the feminine ones nominal. In addition *woman,* in marriage, is treated as the object of the verb, not its subject. He concludes that this linguistic structure reflects the sexual organization of Indo-European society: "This negative lexical situation, the absence of a special verb, indicates that the woman does not 'marry,' she 'is married'. She does not accomplish an act, she changes her condition" (195).

Benveniste is of course concerned with the ancient past, with prehistory, in essence. His assumptions are not affected by the fact that *marry* has allowed feminine and masculine subjects in English since the fourteenth century (a situation which White regards as unnatural, and therefore irrelevant to any discussion of correct usage), or that the Modern French form of the verb, *se marier,* is reciprocal as well as reflexive, indicating the mutuality of the marriage bond. After all, both language and society are capable of change. But Benveniste ignores the evidence that the possible roots of *marry,* Indo-European **mer-* and **mor-,* have produced both masculine and feminine reflexes. In addition, his notion of Indo-European linguistic and social patriarchalism has been challenged by Susan J. Wolfe and Julia Penelope Stanley, who prefer to analyze their data from a feminist rather than a male-centered perspective. Wolfe and Stanley (1981) claim that anthropological as well as linguistic evidence points to an original Indo-European matriarchy that was later supplanted by a male-dominated society. They agree with the *American Heritage Dictionary* in tracing the Indo-European root of the word *marriage* to **mari-,* 'young woman.' However, they feel that its suffixed form, **mari-to,* has been inaccurately construed to mean 'provided with a bride,' in their words, "perhaps because its Latin reflex, *maritus,* meant 'married, a husband.'" Arguing that the participial suffix *-to-* is passivizing and possibly causative as well, Wolfe and Stanley suggest instead that **marito* "may at some transitional stage have designated a 'male attached to a woman,'" someone who has been "womaned" or "made into a mate," and not, as is generally assumed, 'a male who has had a woman attached to him' (231).

Bride and Groom

Like *marry* and *marriage,* the words that refer to men and women as marriage partners and as members of families have also been derived in ways that reveal a sexual bias. While Onions (1966), maintaining sexual neutrality, derives *bride* from an unanalyzable and unattested Germanic root, **bruðiz,* of unknown origin, others see in the word transparent references to the presumed role of the bride variously as caretaker, childbearer, sexual object, property of the husband, and cook.

Celtic *bru,* 'nurse,' because "a bride becomes a nurse." Minshew (1625)

brood, from *broeden,* 'cherish, keep warm, incubate.' Skinner (1671)

Frutis, Italian name for *Venus.* Cited and rejected by *OED*

pruette, 'protected one,' and

kiprutta, 'deflowered.' Cited and rejected by Junius, who prefers a source in

Germanic *bruyen,* 'impregnate,' from Greek *bruein,* 'bring forth' and *'embryon,* 'embryo.' Junius (1743)

Greek *proete,* from *proiemi,* 'to send away,' on the assumption that the *bride* is sent away by her father. Wachter (1737)

Greek *pyrote,* 'purified by fire.' Rejected by Wachter (1737)

Greek *priasthai,* 'to buy, procure, obtain.' Attributed by Ihre (1769) to Helvigius

Welsh *priawd,* or *"priodi,* to render appropriate, to espouse, to marry." Webster (1828)

Latin *privus,* 'one's own.' Wedgewood (1872)

English *brew, broth, bread* are treated as cognates of *bride.* Weekley (1921)

Bridegroom, the masculine equivalent of *bride,* is one of the few English masculines that seem to derive from a feminine. Because such derivation represents to most commentators a reversal of the natural linguistic order, where feminine always comes from masculine, most explanations of the word stress *groom,* emphasizing the husband's presumed duty to control or care for the wife. The status of *bridegroom* is further complicated because the second element of the compound has been altered from the original Old English *guma,* 'man, person,' to *groom,* a word of uncertain origin whose initial meaning in English appears to have been 'lad, boy,' but which eventually developed the sense 'caretaker.'

According to the *American Heritage Dictionary, guma* derives ultimately from a sex-neutral Indo-European word, **dhghm,* 'earthling' (the source not only of the English masculine term but of Greek *khthon* and Latin *humus,* 'earth') and sex-neutral Latin *homo,* 'human being.' Despite the fact that William Somner identified the original, *r*-less form of the English word as early as 1659, many etymologists preferred the later *groom* because, as Skinner observes in 1689, "the man is, as it were, groom, or servant to his bride on the day of marriage." Bailey (1736) also recognizes *guma,* 'spouse of the bride,' but insists that *groom* is more appropriate "because upon the Wedding-day it was the Custom for him to serve at Table." Even Horne Tooke ([1786] 1806), who takes *guma* from Old English *gyman,* 'to lead,' asserts that all the uses of *groom* "denote attendance, observance, care, and custody; whether of horses, chambers, garments, bride, &c."

Noah Webster tried unsuccessfully to restore the *r*-less *bridegoom* in his dictionary of 1828, but the folk etymology that connects *bridegroom* (which is frequently clipped to *groom,* as in the phrase *bride and groom*) with the sense 'caretaker,' or more particularly, 'ostler, or stable attendant,' remains strong even today, producing comments reminiscent of Junius's derivation of *wench* from *wince* and, by implication, *whinny.* Unfortunately, for many present-day male users of English a groom is still an animal tamer (see, for example, the *Harper Dictionary of Contemporary Usage* [1975], s.v. "groom").

Mother and Father

Just as the linguistic roles of men and women in marriage are treated asymmetrically, the etymologies of words for parents and children tend to reflect the different cultural perceptions of male and female members of the family. Because children generally draw their initial language experience from their parents, words for *father* and *mother* are assigned great if often undocumented significance by language commentators. For example, in the *Encyclopédie* (1751, s.v. "lan-gue"), Denis Diderot contends that children of all cultures pronounce *ab, pa, am,* and *ma* as their first sounds. Diderot claims that *ma* is produced first, as it requires less effort than *pa* or *ba,* and he concludes from this that the word *mama* must precede *papa.* Since Diderot as-sumes that the mother is the parent to whom the infant is more at-tached, he finds it only natural that *mama* comes to signify 'mother.'

The notion that the words for mother and father universally derive from natural baby sounds is a common one, though it is not supported by the evidence of infant language acquisition. The *American Heritage Dictionary* traces *father* and its cognates to *papa,* "a child's word for 'father,' a linguistic universal found in many [*sic*] languages," and to Indo-European **pəter,* translated simply as 'father,' while *mother* is said to come from a similarly "universal" babytalk *ma,* whose meaning is more particularized: it is "an imitative root derived from the child's cry for the breast," plus *ter,* a kinship suffix. Onions (1966) is not convinced of the connection between *ma* and *breast,* and gives the derivation *mother* simply as Indo-European **mate·r-,* an exact parallel to his derivation of *father.*

Etymologists have sometimes sought the meaning of the words for male and female parent in their presumed functions. For *mother,* Skin-ner (1671) proposes several Greek ancestors which mean 'to seek after, desire, covet, be eager,' "because of the eager love mothers have for their children." Partridge (1959) prefers the anatomical explana-tion of *mother,* and sees *mama* as a derivative of Latin *mamma,* 'the female breast,' while Shipley (1945), who also inclines toward the anatomical, derives the word either from native Old English *moder,* 'womb,' or from "the sound of suckling." Skinner traces *father* either to a Greek original which means 'feed, provide food for' or to Danish *foder,* 'to procreate,' and Webster (1828) points in support of the feed-ing notion to the derivative noun *fodder.* Mitchell (1908) adds the idea of paternal protection, deriving *father* from *pa,* 'to guard, protect, sup-port.'

In addition to these traditional etymological analyses, a feminist derivation of the word *mother* has been proposed. Wolfe and Stanley (1981) trace *mother* to an Indo-European **ma,* but they take issue with the categorization of IE **ma* into three separate and unrelated roots by both Pokorny (1959) and the *American Heritage Dictionary.*

*Ma[1] is defined by the *AHD* as 'good, timely, seasonable, early,' and is the ultimate source of such words as *mature, Matuta* ('the goddess of dawn'), *matinee, mañana* ('in the morning'), and Latin *manis* ('good'). *Ma[3] is associated with the quality of dampness and produces Old English *mor*, 'marsh, moor,' and Latin *manare*, 'to flow, trickle, emanate,' while *ma[2] is reserved for words associated with motherhood and the female breast. Wolfe and Stanley see no reason not to relate these three Indo-European forms more closely:

> The possibility that all three roots might have been derived from a single source, that there might be a relationship among concepts having to do with the mother's breast, the primal mother whose fecundity replenished the earth at appropriate seasons, and dampness has apparently escaped analysis. [236]

Wolfe and Stanley further suggest a connection between IE *maghu-*, 'young woman,' the source of English *maid*, which is usually derived from *maeg*, 'kinsman,' and the IE roots *magh[1], 'to be able,' and *magh[2], 'to fight,' pointing for support to such words as *Amazon*, Old English *maegden heap*, 'band of female warriors,' and the Germanic proper name *maht-hildis*, 'mighty in battle,' the source of the female names Matilda and Maud. Their reasoning is at least indicative of a new way of looking at the etymology of sex-related terms. While the original meanings of *mother* and *maid* still remain in doubt, we must think carefully before rejecting the argument that separate roots have been postulated for these terms only because of a reluctance on the part of male etymologists to associate women and power.

Children

While mothers are at least seen as essential to family structure, sisters and daughters are treated as far less important than brothers and sons. The word *brother*, for example, suggests to etymologists notions of togetherness, generation, and support. Minshew traces it back to the Hebrew *berith*, 'pact, treaty, or agreement,' as well as to the Greek *phrater*, 'of the same tribe, or group,' while Skinner (1671) feels it refers to one of a *brood*, from Old English *bredan*, 'to breed,' a derivation favored by Bailey, Webster, and Richardson. Sisters, though, are silently excluded from the brood. Wachter favors Celtic *bru*, 'uterus,' as the source of *brother* (but again, not *sister*), and Mitchell, who sees familial function in all the kinship terms, relates the word to Indo-European *bher,* 'to carry, support, or guide,' because "the brother [is] the support, the guide of the sister" (1908, 117).

While *brother* as a word is usually considered independent of its female counterpart, *sister* is generally derived in relation to the masculine sibling. Minshew reflects both the linguistic and biological myths of feminine inferiority when he traces *sister* from Greek *'usera, hystereo,* 'posterior, inferior,' "because the masculine gender is more worthy than the feminine." Casaubon derives the term from the similarly formed Greek *hystera,* 'womb.' Richardson regards sisters as possessions and presents a popular derivation of the word from *swaes,* 'one's own,' though unlike many etymologists Richardson is careful here to use sex-neutral terminology in his account of the word: "Swaestre, or sweoster, may be a female born of his or her own parents, of the same parents of her- or him-self, of his or her own blood." In suggesting *vas,* 'to live, inhabit,' as the source of *sister,* Mitchell is not so meticulous in his pronoun reference. The first person plural, for him, apparently refers to males: "A sister is the woman who lives under the same roof, our companion" (117).

Son and *daughter,* like the other paired kinship terms, are not always treated symmetrically. The male child is usually seen as the normal or direct result of procreation, while the female child is often considered as a specially marked case. Thus *son* is traced by Minshew to the Greek or the Chaldean word for 'son, spirit,' and Martinius derives the German *Sohn* from *saen,* 'to sow,' ultimately from Greek *sperma,* 'seed' (cited in Wachter 1737, s.v.). Wedgewood feels that the word comes from the Sanskrit *su,* 'to beget,' and Mitchell, Skeat, Weekley, Partridge, and the *American Heritage Dictionary* all basically agree in deriving *son* from Indo-European *seu-,* 'to give birth.' On the other hand, *daughter* is not so closely associated with seed or offspring, but is more often traced either to a property term or an anatomical feature. While Onions regards *daughter* as of unknown origin, Skinner traces the word either to Greek *dugates,* 'to deflect, turn aside,' an indication to him of the unnaturalness of female offspring, or to Latin *dos,* 'dowry,' because he considers the dowry to be a major worry for the parents of girls.

Webster sees positive character traits in the possible Saxon roots of *daughter, dugan,* 'to avail, be good,' and *dugoth,* 'strength, grace,' which he relates to Latin *decus,* 'decent.' But Mitchell, for whom sons derive from the Aryan verb *su,* 'to generate,' finds only a suggestion of her domestic chores in the Sanskrit root of *daughter, dud, dhugh,* 'to milk,' a notion favored by Weekley as well as by Shipley, who insists that the daughter is "the milker of the family."

REVISIONIST ETYMOLOGY

Wolfe and Stanley note that both Pokorny and the *American Heritage Dictionary* present a number of different Indo-European roots that appear in the identical form **seu-*. The *AHD* derives *son* from **seu-*[3], 'to give birth,' while *sister* is traced to **seu-*[2], the pronoun of the third person and the reflexive. **Seu-*[1] means 'seethe, boil,' and **seu-*[4], defined as 'to take liquid,' is the source of our English words *soup, sop,* and *suck.* Wolfe and Stanley suggest that these four etymons have a common core of meaning that might be more elegantly arranged from a feminist perspective. Acknowledging the etymologists' apparent commitment to connect family and physiology, they argue that *son* and *sister* could easily derive from the roots which produce *suck* and *seethe:* "Perhaps both kinship terms have their origin in the concept of 'warm liquid' or 'those who produce milk'" (1981, 234). Such a derivation not only unites previously distinct words, but also places the female, rather than the male, at the center of the family structure and derives a good part of that structure from the female, not the male. This redresses an imbalance that has existed, at least in terms of etymology, for several centuries, and at the same time it restores some small degree of semantic productivity to Eve's daughters.

Although Wolfe and Stanley's arguments remain controversial, it is clear that even today's more scientific etymology has been influenced by a tradition which tacitly assumes the linguistically feminine to be secondary or derivative, more limited to reflections of social or physiological form and function, and that this assumption is based on a cultural stereotype which underlies the grammatical one. We should expect that the gender-related distortions of etymology will be reassessed in an era of feminist theorizing about language. It is not surprising, given the antifeminist evidence cited in this chapter, if new etymologies reflect an opposite, ultrafeminist extreme. What we can ultimately hope for, though, is a critical reexamination of the subject whose history has been sketched here, a reassessment that will bring about a less biased investigation into the origins of our words.

CHAPTER 4

An Alien Tongue

*The differences between the speech of
the sexes . . . may have been due to
the capture of alien women.*
James G. Frazer

The differential treatment of gender-related words by etymologists is only one aspect of a broader notion that has been a commonplace for centuries. That women's speech differs from men's is accepted in much the same way that the physiological differences between the sexes are accepted, and because language is perceived to be an innate and essential part of our humanity, sex differences in language are treated as natural, genetic, only to be expected, and frequently to be enforced. Unfortunately, difference in language is often equated with defectiveness. In the past the critics of language, almost always men, have accepted the notion that biology is destiny—or more specifically, that physiology is somehow reflected in philology—and they have reacted in a negative or patronizing manner to what they perceived to be the different or unfamiliar speech of women.

Complicating matters still further is the fact that linguists disagree on the specific features of men's and women's speech. Men describe what they consider women's English in ways that are often illogical and contradictory, basing their ideas on stereotyped notions of human behavior rather than accurate observations of language. Consequently it has become the paradox of Eve, and of her language, that she is seen both as the source of trouble and the wellspring of hope. At the same time that Milton blamed Eve for using words to corrupt Adam, some writers were lamenting women's inability to use English well enough to convince anybody to do anything, while others saw in women's English the source of our literary and linguistic salvation. Women were simultaneously praised for conserving the traditional forms of language and condemned for innovating upon them. Some experts judged women's pronunciation to be exemplary; others mocked it as ignorant, abrasive, and sloppy. Women were thought to be either tasteful or prudish in their rejection of the coarse vocabulary of men, and the vocabularies of women were either stigmatized as limited and affected, or celebrated as copious and refined. Many commentators on the English language considered women to be poor spellers; others found them to be better spellers than men, as well as natural letter writers and novelists. Several male novelists, on the other hand, protested that women's language skills were shamefully inadequate, and male literary critics frequently trivialized the work of women writers.

Men were told that women should be ignored because they were incapable of logical thinking or abstract, mathematical reasoning. Paradoxically, men were also advised to listen to women, whose use of language was said to bring polish and civilization to an otherwise rude and barbarous tongue. But barbarous or not, English was always regarded by its commentators as a masculine language, superior in almost every respect to the effeminate French or Italian. And usage critics invariably encouraged the speakers and writers of English, both men and women, to avoid those few aspects of the language— items of vocabulary or idiomatic expression—that had come to be labeled as feminine or effeminate.

While the refined and civilizing conversation of women was frequently the subject of sincere praise, women were also characterized as gossips, prattlers, scolds, and shrews. Since the fourteenth century, works of literature as well as etiquette books have advised women to speak as little as possible, partly because it was assumed that women would naturally misuse the language and partly because discourse was seen as the prerogative of men alone. In the most extreme cases, women were counseled to keep silent. It was their duty to listen to and obey their fathers and husbands, and they were sternly warned against corrupting the language of their children. Thomas Wilson, illustrating the technique of repetition in his *Arte of Rhetorique* ([1553] 1962), echoes the common feeling among men that women should be seen and not heard:

> What becometh a woman best, and first of al: Silence. What seconde: Silence. What third: Silence. What fourth: Silence. Yea if a man should ask me til' dowmes day, I would stil crie, silence, silence, without the whiche no woman hath any good gifte, but hauing the same, no doubt

she must haue many other notable giftes, as the whiche of necessitie do euer folow suche a vertue. [227]

Harriet Lane, writing almost four hundred years later, advises women in *The Book of Culture* (1922) that silence can speak more eloquently than words: "You can make your eyes, your smile speak for you and say more, perhaps, than words could express" (cited in Kramarae 1975, 8).

SILENCING WOMAN

The silent woman has actually been held by many language commentators to be the ideal woman, and tracts that codify the behavior of women often praise silence as one of the highest virtues that the sex may aspire to. In the popular *De Institutione Christianae Feminae* (1523), written by the Spanish humanist Juan Luis Vives and translated by Richard Hyrd as *A very frutefull and pleasant boke called the instruction of a Christen Woman* (1531), Vives laments the fact that men grumble about women's ignorance but do nothing to educate them, and in some cases even prevent them from learning. Yet for Vives the ideal woman does not speak; he regards the ever-silent Virgin Mary as an example of appropriate verbal behavior.

Vives asserts that silence is a woman's noblest ornament, and he warns his female readers not to speak when men are present, for verbal intercourse leads inevitably to sexual intercourse. Vives explains that a woman can defend her chastity "stronger with silence than with speche"(O 3 verso–O 4 recto), and he counsels that children of opposite sexes, including brothers and sisters, should not play and talk together, even in the presence of a chaperone, in order to preserve their purity.

The myth of the loquacious woman and that of the ideal, silent woman are intertwined: for Vives, as for many commentators on language, a woman who speaks at all is one who speaks too much. Obviously speech is a necessary part of everyday life for men and women; thus, the notion that women's silence is golden places them in the cruelly paradoxical situation of being required to speak yet being criticized or even punished for speaking. Although men are also warned against the misuse of language, women's speech is often singled out for special blame. In *The Accidence; or First Rudiments of English Grammar, Designed for the Use of Young Ladies* (1801), Ellin Devis subscribes to the notion that women should be muffled. She accepts a double standard of morality for the sexes and warns that improper verbal behavior gives women more than men a bad name: "A forward-ness to talk, and a multitude of words, is no advantage to the character of any person, especially women; whose greatest reproach, in the apostle's censure of them, was, to be tatlers, and busy-bodies" (136).

The Presbyterian theologian Alexander T. McGill also marks women's language for censure when he takes the dangers of speaking as the topic of his address to the Literary Societies of Oxford (Ohio) Female College in 1858. In a tone more evangelical than literary, McGill calls the tongue women's special infirmity, which "cannot be tamed by any art of man" (1858, 5–6). McGill advises his listeners that silence is golden, that a woman should be "swift to hear, slow to speak," and that "idle and inadvertant words are the bane of social peace" (6–7). Furthermore, he tells the assembled members of the literary societies, all of them women, that men do not want women to read novels, whose morality is often suspect, and he recommends to his audience of *litteratae* that they curb their reading as well as their speech (16).

ALIEN WOMEN

Though men set up the silent and illiterate woman as an ideal, even the staunchest antifeminists admitted that women did have to use lan-guage now and then. But many observers were reluctant to allow women full membership in the speech communities of men. Just as Eve was not Adam, her use of language was seen as different from Adam's. In some cases, women have even been thought to use not just distinct varieties of the same language, but different languages alto-gether. For example, in his account of the languages of Eden, *Die Sprachen des Paradieses* (1683), the Swedish writer Anders Kempe implies that Eve's language is not that of Adam. According to Anders Kempe, God speaks to Adam in Swedish, Adam replies in Danish, and the serpent tempts Eve in French, a language she apparently understands only too well (cited in Müller [1860] 1866, 142n).

Women's speech has been perceived not just as different, but as dangerous. In *Remaines, Concerning Britaine* (1614), a sometimes apocryphal linguistic history of the British Isles, William Camden describes the threat posed by the language of alien women to the survival of native Celtic speech. According to Camden, when the Celtic Britons were forced from their homeland in the wake of the fifth-century Germanic invasions, they took drastic measures to ensure the continuity of their linguistic heritage. Crossing the English Channel, they "passed hence into *Armorica* in *France,* and marrying strange women there, did cut out their tongues, lest their children should corrupt their language with their mothers tongues" (30). Such an extreme case is not to be taken as historical truth, but it does reveal an assumption on Camden's part that men have both the right and the duty to limit access to language to the point where women may with justification be irrevocably silenced. What is perhaps more important, Camden's account reveals a fear of the power of women's language to control linguistic development and change through a monopoly of the process of language acquisition in the young.

In addition to such quasi-historical accounts of male–female language conflict, anthropological evidence was brought to bear on the question of the alien language of women. In 1654 J. B. Du Tertre, writing of the Carib Indians of the Lesser Antilles, claims that "the women have a language quite different from that of the men, and it would be a sort of crime to speak otherwise among themselves, when they are not obliged to converse with the men" (quoted in Frazer 1900, 81). It was commonly assumed that this situation came about when the Caribs, in their invasions of the islands, wiped out the native male Arawaks and married the remaining females. However, some observers were able to relate such sex-linked linguistic variation as existed among the island Caribs to more complex social factors. Father Labat, in 1742, describes three distinct forms of communication among the Caribs: a general language, spoken by all but considered to be the special preserve of the men; a woman's language, understood by men though they avoid using it or admitting that they understand it; and an invented jargon known only to male warriors, especially the old men, used for secrecy and not understood by women or boys (Frazer 1900, 81–82).

The Danish linguist Otto Jespersen (1924a) suggests that early travelers and missionaries exaggerated reports of cultures in which the women spoke languages entirely distinct from the men's. Examining the evidence collected by De Rochefort in 1665, he discovers no sex-related grammatical differences among the Caribs. Jespersen does identify a small number of lexical items—roughly ten percent, consisting mostly of kinship terms, the names of the parts of the body, and such isolated words as *friend, enemy, joy, work, war, house, garden, sun,* and *moon*—that differ according to whether a man or a woman is speaking, but he concludes that while men and women may exhibit linguistic differences, a separate women's language does not in fact exist (238).

VERBAL CRIME AND PUNISHMENT

Jespersen attributes the development of sex-related dialects not to intermarriage between Carib men and Arawak women, but to social restrictions imposed on the Carib women: they may not eat until the men are done, they must wait on the men like slaves, and they may not utter their husbands' names. Jespersen suggests that both the men's hunting jargon and the women's dialect result from verbal taboos. He cites examples of sex-linked verbal taboos among the Bantu to support this view, noting that in some cases the ultimate penalty must be paid for a linguistic transgression:

> With the Zulus a wife is not allowed to mention the name of her father-in-law and of his brothers, and if a similar word or even a similar syllable occurs in the ordinary language, she must substitute something else of a similar meaning. In the royal family the difficulty of understanding the women's language is further increased by the woman's being forbidden to mention the names of her husband, his father and grandfather as well as his brothers. . . . If a woman were to contravene this rule she would be indicted for sorcery and put to death. [1924a, 239]

Death may seem a high price to pay for a violation of language etiquette that may be little more than a slip of the tongue, and Zulu linguistic conventions may strike us as primitive and irrelevant to the situation of modern English, but women's unrestricted use of language is regarded as a threat in so-called civilized, though male-dominated, societies as well. In seventeenth-century New England, for example, where manners were equated with morals, both men and women were publicly punished for such breaches of linguistic etiquette as cursing, swearing, and name-calling. However, as Connie Eble reports, women were the particular objects of the language codes:

> Women were admonished to suffer in silence, and the penalties for failing to heed this instruction were severe. The ducking stool was the punishment for *common scolds,* "troublesome, angry women, who by their brawling and wrangling amongst their neighbors, break the public peace, increase discord, and become a public nuisance to the neighborhood." (Jacob's Law Dictionary) In Plymouth slanderers were put into the stocks wearing signs announcing their offense; in Maine women were gagged for gossiping; in New York a cleft stick on an angry tongue brought silence. (1976, 469)

Despite such obvious exceptions, women's language behavior was generally codified in courtesy or etiquette books rather than in the legal statutes of American and European society. Women were discouraged, for example, from the verbal expression of anger, particularly against their husbands. Diane Bornstein (1978) notes that in the fourteenth-century English poem "The Northern Mother's Blessing" the mother advises her daughter to answer her husband-to-be meekly and with fair words, to be sweet of speech, and to laugh softly, so that men do not hear her. Although punishments for inappropriate behavior were not prescribed, examples of what became of women who strayed from the linguistic straight and narrow show that both verbal and physical abuse were considered appropriate responses to infringements of language taboos. In the medieval French *Book of the Knight of the Tower* (translated into English by Caxton in 1484), we are told by an approving narrator of a husband who breaks his wife's nose when she vents her anger. According to Bornstein, women who violate the common prohibition against arguing and scolding can expect men to respond with sexual insults. The Knight of the Tower tells several stories about women who argue with men over a variety of issues which have nothing to do with sex. The men involved, however, may accuse their interlocutors of unfaithfulness, harlotry, and witchcraft (133).

A woman's language is also equated with her sexuality in Richard Allstree's *Ladies Calling* (1673), where linguistic behavior is treated in the section on modesty. According to Allstree, modesty of discourse imposes a taboo against loud speech for women and requires that "a Womans tongue should indeed be like the imaginary Musick of the Spheres, sweet and charming, but not to be heard at distance" (Eble 1976, 470). Cheris Kramarae reports that nineteenth- and twentieth-century etiquette books frequently advise women to lower the pitch as well as the volume of their voices. Women are directed to modulate their tones, enunciate clearly, listen well, and learn about male topics of conversation. These behavior tracts take the position that women do not and should not talk like men, and in their attempt to preserve a separate women's language they catalogue the taboos that apply to women's speech, advising women to avoid slang, gossip, emotional speech, and excessive loquacity.

Western women are stereotyped as gossips who are only too eager to tell everything they know, and both medieval courtesy books and modern treatises on etiquette strongly reprove this behavior. In one of the Knight of the Tower's exempla, a wife is publicly ridiculed for failing to keep her husband's secrets. But, according to Bornstein, the most successful of all the taboos placed on women's speech were the restrictions against cursing and joking (135–36). The late fourteenth-century *Menagier de Paris* presents the exemplary warning of a woman called a whore because of her jesting, and Richard Allstree evokes the notion of Eve as the source of the fall from grace when he equates a woman's use of oaths with the literal sounds of damnation: "Out of a woman it hath such an uncouth harshness, that there is no noise on this side [of] Hell can be more amazingly odious" (Eble 1976, 470). Even today women are censured and occasionally dismissed from their jobs for using obscenities or other types of *unladylike* speech that would be tolerated from the mouths of men, a double standard of linguistic behavior that has characterized attitudes toward sex-linked language variation from the outset.

EFFEMINATE LANGUAGE

If etiquette books encourage women to use language differently from men we may suspect that, at least to some extent, women and men naturally speak in fairly similar ways. After all, taboos against certain types of usage arise to discourage language that is otherwise almost certain to occur, and the imposition of a taboo is an overt attempt to control social behavior. Sex-linked linguistic taboos establish a double standard by which what is tolerated in one sex is prohibited to the other. As Bornstein puts it, "all forms of aggressive, assertive, hostile, and vigorous language were defined as acceptable for men and placed under taboo for women" (136). According to the clergyman and educator Andrew Peabody, women must curb not just their tongues but their laughter and, by implication, their entire range of sound production: "Man may indulge in any latitude of expression within the bounds of sense and decorum, but woman has a narrower range— even her mirth must be subjected to the rules of good taste" (1867, 103). But there are usage taboos for English-speaking males as well as females. Stuart Berg Flexner, in his preface to the *Dictionary of American Slang,* suggests that men "tend to avoid words that sound feminine or weak" (1975, xii). And there is a general proscription against what is usually termed *effeminate* usage that applies both to men and women.

Men frequently react to the idea of women's speech with fear and derision. Du Tertre reports that Carib women "mock at the men when the latter use the feminine manner of speech" (Frazer 1900, 81), and De Rochefort finds that Carib women "have words and phrases which the men never use, or they would be laughed to scorn" (Jespersen 1924a, 237). The reluctance of men to be identified with what is regarded as women's English is also strong. For example, women are often thought of as careful pronouncers of words; the lexicographer Frank Vizetelly, invoking this stereotype in order to debunk it, recounts the story of a young actor who defends his slovenly enunciation because "he feared that people would think him effeminate if he gave his vowels and consonants their due" (1929, xxi). Gossip in men may receive the same censure. Some advisors on etiquette forgive women's gossip because it is presumed to be so much a part of their nature. However, according to *Esquire's Guide to Modern Etiquette* (1969), "when a man gossips he courts a double penalty: he throws suspicion on his manhood as well as on his manners" (87).

Women are often assumed to be overly finicky about usage as well as pronunciation. Initially the question form *aren't I?,* which arose during the nineteenth or early twentieth century as an alternative to the highly stigmatized *ain't I?,* was not well received by usage critics who associated this too-polite innovation with the speech of women.

Some commentators went so far as to prefer the colloquial _ain't I?_ over the upstart, euphemistic, and hypercorrect _aren't I?_, called by linguist George Philip Krapp, in his _Comprehensive Guide to Good English_ (1927a), "a kind of kittenish feminine English." There is still in the American popular mind a notion that _ain't,_ for all its faults, is masculine, while _aren't_ is not simply feminine, but effeminate. In Thomas Berger's novel _The Feud_ (1983), Tony, a high school student, finds that good grammar must take a back seat to his public sexual identity. Tony defends his use of the masculine _ain't_ against his girlfriend Eva's objection that it is a sign of ignorance: "I don't like to talk like a girl. Somebody might think I was a pansy" (196).

According to J. M. Steadman (1938), the proscription against effeminate diction is one of the strongest language taboos among college students. Steadman found some forty-four words that both sexes considered effeminate, including the following, listed in order of descending frequency: _darling, gorgeous, adorable, lovely, precious, sweet_ (describing a person), _charming, luncheon, exquisite, dear, divine, gracious,_ and _stunning._ Also considered effeminate, though by only a very few of the students, were _simply, marvelous, naughty, limb_ (for leg), _glorious, dreadful, chic, doily,_ and _gobs._

Steadman attributes the sexual taboo placed on certain elements of the English vocabulary to three factors: a basic American fear of culture that is produced by the social dominance of the middle and lower classes; the American focus on individualism; and the democratic downward leveling of standards. But perhaps most important, for Steadman's purposes, is his citation of James Truslow Adams's opinion that the frontier equated culture with effeminacy. The schoolteacher has often been pictured as the lone bastion of culture on the frontier, and the schoolteachers' concerns, particularly their linguistic concerns, have frequently been stereotyped as effeminate. Many language commentators who found their own schooling unenjoyable have placed the blame for effeminate language directly on the stereotype of the schoolteacher, or more precisely, the _schoolmarm_—characterized either as a woman or an effeminate man—who is supposed to have instilled in generations of unsuspecting youngsters an unhealthy concern for hypercorrectness in pronunciation and grammar at the expense of ease and naturalness of expression. Such attitudes are not limited to the nineteenth century. Patricia Sexton (1979) complains that American boys are feminized by their school experience, that is, their "normal male impulses are suppressed or misshapen by overexposure to feminine norms." Sexton is particularly troubled by the way our schools instill effeminate vocabulary in their male charges:

> School words tend to be the words of women. They have their own sound and smell, perfumed or antiseptic. Boys usually prefer tough and colorful short words—while teachers and girls lean toward longer, more floral, opaque synonyms. School words are clean, refined, idealized and as remote from physical things as the typical schoolmarm from the tough realities of ordinary life. [25–26]

Even so apparently innocuous a form as underlining for emphasis (or italic type in printed works) has been stigmatized as a feminine or effeminate linguistic form, because of the stereotype of women's language as emotional. Otto Jespersen (1924a) claims that women typically use parataxis rather than hypotaxis when constructing sentences; their clauses are joined through coordination, which gives equal grammatical rank to the elements linked by its conjunctions *and, or, but,* etc. (Subordination, in contrast, distinguishes more important information from lesser points by giving greater grammatical weight to key elements; moreover, subordinating conjunctions such as *although, after, if,* and *because* can signal complex relationships between units of information.) In other words, if we are to accept Jespersen's assertion about women's reliance on parataxis, women tend simply to compound ideas and details. Jespersen finds that, as a result, women mark the gradation between their ideas not grammatically, through the use of constructions that pattern ideas with logic and emphasis, "but emotionally, by stress and intonation, and in writing by underlining" (251). In his essay "Grammar and Style," Hugh Sykes Davies (1964) advises against this literal or graphic expression of emotion:

> Underlining is generally described as 'feminine,' by which it is to be inferred that no real man would make use of it, for fear of being thought womanly, while no real woman would use it either, because it is unmanly. [19]

For Davies the writing of both women and men must be "manly"—it must bear no trace of the feminine or the effeminate. Such a proscription may seem at first to work against the efforts of the etiquette mongers to maintain separate dialects for the separate sexes, but in effect it does little more than reinforce the sex-linked language stereotypes which already exist, while at the same time marking the "feminine" variant—gossip, for example—as undesirable even for the women for whom it is supposed to be natural. Women are being told that they must not use language as men do, yet they must not use the language attributed to women either. Like Thomas Wilson, men writing about women's language frequently and irrationally reach the conclusion that silence is the only logical and safe solution to the paradox of Eve.

A MASCULINE TONGUE

In specific matters of intonation or idiom the so-called masculine has frequently been judged worthier than the feminine, but we also find whole languages praised as masculine and others condemned as feminine or effeminate on the basis of pronunciation, vocabulary, and even grammar. Those who have preferred English over the past few centuries have often described it as a man's language, monosyllabic, consonantal, direct, and unemotional, in contrast to feminine tongues, which are characterized as polysyllabic, vocalic, devious, and hyperbolic. Richard Carew, in his essay "The Excellencie of the English Tongue," published in William Camden's *Remaines* (1614), prefers the "apt and forcible" English interjections *ah, oh, alas,* and *alacke,* to effeminate Italian *deh* or French *hélas* (37). Carew compares French unfavorably to a vain woman, "scarce daring to open her lippes for feare of marring her countenance." English is for him a manly tongue, while German is perhaps a bit too brutish for his taste, being "manlike but withall verie harsh," excessively consonantal and always ready for a fight (43).

John Brightland goes so far as to suggest that feminine languages are threats to public morality. In his *Grammar of the English Tongue* (1711), Brightland warns that the monosyllabic purity of our masculine English must be defended against "the Adulterous Charms of any strange Tongue." Specifically, we must avoid any further borrowing of polysyllabic vocabulary from the romance languages (A 4 recto–A 5 recto). On the other hand, supporters of borrowing generally see the source language as positive, and therefore masculine, not feminine. For example, V. J. Peyton is convinced that our masculine English does well to take so much of its vocabulary from Latin, which he calls a "learned and masculine language" ([1771] 1970, 5).

In *Growth and Structure of the English Language* ([1905] 1923), Otto Jespersen sees masculinity as the most striking characteristic of English: "it seems to me positively and expressly *masculine,* it is the language of a grown-up man and has very little childish or feminine about it" (2). Even the English of women is described as masculine. The eighteenth-century grammarian James Buchanan sees no irony in dedicating his *British Grammar* (1762) to Queen Charlotte of Mecklenburg, who arrived in England only the year before to become the wife of George III, and whose English he calls as manly as the next man's. And Jespersen remarks that English women speak in monotones like men, without the pitch variation he finds so common in the speech both of primitive and southern European women. They even write like men: "an English lady will nearly always write in a manner that in any other country would only be found in a man's hand" (2).

THE PHONETIC STEREOTYPE

One gender stereotype, popular until recently, assumes that the speech of women and, by extension, the feminine, romance languages abound in vowels, while the speech of men and the masculine, Germanic tongues are predominantly consonantal. Jonathan Swift ([1712] 1957) describes a no-doubt fictitious experiment in which he asked an equal number of men and women to write a random series of nonsense letters. The men wrote down more consonants than vowels, creating a gibberish sounding like "High-Dutch," while the women, favoring vowels and liquids, produced a string of letters that resembled Italian. Swift concludes that the softer, vocalic speech of women may have a refining influence on conversation, though he is unwilling to grant them any larger role in language reform (13).

Swift's contemporary, the Anglo-Saxon scholar Elizabeth Elstob, rejects the idea that women's language is vowel-ridden. In her *Rudiments of Grammar for the English-Saxon Tongue* (1715), Elstob argues that there are many examples of women "whose writings abound with Consonants; where Vowels must generally be understood, and appear but very rarely" (xi). Despite this protest, the stereotype persisted among expert and layman alike. The obscure American spelling reformer Benajah Jay Antrim assumes, in *Pantography* (1843), that vowels are feminine, "because they are the soft and delicate voices," and consonants masculine, "because they are more harsh and irregular" (iv). In *Lectures on the Science of Language* (1864), the linguist Max Müller expands on this same notion. Müller implies the inferior status of feminine languages, which he deems more vocalic and less conservative than their masculine counterparts—a reverse of the stereotype that women are more conservative in their use of language—and his comments suggest a view in which the feminine languages, by altering or discarding elements of the original language that are preserved in the masculine, actually derive from their male counterparts in a genesis that should by now be all too familiar:

> Several languages divide themselves from the first into two great branches; one showing a more manly, the other a more feminine character; one richer in consonants, the other richer in vowels; one more tenacious of the original grammatical terminations, the other more inclined to slur over these terminations, and to simplify grammar by the use of circumlocutions. [38]

The masculine/feminine language pairs that Müller discusses include Aeolic and Ionic Greek; High and Low German; the Goidelic and Cymric branches of Celtic; and the Sanskrit and Prakrit languages of India. Müller finds it possible that, as Jakob Grimm suggested, these masculine/feminine divisions originated in the separate dialects spoken by men and women while engaged in their sex-differentiated tasks: the "stern and strict dialects . . . represent the idiom of the fathers and brothers, used at public assemblies; while the soft and simpler dialects . . . sprang originally from the domestic idiom of mothers, sisters, and servants at home."

Otto Jespersen ([1905] 1923) accepts the phonetic stereotype, characterizing English as consonantal, and therefore masculine, in contrast with Hawaiian, which requires open syllables (that is, syllables ending in vowels) and forbids consonant clusters, giving an overall impression—according to Jespersen—of a vocalic, "childlike and effeminate" language (4). In addition to its preponderance of consonants, Jespersen characterizes the masculine style as brief, concise, and terse, "while women as a rule are not such economizers of speech"

(5). Predictably, Jespersen finds that English is brief, concise, and terse. In contrast to Müller's suggestion that loss of inflection is due to women's influence, Jespersen sees English grammar as masculine, simplified by the loss of its original, and by implication *feminine,* inflections. Furthermore, were it not for foreign borrowings, English would have a vocabulary approaching the manly monosyllabic ideal of Chinese. Jespersen finds that English idiom encourages the reduction of phrases to single words. Thus *thank you* becomes the terser, more manly *thanks,* and such English proverbs as *first come, first served,* devoid of pronouns or function words, demonstrate the structural and masculine leanness of the language.

English, like the Englishmen who use it, does not like to show emotions, and this, according to Jespersen, is a trait "certainly found more frequently in men than in women" (9). In a more recent example, language historian George H. McKnight (1923) finds a connection between what he sees as the tendency of women to hyperbolize and a related stereotype of French as overly passionate:

> The exaggerated mode of expression is more characteristic of the vocabulary of women than that of men. It will be noted also that the French language is more given to exaggerated expression of feeling than is the English. In fact many of the English words of greater intensity, such as *adore* and *enchanted,* are to be explained as Gallicisms. [274]

According to Jespersen, English also has few of the childlike or effeminate diminutives—Jespersen calls them "fondling endings"— that characterize other languages, and its word order, permitting few inversions and encouraging ellipsis, is forthright and distinctly virile. Unlike other languages with flexible word order, and, by implication, unlike women whose language is at best vague, at worst devious, English says what it means: "Words in English do not play hide-and-seek, as they often do in Latin, for instance, or in German" (11).

Finally, English has an undeniably rich vocabulary, which Jespersen regards as another masculine trait. Although he has no empirical evidence to back up his claim, except a vague sense that "novels written by ladies are much easier to read and contain much fewer difficult words than those written by men," Jespersen believes that women have smaller vocabularies than men (17). He can find only one womanish aspect of English to stand up against his catalogue of masculinity, and that is the British and American disposition toward prudery. However, Jespersen concludes that this is simply an overzealous attempt to ensure purity. He does not doubt that purity is a masculine virtue, and just as Brightland equates femininity in language with adultery, Jespersen finds English to be not only more masculine but also purer and more literally virtuous than most of its neighbors: "There can be no doubt that the speech of the average Englishman is less tainted with indecencies of various kinds that that of the average continental" (249). Despite the strong sense of English as a masculine tongue, women's use of the language was often considered a direct threat to its virility.

CHAPTER 5

Women's Words

There is a danger of the language becoming languid and insipid
if we are always to content ourselves
with women's expressions.
Otto Jespersen

Evaluating their language in the international arena, British commentators judge English superior to what are described as the weaker, gentler, less rational, or more effeminate languages. But when English speakers are at home they are less reticent to find fault with their own language, and women's language is often treated as a special case requiring particular attention.

Many writers attribute the supposed defects of women's language to their inadequate training in English. Early dictionaries like Robert Cawdry's *A Table Alphabeticall* (1604) and Henry Cockeram's *Dictionarie* (1623) classed women with illiterates and foreigners. Thomas Blount's *Glossographia* (1656), directed to "the more-knowing women and less-knowing men," assumes the inadequate background of even his educated women readers, and John Kersey evokes the stereotype of women as poor spellers in his *New English Dictionary* (1702), "designed for the benefit of Young Scholars, Tradesmen, Artificers, and the Female Sex, who would learn to spell truely" [*sic*].

Grammar and usage books also singled out women's language as flawed (Stanley 1978; Sklar 1983). In *The British Grammar* ([1762] 1968), James Buchanan contends that women exhibit improper pronunciation, lack "a natural, easy, and graceful Variation of the Voice," and can write neither grammatically nor elegantly. Buchanan further accuses "Females and mean Authors" of introducing into English such errors in verb formation as *I have wrote; he was drove; he has did;* and *his tooth is drew.*

Michael Maittaire (1712) questions the assumption that women cannot or should not be educated in the ways of their native language:

As for that tender Sex, which to set off we take so much care and use such variety of breeding, some for the feet, some for the hands, others for the voice; What shall i call it, cruelty or ignorance, to debar them from the accomplishments of Speech and Understanding; as if that Sex was (as certainly we by experience find it is not) weak and defective in its Head and Brains. [vi]

Similarly, in *The Many Advantages of a Good Language to Any Nation* (1724), Thomas Wilson complains that because women's education is neglected, "many a pretty Lady by the Silliness of her Words, hath lost the Admiration which her Face had gained" (37). Wilson is optimistic about correcting "those improprieties in Words, Spelling and Writing, for which [women] are usually laugh'd at," but like his colleagues, he assumes that men control language standards, and he writes for a male audience: Wilson contrasts "the female Sex" with "our Sex," and argues that the best way to correct such shortcomings of English as its effeminate pronunciation is to make "our" language easily understood by women, so that they in turn may train "our" children correctly (38).

Joseph Addison, also writing for men in *Guardian* 155 (1713), believes that the stereotypes of women's speech are true. He maintains that women have a *"Copia Verborum,* or plenty of Words,"* and an education could provide them with something important to say, freeing them from their reliance on what Addison regards as a staple of women's conversation, gossip:

If the Female Tongue will be in Motion, why should it not be set to go right? Could they discourse about the Spots in the Sun, it might divert them from publishing the Faults of their Neighbours: Could they talk of the different Aspects and Conjunctions of the Planets, they need not be at the Pains to comment upon Oglings and Clandestine Marriages.

Addison is critical of men's language as well. He urges that women become literate because men are not, and feels that women are already better spellers and occasionally better scholars than "the beaus." Addison offers in what is supposed to be a compliment the opinion that women can transcend stereotypes and triumph over their linguistic limitations: "There have been famous Female *Pythagoreans,* notwithstanding most of that Philosophy consisted in keeping a Secret, and that the Disciple was to hold her Tongue five Years together."

Eighteenth-century attempts to correct women's pronunciation and vocabulary were designed to make English-speaking women more ladylike, not more like men. Women were attacked then, as they are now, for speaking in a womanish fashion (though documentation of just what constitutes women's speech, then as now, is always vague). At the same time women were being told to speak the way women should, a style separate from the men's, and certainly not equal. Francis Grose goes so far as to admonish women to suppress what knowledge they do have so that they will not seem superior to men. He recommends that a woman should never claim to understand technical words, but should instead ask a man to explain them to her (Tucker 1967, 78). Similar advice that women should mask their linguistic abilities so as not to compete with men can be found in the etiquette books of today. Paradoxically, women are expected to be silent because they do not know enough about words and because they know too much.

WOMAN'S VOICE

While it appears that men are ready to find fault with almost anything that women say or write, the two areas of women's language use that have come under the sternest censure are those of voice quality and diction. Some men see woman's voice as a reminder of her secondary status. For example, Midrashic accounts claim that women's voices are shrill, while men's are not, because man was formed from earth and woman from a man's rib: when soft meats are cooked, the explanation goes, no sound is heard, "but let a bone be put in a pot, and at once it crackles" (Ginzberg 1909, 1:67). In a less fatalistic though equally negative view, etiquette books treat the stereotypically high-pitched feminine voice as an irritating defect which can be overcome with practice (Kramarae 1975, 14).

Woman's voice has been the object of pseudoscientific comment as well. Havelock Ellis ([1894] 1929) believes that the higher, shriller voice of woman has determined the nature of the grammatical feminine endings in French and other languages which exhibit grammatical gender (104). Ellis cites the opinion of Delaunay that voice pitch and the size of the larynx are directly related to sexual activity. Thus he claims that prostitutes have lower, more masculine voices, and that promiscuity in tenors endangers their singing careers. As a man, Ellis finds that evolution favors the development of masculine rather than feminine vocal characteristics, and as a European he concludes that Europeans, who are the most advanced peoples of the earth, have the largest larynxes and deepest voices (101–02).

THE SPEECH OF AMERICAN WOMEN

While some writers proclaimed that women's voices were inferior to men's because of their higher pitch, others assumed that women, because they were more refined and civilized than men, had in general a superior quality of voice. In *Notions of the Americans* (1828), written after a long stay in England, James Fenimore Cooper praises the voices of American women as "particularly soft and silvery" and claims that the natural harshness of the English language "is made softer by our women" (2:133). But in the ten years after his return to the United States, Cooper develops a distaste for the voices of American women, and he faults them for failing to uphold the tradition of feminine vocal excellence ([1838] 1956, 116).

Richard Grant White also finds the voices of American women inferior to those of their British counterparts. In *Every-Day English* (1881), White complains that American women are overly emphatic, stressing almost every word they utter. Although British women may be more likely to use bad grammar, even the women of the lower classes "will delight you with the rich, sweet, smooth, and yet firm and crisp tones." American women, on the other hand, are physically attractive, but one's initial impression is quickly altered when they open their mouths to produce "a mean, thin, nasal, rasping tone, by which at once you are disenchanted" (93–94).

The novelist William Dean Howells (1906) also singles out the speech of American women for special blame. He praises the superiority of women to men, and of the American woman to almost all others of her sex, in beauty, mind, manners, money, singing voice, and the excellence of her thoughts, but not in speech: "She sometimes spoke through her nose, she twanged, she whiffled, she snuffled, she whined, she whinnied the brilliant things which she was always incontestably saying." Howells fears that the speech of American men can never be improved "because nothing good is to be expected of them until their mothers and wives reform" (930–31).

Following Howells's lead, Henry James (1906–07) used the forum of *Harper's Bazaar* for a vicious attack on the pronunciation of American women, who he claimed speak not as ladies but as they like. Like Howells, James acknowledges that the verbal ability of American women is unsurpassed, but it is a pity, he adds, evoking the stereotype of feminine loquacity, that any class of persons should talk so prodigiously before they have learned to speak (41:115). James finds the pronunciation of American women a reflection not of their freedom of spirit, but of an anarchy that borders on insanity, and he feels that a perverted sense of social equality has led Americans to regard it as their duty to sink to the lowest possible linguistic level. According to James, there is in America "an innumerable sisterhood, from State to State and city to city, all bristling with the same proclamation of indifference, all engaged in reminding us how much the better sisters may, occasion favoring, speak even as the worse" (40:1105).

In short, James charges that the speech of American women is common, loose, flat, without tones, form, charm, or direction. He claims that their speech is so irregular that it can scarcely be described: "To attempt to represent it by imitative signs is, besides being a waste of ingenuity, to impute to it a consistency which is really the last thing it owns. We rather avert our ears from it" (40:1106). He describes a dialogue, from his point of view a monologue, with an "interlocutress" who holds the opinion that the imposition of a standard pronunciation represents a form of sexual oppression that American women will not tolerate. According to James, American women prefer to reduce their words, when speaking them, to a phonetic minimum:

> Intelligibly expressed, my young lady's attitude was that discriminated sounds, indicated forms, were at the best such a vocal burden that any multiplication of them was to be viewed with disfavor: I had indeed to express this *for* her, but she grunted (her grunt had, clearly, always passed for charming) an acceptance of my formula. . . . Syllables and consonants . . . might be almost unlimitedly sacrificed without absolute ruin to a rough sense. [41:113]

American women are imprisoned in their poor, minimalized speech, a situation which James characterizes as an affront to the national honor. Yet according to James the supposed degeneration of women's speech is a direct result of their growing importance in American society, for women regard their power to reduce words to insignificant grunts as a sign of their increasing social liberation:

> Anything that would sufficiently stand for the word, and that might thereby be uttered with the minimum of articulation, would sufficiently do, wouldn't it?—since the emancipation of the American woman would thereby be attested, and the superstition of syllables, of semitones, of the beginning of a sound, of the middle of it, and of the end of it, the superstition of vain forms and superfluous efforts, receive its quietus. [41:113]

James warns that, if Americans continue to be led by the example of their women, "the word, stripped for action . . . [will] become an inexpensive generalized mumble or jumble, a tongueless slobber or snarl or whine, which every one would be free, and but too glad to answer in kind." And he echoes the admonition so popular with the amateur language reformers of any age: if something is not done soon, American English, and by implication civilization as we know it, will inevitably degenerate into "the moo of the cow, the bray of the ass, and the bark of the dog" (41:113).

In contrast to the misdirected emancipation of the dialect of American women, James praises the long-lost Puritan speech of New England, which symbolized a paternalistic and therefore well-ordered society, in which women knew their place. New England dialect was "the highest type of utterance implanted among us. . . . [It was] the expressional effect of the few capable of taking care of themselves, and of keeping themselves in hand—capable even of keeping their wives, their daughters, their sisters" (41:20–21).

PRONOUNCED SEXUAL DIFFERENCES

In addition to differences in voice quality and pronunciation, or tone as James calls it, language commentators have observed specific examples of sex-linked variation in pronunciation. Despite the stereotype that women are more conservative about language matters than men, women have often been blamed for innovation in the area of pronunciation. As early as the sixteenth century, English writers noted differences between the pronunciation of men and women, and they favored the masculine form even when—or perhaps especially because—it was losing ground to the innovative form attributed to women. Sir Thomas Smith, one of the earliest English spelling reformers, complains in 1568 of the affected speech of women, and Richard Mulcaster, in his *Elementarie* ([1562] 1925), distinguishes a pair of sex-linked vowels, implying the superiority of the masculine, though it is the pronunciation attributed to women that has become standard in Modern English:

> Ai [that is, /ai/, as in *fine*], is the mans diphthong, & soundeth full: ei [that is, /e/, as in *faint*], the womans, and soundeth finish in the same both sense, and vse, *a woman is deintie, and feinteth soon, the man feinteth not bycause he is nothing daintie.* [132]

Similarly, in his *Logonomia Anglica* ([1619] 1972), Alexander Gill complains that some women affect an improper "diphthong" in pronouncing [æ:], from Middle English [a:], as [e:]. When shopping for fabric, instead of buying *laun* and *kambrik* they buy *len* and *kembrik* (17; in the "improper" pronunciation, the vowels rhyme with *lain* and *came*). Again it is the stigmatized, allegedly feminine pronunciation of *cambric* that predominates in Modern English.

More recently, and more impressionistically, Otto Jespersen (1924a) finds that the tongue-trilled *r* of English and other languages was lost or weakened through women's refining and confining influence. Jespersen claims that the tongue-trilled *r* is "natural and justified when life is chiefly carried on out-of-doors, but indoor life prefers, on the whole, less noisy speech habits, and the more refined this domestic life is, the more all kinds of noises and even speech sounds will be toned down" (214). He blames the innovative pronunciation of French women for the loss of the original *r* in *chaise,* 'chair,' a domestic object which Jespersen describes as "belonging more naturally to the speech of women." The English word *chair* derives from the older French *chaire,* retained in Modern French only in the sense of pulpit or professorial chair, specialized meanings that Jespersen places in the realm of the male.

In addition to such phonetically innovative behavior, Jespersen identifies a conservative tendency in Southern English women, who preserve the aspiration of words with initial *wh-* [hw], for example, *which* and *whether,* whereas the less conservative men pronounce only initial [w], making no phonetic distinction between these words and *witch* or *weather.* Jespersen also cites the opinion of the English phonetician Daniel Jones that men pronounce *soft* with a long vowel, while women use a short one, and that women turn the vowel of *girl* into a diphthong. Jespersen feels that British women are likely to pronounce *waistcoat* as it is spelled, while men, who use the word more often, shorten it to the historically correct [wɛskɪt]. But Jespersen concludes that such differences in pronunciation, though they do exist, are essentially trivial: "From the phonetic point of view there is scarcely any difference between the speech of men and that of women" (243–45).

VACANT CHAMBERS OF THE MIND

Jespersen ([1905] 1923) does believe that significant sex-linked variation occurs in the area of word choice, and he attributes this to limitations in the experience of women and to the different organization and capacity of the male and female minds. Although Jespersen admits that English-speaking women are apt to experiment with pronunciation, he considers them lexically conservative. They avoid hard words, neither understand nor make puns, and leave innovation— both the coining of new terms and the revival of discarded ones—to men, who are semantically less banal.

According to Jespersen, women's limited vocabulary contributes to their supposed volubility, while men's superior knowledge of words proves an impediment to smooth speech:

> Women move in narrower circles of the vocabulary, in which they attain to perfect mastery so that the flow of words is always natural and, above all, never needs to stop, while men know more words and always want to be more precise in choosing the exact word with which to render their idea, the consequence being often less fluency and more hesitation. [16–17]

Havelock Ellis (*Man and Woman* [1894], 1929), from whom Jespersen gets many of his ideas about the sexes, acknowledges women's linguistic excellence in only one area, the writing of fiction, because of all the arts fiction makes the fewest "serious artistic demands . . . inasmuch as it is simply a version of life." Ellis describes the speech of lower-class women as novelistic in style: "In the poorest and least cultured ranks the conversation of women consists largely of rudimentary novelettes in which 'says he' and 'says she' play the chief parts," and he thinks letter writing even better suited to a woman's literary methods, which are based on "spontaneity, carlessness of form, [and] a very personal and intimate frankness" (372–73).

Jespersen admits that women are faster readers than men, though he is quick to point out that there is no connection between speed and intelligence. Again he draws on Havelock Ellis, who claims that women, like children, have minds that are organized more simply than those of men, and both Ellis and Jespersen attribute women's superior reading rate to their lack of knowledge of the world:

> With the quick reader it is as though every statement were admitted immediately and without inspection to fill the vacant chambers of the mind, while with the slow reader every statement undergoes an instinctive process of cross-examination; every new fact seems to stir up the accumulated stores of facts among which it intrudes, and so impedes rapidity of mental action. [Jespersen 1924a, 252]

For Ellis, both types of mental organization—the simple, childlike, feminine, and the complex, adult, masculine—have their advantages. Women are able to react to situations more quickly. Because of this they are more prone to error, but they are also apt to use their facility with language to save the day. The positive manifestation of this ability Ellis calls tact, the negative one lying, and although he hesitates to endorse the stereotype that women are greater liars than men, Ellis does note that some researchers have claimed "the method of obtaining results by ruses (common among all the weaker lower animals) is so habitual among women as to be . . . 'almost physiological'" (399).

Jespersen is not quite so generous in his analysis of the situation. In order to demonstrate that excessive loquacity in women is related to the vacant chambers of their minds, he cites one of Jonathan Swift's "Thoughts on Various Subjects" (though the satirist is concerned with prattling and empty-headedness in *both* sexes):

> The common fluency of speech in many men, and most women, is owing to the scarcity of matter, and scarcity of words; for whoever is a master of language, and hath a mind full of ideas, will be apt in speaking to hesitate upon the choice of both: whereas common speakers have only one set of ideas, and one set of words to clothe them in; and these are

always ready at the mouth. So people come faster out of a church when
it is almost empty, than when a crowd is at the door. [quoted in Jespersen 1924a, 252–53]

Not only does Jespersen persist in the absurd claim that women
have fewer ideas and fewer words with which to express them, he
insists that women also tend to speak without thinking. As a result,
women exhibit "the linguistic symptoms of a peculiarity of feminine
psychology," and are more likely than men to use "stop-short" or
"pull-up" sentences such as _Well I never!_ or _I must say!_ They are also
more likely to use what we now call skip connectors, pronouns that
refer not to the person last mentioned, but to "somebody else to whom
[the woman's] thoughts have already wandered, while a man with his
slower intellect will think that she is still moving on the same
path" (251).

EVE'S SLANG

The idea that women know fewer words than men and are less creative
linguistically is related to the general stereotype of women's conservatism in matters of language. In his preface to the _Dictionary of American Slang_ (1975), Stuart Berg Flexner argues that "most American
slang is created and used by males." Slang reflects the concerns of
American men: "Many types of slang words—including the taboo and
strongly derogatory ones, those referring to sex, women, work,
money, whiskey, politics, transportation, sports, and the like—refer
primarily to male endeavor and interest" (xii). This masculine creativity is the result of the greater range of experience supposedly available
to men. According to Flexner, women, most of whom stay at home,
do not develop their own slang, but learn it instead from their husbands. Moreover, he maintains that women's words for clothing, hair-
styles, and household gadgets are created by the men who determine
styles and make or sell these products, not by the women who buy
and use them. Flexner finds that even working women, because they
have shorter careers or are less involved in their jobs, do not develop
much in the way of slang, and he insists that even when women get
together in groups, "they do not often talk of the outside world
of business, politics, or other fields of general interest where new
feminine names for objects, concepts, and viewpoints could evolve"

(xii). Flexner believes that men use slang for its shock value, its expression of action or violence. They relish the hyperbole so common in slang; taking a position contradicting that of Jespersen, Flexner finds that men "do not see or care to express fine shades of meaning" as women do.

Flexner lists the few female subgroups that do contribute to American slang as airline stewardesses, beauty-parlor operators, chorus girls, nurses, waitresses, and prostitutes. But David Maurer ([1939] 1981), an authority on the language of the American underworld, believes that prostitutes, whom he clearly dislikes, are not capable of the same kinds of innovative thought and lack the technical vocabulary found among the predominantly male criminal elements who merit his admiration, that is, thieves, confidence artists, narcotics addicts, and pickpockets. Maurer attributes the absence of prostitute slang to a combination of low intelligence and adverse working conditions. Echoing Jespersen's "vacant chambers" theory, he characterizes prostitutes as egoless, ignorant, socially inept, and incapable of innovative thought. Maurer considers the work of the prostitute to be less technical than that of other underworld professionals, and he assumes it is natural for the prostitute, like women in general, to be prohibited from developing a language of sexuality: "Her vocabulary for discussing technique is no more adequate than that of the average semiliterate farm wife" (114–15). Maurer finds fewer than fifty words—and he labels these "colorless"—that qualify as belonging to the prostitute's argot, and an additional thirty or so that are used by men to refer to prostitution, though they are not used by prostitutes themselves.

Other scholars suggest the more credible position that prostitutes are not linguistically deficient. Unfortunately no complete study of the slang of prostitutes, either female or male, exists, and it is quite likely that the general slang of women is not nonexistent, as has been maintained, but has instead been ignored by—or hidden from—primarily male investigators.

SEPARATE BUT NOT EQUAL

Summing up his opinions of sex-linked language variation, Havelock Ellis ([1894] 1929) labels males as abstract, rational, aesthetic, and creative; females as concrete, emotional, practical, and receptive. He cites one study in which the psychologist Joseph Jastrow asked a group of fifty male and female students to write a list of one hundred unconnected words. Jastrow found that the men's words came, in descending order of frequency, under the categories of the animal kingdom, proper names, verbs, implements and utensils, adjectives, the vegetable kingdom, abstract terms, meteorological and astronomical terms, occupations, callings, conveyances, other parts of speech, and geographical and landscape features. Women had a greater tendency to refer to wearing apparel and fabrics, interior furnishings, foods, buildings and building materials, the mineral kingdom, stationery, educational subjects, the arts, amusements, and kinship. The greatest difference appeared in the area of food: women used 179 words to refer to food, men only 53. Jastrow concluded that women are more concerned with their immediate surroundings, finished products, the ornamental, the individual, and the concrete, while men refer more readily to the remote, the constructive, useful, general, or abstract (Ellis 380–82). Such absurd and impressionistic classification still informs our thinking about the English vocabulary, particularly the lexicon of women.

Language commentators have little trouble naming what they feel to be women's words, though like their assessments of the personality traits of men and women, their lists are usually impressionistic and have little validity. Jespersen identifies a variety of alleged women's words and expressions. Among these are *to be sure, whoever,* and *whatever.* Jespersen cites *pretty* and *nice* as women's adjectives, and *vastly, quite, so* and *such* as adverbs peculiar to the female sex. Although he assumes women to be more emotional, Jespersen finds that it is men who use the stronger *Who the devil* or *What the dickens.* Jespersen's women do not swear, and consequently he holds them responsible for the creation of such euphemisms as *the other place* and *a very hot* or *a very uncomfortable place* as substitutes for *hell.* Women use such euphemistic expressions as *Good gracious, Gracious me, Goodness gracious,* and *Dear me,* while men will say *Good heavens* or *Great Scott,* though Jespersen forgets for the moment that these last two, as well as *What the dickens?,* all so-called masculine expressions, are also euphemistic in their origin.

As early as the eighteenth century commentators singled out women's words for special treatment. Writing in *The World* in 1754, Lord Chesterfield acknowledges the role of women in the formation of the English vocabulary and the dilemma posed by their lexical creativity (a creativity which is denied by the more recent commentators on grammar and gender trained in the antifeminist tradition of Delaunay and Ellis). Chesterfield warns Samuel Johnson that any sign of approval in his forthcoming dictionary of "those words and expressions, which, hastily begot, owe their birth to the incontinency of female eloquence" will be censured by his learned readers, while any attempt on Johnson's part to "banish and attaint many of the favourite words and expressions with which the ladies have so profusely enriched our language" will be met by indignation. Acknowledging that "language is indisputably the more immediate province of the fair sex," Chesterfield offers Johnson the chance at a compromise: add to the dictionary a supplementary glossary of women's words, on the model of Latin dictionaries which contain appended lists of discarded pedantic words. As examples of feminine vocabulary Chesterfield cites *flirtation* (a word which, together with *frightful,* is stigmatized by Johnson as cant), *to fuzz,* "dealing twice together with the same pack of cards, for luck's sake, at Whist," and *vast* and *vastly,* two words which according to Chesterfield mean "any thing" (606–07).

The following list provides a sampler of words that have been ascribed to women:

ah!, oh!, such, so, somehow, fine, and pronominal *one* (18th century). Tucker (1967, 79)

ruck, 'covered.' Horne Tooke ([1786] 1806 2:188)

implicit (mid 19th century). Thomas De Quincey ([1840–41] 1897)

splendid, 'pretty'; *horrible,* 'unpleasant'; *thousands,* "any number greater than two." Peabody (1867, 14)

unwell, used by women primarily as a euphemism, presumably for menstruation. Hall (1873, 125)

person, 'woman'; *nice,* 'fine'; *common,* 'vulgar.' Greenough and Kittredge label this last "effeminate" ([1901] 1920, 54).

perfectly, because, lovely, darling, sweet, horrid, mean, nice, dear, just-too-sweet, poor thing, minx, cat. Parsons (1913)

just, so, too. Weseen (1928)

horrid, "now restricted to the most effeminate vocabularies." Jefferson,
Peckham, and Wilson (1931)
cute, a "feminine counterword of approbation." Whitford and Foster
(1955)

The linguist Edward T. Hall, following the widely held presumption that women are more concerned than men with refinement in language, attributes to women the usage distinction that is often maintained between *can,* to denote ability, and *may,* to denote permission. Although his theory is not supported by any evidence or by the standard language histories, Hall claims in *The Silent Language* ([1959] 1968) that originally

> men and boys said "can," women and girls "may." "May" naturally sounded more refined to the women so they insisted on foisting it on the men along with a lot of gobbledygook about possible and not possible. At the present time, what with the women trying to be like the men and the men doing more and more things women used to do, the may–can now is so mixed up it's almost impossible to develop any rules. It is possible for either to be applied in a great many situations. [120]

The etymologist Wilfred Funk (1950) asserts that women not only talk a lot but also have their own unenviable vocabulary, which contains such trivializing adjectives as *adorable, sweet, precious, cunning, darling, cute, stunning,* and *itsy bitsy.* In addition, Funk finds that women are prone to hyperbole because of their emotional makeup. They use *terribly, awfully,* and *frightfully* because they "boil at lower temperatures than men" (249).

Funk goes so far as to allow women the right to their own distinctive words. Another linguistic writer, Mario Pei (1969), is not so generous. Pei lists as women's words *sweetie, honey, dear heart, doll, all rightie, natch, darling,* and *hi, love!* Pei accuses women of using French color terms like *beige, mauve, taupe,* and *ecru,* which mean nothing to men, and he claims that men always avoid such feminine clothing terms as *hanky, panties, undies, nappies, scanties, nightie,* and *powder room.* Pei attributes to women the use of extravagant adjectives, including *wonderful, adorable, heavenly, divine, dreamy, sensational,* and *hysterical* (in the sense 'really funny'), and he suggests—without offering any substantiating evidence except the implicit connections between Eve, carnality, and linguistic diminutives—that feminine influence may stand behind the derivation of the adjective *sexy*. Pei does not hesitate to use the eighteenth-century grammarian's tactic of excluding women from his audience when he complains, "What women use among themselves is their own business, but must they inflict it on us?" Like Ellis and Jespersen, Pei does not even consider women to be adults: "A thoroughly masculine and adult vocabulary could form the subject of a chapter, too; but then our book might be banned in Boston" (33-44).

SILENCE IS BRAZEN

With few exceptions, the views of women's language described in chapters four and five have been negative ones, based like the negative and derivative etymologies of chapter three on stereotypes of women's and men's verbal behavior that have little or no connection with actual language use. The praise that is occasionally given to the speech and writing of women is often damningly faint. For example, Otto Jespersen concludes his impressionistic list of women's linguistic failures with the questionable compliment that women represent the golden mean: they are more average when it comes to language, while men are at the extremes, being greater orators but also greater imbeciles, stutterers, and stammerers (1924a, 253).

Some commentators, for example Max Müller and Wilfred Funk, acknowledge women's right to their own language, but legitimizing woman's language is often a tactic to prevent her from acquiring man's language. Elsie Clews Parsons (*The Old-Fashioned Woman,* 1913) notes that in eighteenth-century England men and women at parties would separate, each talking their own talk. She adds that American men and women also have separate dialects based on their separate interests: the women, for example, read poetry, but the men read only politics. Furthermore, according to Parsons, the fact that women do not voluntarily participate in the daily activities of men leads to a lack of communication between the sexes:

> Taking little or no part in men's callings or games, the ladies are apt to be inattentive listeners when 'business' or 'shop' or 'sport' are under discussion. No wonder a man is given to saying there are so few things you can talk to a woman about. [130]

Parsons does not feel it incumbent upon men to become conversant with the household words consigned to women, for those words are neither standard nor powerful. In her view, the exclusion of women from the language of men is not entirely voluntary. It represents a Western refinement of the almost universal practice among primitive cultures of keeping women ignorant of the languages of power by creating taboos that deny them access to certain areas of verbal intercourse: sacred words or dialects are kept secret from women, as are the vocabularies of hunting and fishing, sailing and mining, war and trade. Women's language, in this exclusionist view, consists of scraps and leftovers.

In medieval Europe, women were steered away from Latin, the language of politics and the church. Even in modern times (that is, circa 1913), Parsons reminds us, special reading material, censored by parents or husbands, is prepared for women, and special periodicals or sections of newspapers (which are otherwise regarded as men's reading matter) are devoted to what are supposed to be women's interests. Parsons claims that novels are primarily women's literature, and she notes that, although women may read material intended for men, it is assumed that men will not be interested in reading what is written for women. Furthermore, she notes that slang and profanity remain the province of men, and women must apologize when they use unfamiliar or technical terms to disarm male criticism of their lexical trespass. Parsons maintains that men have a secret language of sex, whereas women "have no words, secret or otherwise, to describe some of the simplest sex characteristics and expressions" (156). She reports that in 1837 a group of New England clergymen even sought formally to prohibit the naming of the sexual organs and functions by women, arguing that the awareness and use of such words tended toward the erosion of virtue.

Parsons concludes that this sex-linked linguistic separatism also prevents women from developing special terms to describe their own interests, thus weakening their already restricted dialects. Although she does feel that American women use more color terms than men and have a fashion vocabulary that men claim not to understand, Parsons finds that men are attracted to technical terms, while women run from them; thus she implies that men, not women, are the progenitors of language, a statement altogether out of keeping with Parsons's otherwise feminist approach to anthropology.

Max Müller (1864) also recognizes the exclusion of women from certain aspects of language, but he allows women a greater role in language development than Parsons does. While he does not have as high an opinion of the feminine in language as of the masculine, Müller does concede that women influence the progress of language, and he admits that their idioms are to be found in public as well as domestic language. Müller cites Dante's opinion that the first attempts at using the vernacular Italian language owed much to "the silent influence of ladies who did not understand the Latin language," and he also points out that although women and servants in the early Sanskrit plays used the less favored Prakrit dialect, while men and gods used Sanskrit, Prakrit eventually became the standard literary language (38).

These representations of women's English clearly show that it is usually considered to be the language of a socially powerless or subordinated group. Describing women's dialects as self-fulfilling women's-language traps, the linguist Suzette Elgin (1980) argues that women find themselves using the subordinated type of language that has been stereotyped as women's language because they themselves are more frequently subordinated in American society. But Elgin warns women that attempts to rid their speech of its "'female' characteristics" will backfire, resulting in a style of language that is embarrassing or ridiculous, and that will cause women to feel more rather than less subordinated (289–90).

Another contemporary researcher, Cheris Kramarae (1981), is not surprised that linguistics has treated the language of women as inferior, since "it is customary for science to support the dominant values of society by justifying those values, including women's subordinate social roles" (vi). One theory which Kramarae discusses places women in a socially muted group. They are inarticulate "because the language they use is derivative, having been developed largely out of male perceptions of reality" (2). According to this muted-group theory, which is popular with a number of feminists, women have been excluded from the process of word formation, and gaps in the male-created language prevent women from articulating their experience. Furthermore, the role of women in the history of the English language is largely ignored by scholars.

The muted-group theory implies a trickle-down mechanism for language standardization and change, but such an interpretation ignores the fact that women are linguistically creative. Though some prestigious language features are imitated by lower-status speakers and writers, there is also a strong tendency for linguistic forms to trickle up, to make their way from stigmatized to nonstigmatized groups. As M. L. Samuels (1972) has said, all new linguistic forms are initially nonstandard in that they represent departures from existing norms (177). The muted-group theory also ignores the role that women are presumed to play in language acquisition.

While it is true that the standard language histories fail to document the contributions of women to the development of the English language, some of them do discuss certain stigmatized features that have been attributed to women's language—for example, particular vowel pronunciations or the development of euphemisms—that have since become standard, although as we have seen it is more likely for discussions of women's language to be used to reinforce presumed though undocumented gender differences. The result is the doubly cruel irony of double jeopardy. Women are accused of lexical conservatism and the inability to produce new vocabulary, yet at the same time their speech is criticized for containing an innovative use of words that men—real men, and women who want to be like them—would never use.

Women are reminded by men that their language is a nonstandard dialect, possibly of alien origin, and they are encouraged to develop a passion for correctness that involves both the rejection of what is supposed to be their natural feminine dialect and the adoption of a supposedly masculine standard English that would represent for women an alien tongue. The problem is compounded because it is based not on actual language production but on stereotype: it is difficult to find with much certainty either spoken or written dialect features—whether of pronunciation, voice quality, choice of word or idiom, syntax, or anything else—that can be safely labeled male or female independent of the social constraints that are placed upon the sexes.

Furthermore, the linguistic insecurity or self-hatred created by a situation in which one must trade a native dialect for an adopted one can lead any subordinated social group—for example, women, students, immigrants, and racial or religious minorities—either to hyper-correction, the creation of new and by definition nonstandard linguistic forms by those who are trying as hard as they can simply to be correct, or, in the opposite direction altogether, to silence, that most alien of tongues.

CHAPTER 6

Grammar and Gender

All Nouns the Male, or Female Gender have,
As Nature first to things the Sexes gave.
James Shirley

The most blatant attempts to connect linguistic form with stereotyped characteristics of the sexes are found not in the pseudobiblical theories of pronoun origin, or the far-fetched etymologies of words, not even in the impressionistic descriptions of the differences between the language of men and women, but in the study of the phenomenon of grammatical gender. This particular type of morphological variation in nouns, pronouns, adjectives, and articles is described in terms of the sexual categories masculine, feminine, and neuter, and this fact has colored the way commentators have looked at linguistic representations of reality.

In his essay *On the Origin of Language* ([1772] 1966), the philosopher Johann Gottfried Herder traces grammatical gender to a primitive animistic world view. According to Herder the first humans, in their attempt to make sense of the world and of their existence, personified the animals and plants, the inanimate earth, rocks, and water, and the natural and supernatural forces around them as women and men, as gods and goddesses working evil or good. Since everything in the universe was anthropomorphized, all the nouns in the first human language were assigned both gender and divinity, and according to Herder, "the oldest dictionary was thus a sounding pantheon, an assembly of both sexes" (133). In *A Course of Lectures on Oratory* (1777), Joseph Priestley accepts this animistic theory, adding that gender first occurs in the languages of the warmer and what he presumed were the more sexually active southern parts of Europe.

THE GENITALS OF SPEECH

In the previous chapters we saw how commentators on language felt compelled to interrelate language and supposed sexual characteristics. They go so far as to associate the origins of language with the sexual differentiation of the human species through the Genesis story of the creation of woman. It is no wonder that those who deal with grammar and gender are least able to escape the temptation of connecting language with sex. For example, Herder, equating grammatical gender with the human sex organs, sees gender as the direct linguistic representation of the sexual distinctions between males and females. He even identifies the category of gender as a mechanism for perpetuating these distinctions, increasing and multiplying them in a manner analogous to that of human sexual reproduction: "The attribution of sex through language [is] . . . an interest of mankind, and the genitals of speech are, as it were, the means of its propagation" ([1772] 1966, 134).

This association of grammatical gender with human generation was introduced as early as Priscian's sixth-century Latin grammar, and it was developed by medieval grammarians and accepted by their successors. Richard Johnson ([1706] 1969, 13) derives the word *gender* (whose original meaning 'kind, or sort,' had nothing to do with sex) from Latin *genus,* 'birth, species,' and from *gigno,* 'to beget,' a direct reference to the physical act of engendering. Even in English, which lost grammatical gender marking in its noun system, the need to personify inanimate nouns and to mark human agent nouns in terms of biological or referential gender remains strong. As Herder intimates, such categorization serves in part to *propagate* linguistic sex differentiation.

All in all, the history of gender has never been satisfactorily explained, and no attempt will be made here to remedy that situation. Instead, we will examine the various accounts of gender marking in English nouns and pronouns, and the discussions of the theory of grammatical gender in the Indo-European languages, in order to see how ideas about sex have been translated into ideas about language. Basically, the notions of grammar and gender fit the pattern we have encountered up to now: although women are considered responsible for language acquisition in infants, and the first words of babies are traditionally thought to refer to the nourishing mother and her breast, the masculine gender is treated both as primary in creation and order of importance, and as inclusive of the other genders, whereas the feminine, like Eve herself, is regarded as a less important, subsequent and dependent linguistic development. For example, arguing that gender differentiation among words is a natural, perhaps a universal linguistic process, the anthropologist Karl R. Lepsius (1880) assumes that feminine nouns are created from masculine originals by means of a suffixing rib, as Eve was created from Adam, and that they must forever bear this suffix as the linguistic mark of Eve:

> Because it is man who creates language, we generally find that the differentiation of genders is achieved by separating out the feminine. If the masculine is also given a special form, that is a bonus. In the Hamitish languages the feminines are often doubly marked, with a suffix as well as a prefix or preceding article. [xxii–xxiii]

The fact that the linguistic masculine is occasionally marked does not represent for Lepsius an attempt to balance the system of gender representation, but an incidental redundancy that may safely be ignored.

The first theories of grammatical gender rely heavily on the connection between grammar and physiology, though early grammarians also recognize that gender may be a function of the form of a word rather than its meaning. Aristotle tells us in his *Rhetoric* that the first of the Greek grammarians to isolate the category of gender was Protagoras, who classified names as masculine, feminine, and inanimate according to the sex, or lack of sex, of their referents. Aristotle himself distinguished between natural gender, which was simply a reflection of sex, and grammatical gender, which was independent of reproductive physiology; he is the first grammarian to classify nouns according to their terminations rather than their referential meaning. However, some of the Greek grammarians allowed their notions of sex to direct their views of language. For example, Protagoras unsuccessfully urged changing the gender of *menis,* 'anger,' and *peleks,* 'helmet,' from feminine to masculine because he felt that they referred more appropriately to males (cited in Robins [1951] 1971, 15–16).

Early Latin grammars copied the Greek classification system, accepting the connection between gender and sex by adapting the Latin terms for man and woman to serve as gender classifications: Varro uses *virilis* for the 'man-ly' and *muliebris* for the 'woman-ly' gender. After the second century, these were replaced with the modern terms *masculinum* and *femininum*, although the nineteenth-century Saxonist William Barnes tried unsuccessfully to substitute for this latinate grammatical nomenclature what he considered to be more appropriately native-sounding gender names, *the stronger, or carl sex* and *the weaker, or quean sex* (Baron 1982a, 30).

GENDER AND GENERATION

In the *Institutionum Grammaticarum,* the standard European treatise on Latin grammar from the sixth to the eleventh century, Priscian treats grammatical gender much as Herder does some thirteen hundred years later, as a reflex of the natural division of the sexes and of their reproductive function: "As in nature, there are two principal genders, masculine and feminine. The genders may be said to come from that which is actually capable of generation, namely that which is masculine and feminine" (1855, 141).

The medieval grammarian Thomas of Erfurt, one of a group known as speculative grammarians, or Modists, because they analyzed language as a set of *modes* of signifying, connects the categories *masculine* and *feminine* with the supposed active and passive roles that males and females play in sexual reproduction and, by extension, in other activities as well. According to Thomas, whose *Grammatica Speculativa* ([ca. 1300] 1972) was the most widely reproduced and discussed Latin grammar in the Middle Ages, the masculine gender is the mode of signifying active agency and the feminine is the mode of signifying the patient, or passive acceptance of an act. Thomas elaborates the generative notion of gender introduced by Priscian, using an implicit metaphor for sexual intercourse and procreation. For Thomas the male is both the agent and the progenitor, *generans,* the actual and active creator of the homunculus which becomes the child, and the female, whose role in the reproductive process was not understood until much later, is nothing more than the passive recipient, *patiens,* the incubator and bearer of what is created solely by the male.

According to Thomas *vir,* 'man,' and *lapis,* 'stone,' are active in meaning, and therefore masculine, while *mulier,* 'woman,' and *petra,* 'rock,' are passive and feminine (59). The grammatical commentary of another Modist, Martin of Dacia, shows that the distinctions for *lapis* and *petra* are based on fanciful etymologies which purport to reflect the sex-linked relationships that pertain between feet and stones. Martin derives the masculine *lapis* from the active phrase *laedens pedem,* 'injuring the foot,' and the feminine *petra* from the passive *pede trita,* 'worn or trodden by the foot' (1961, 35–36). Other grammarians explain that *dies,* 'day,' may be construed as either masculine or feminine because the day either acts to expel the night, or passively allows the night to drive it away. However *nox,* 'night,' is always feminine because as we are told in Genesis, in the beginning everything was in darkness which is, after all, night, and this darkness passively suffered the movement of the stars and planets (Thurot [1869] 1964, 202–03).

The Modists' notions of active and passive also play a role in discussions of the metaphorical gender assignment of English nouns. In the introduction to his translation of Plato's *Cratylus* (1793), Thomas Taylor argues that the gender assigned to inanimate objects represents an essence in their nature that parallels human sexuality, and he demonstrates this by showing how rivers and marshes, and intellect and soul, behave just like human men and women in the act of intercourse:

> Those ancient founders of names did not rashly and without design denominate marshes of the female genus, but rivers of the male . . . but they characterized the former by the feminine genus, because like the soul they are certain receptacles; and called the latter by a masculine appellation, on account of their entering into and mingling themselves with the former. In like manner they assigned the masculine genus to intellect, and marked soul with a feminine appellation; because intellect diffuses its light upon soul, which, in consequence of receiving it from thence in her inmost penetralia, is most truly said to be filled and illuminated by intellect. [xix–xx]

GENDER IN ENGLISH

The vernacular grammars took their notions of gender directly from classical models. Some grammarians even tried to apply gender agreement rules to Modern English. For example, Daniel Duncan's *New English Grammar* ([1731] 1967) includes a rule requiring the English adjective to agree in gender with its noun, although Duncan recognizes that, unlike Latin, English adjectives are not marked for gender and cannot show such agreement; he also complains that the apparently random assignment of gender to Latin nouns "gives no little Trouble to the Learner to get Master of."

In some eighteenth-century grammars, however, more scientific notions of gender were beginning to appear, and a clear sense of the superiority of modern knowledge to ancient speculation makes itself felt. English grammarians favor the English system of natural gender for animate nouns and metaphorical gender for some inanimate or abstract nouns because it is more rational and flexible than the arbitrary grammatical gender of such languages as Latin or French. But with the celebration of natural gender comes a renewed association of linguistic gender with physiology. Benjamin Martin writes in his *Institutions of Language* (1748) that the inconsistencies of Greek and Latin grammatical gender arose because the ancients did not know that plants had sex or that animals could be sexless, and therefore erred in their attempts to assign natural gender to words. As James Beattie puts it in his *Theory of Language* ([1788] 1968), "the sexual arrangement of vegetables is a modern discovery, hinted at by Aristotle, but unknown to the authors of language" (141).

Furthermore, according to Beattie, all animates have sex, and therefore gender, "but the sex of all is not equally obvious, or equally worthy of attention." As a result, gender may be represented in two ways: sometimes the male is called by one word, the female by another (for example, *man, woman,* or *king, queen*), while at other times—presumably times when sex is less obvious or important—the feminine is derived from the masculine by suffixation, or as Beattie puts it, "the name of the male is altered only in the termination when applied to the female."

Propagating Gender

Despite a general tendency to restrict gender as far as possible to male and female animates, and the suggestion by a number of grammarians that neuter was not a gender at all, a few writers sought to proliferate gender categories. In his proposal for a universal language, *Logopandecteision* ([1656] 1970), Thomas Urquhart assigns gender to verbs as well as nouns and adds four new categories to the seven traditional genders of the Latin grammarians in order to distinguish gods from goddesses and male from female animals.

The Scottish editor and grammarian James Anderson (1792)

sought to extend the system of pronominal gender as well. Although he grumbles that "the doctrine of *genders* is indeed one of the most intricate, and . . . one of the most absurd, in grammar," Anderson presents his own complex and highly idiosyncratic theory of gender in a series of "Grammatical Disquisitions." Anderson rejects the notion that a simple grammar is a better one. He prefers a complex representation of linguistic categories, and would therefore like to see actual gender distinction in the first and second person pronouns, claiming that "such a variation might, if it had been practised, be the source of much elegance and refinement in language" (122). He proposes to extend the category of neuter from the third person to the first and second persons. Even though inanimates do not speak and are not usually spoken to, Anderson considers that such an extension would be useful for the expression of contempt.

A perfect language, according to Anderson, would have gender distinctions even in the plural, and he offers thirteen such distinctions, which he considers necessary for linguistic perfection. To the traditional masculine, feminine, and neuter Anderson would add the *indefinite* gender, "where the sex of the parties is either not known, or immaterial, and therefore not necessary to be known, or where it is wished to be concealed," and the *imperfect* gender, useful both in countries where eunuchism prevails and for purposes of insult. He would also refine the neuter category to include inanimates as well as "animals that have no sex at all, those whose sex is not apparent, and others still in which, though the sex be known, it is not at all considered" (195). And, finding the generic use of *he* inadequate because "the effect is confined to the *male,* which ought to include the *female,*" Anderson would create a true common-gender pronoun to represent such indefinites as *friend, servant,* and *neighbor.*

Anderson further proposes to remedy the defective plural by adding such categories as the *matrimonial gender,* for "males and females known to be such, though not meant to be separated"; the *masculine imperfect,* for "males only, part perfect, and part castrated, known and meant to be distinguished, but not separated"; the *feminine imperfect;* the *mixt imperfect;* the *masculine mixt,* to represent "males and inanimates conjoined"; the *feminine mixt;* the *united,* for masculines, feminines, and inanimates, conjoined; and the *universally indefinite,* which is to be used for "males, females, or inanimates, either separated or conjoined, where no distinction of gender was meant to be adverted to in any way. This is precisely the power of our present pronoun *they*" (198). Anderson has been considerate enough not to burden us with all the categories that have occurred to him—he writes, "some lesser distinctions are omitted to avoid the appearance of unnecessary refinement"—and he concludes that the creation of pronouns to represent all of his thirteen genders would give any language "a variety of phraseology, and a clear, precise, nervous perspicuity of expression with which we are as yet entirely unacquainted" (199).

Fortunately, most English grammar texts in the eighteenth and nineteenth centuries did not worry their readers too much when it came to gender. Few devoted more than one or two paragraphs, together with some illustrative lists, to the explanation of English nominal gender, and most books did not discuss pronoun gender to any great extent. The work of Lindley Murray serves as a good example. In his *English Grammar* ([1795] 1968), Murray, who was not concerned with illogicalities in languages with grammatical gender, says simply that "gender is the distinction of sex" and describes four principal methods of distinguishing *sex* in the English noun system:

> 1st, By different words; as, man, woman; boy, girl; son, daughter; gander, goose; cock, hen.
> 2d, By a difference of termination; as, duke, duchess; count, countess; poet, poetess; hero, heroine; actor, actress; executor, executrix.
> 3d, By adding an adjective or pronoun to the substantive; as, a male child, a female child; a he-goat, a she-goat; a he-ass, a she-ass.
> 4th, By prefixing another substantive to the word; as, a cock-sparrow, a hen-sparrow; a man-servant, a maid-servant. [25]

THE MOST WORTHY GENDER

Grammarians have treated the masculine gender as primary in order of creation and in importance, both in the natural world and in the sentence. Eighteenth- and nineteenth-century English grammars set forth the doctrine of the worthiness of the genders, borrowed from Latin, to justify the use of masculine nouns and pronouns to stand for both the sexes. Even today, many linguists assume that the masculine is the normal, or unmarked, gender and that all English nouns are masculine unless specially marked.

In Latin, adjectives agree with nouns in gender, number, and case. Latin grammars introduce the notion of gender worthiness in order to deal with situations in which an adjective must agree with a coordinate noun phrase containing nouns whose genders differ. William Lily ([1567] 1945) gives this example: *Rex & Regina beati,* 'The King and the Queen are blessed,' to show that the adjective *beati,* which is masculine plural, agrees in number with the pair of nouns, *rex* and *regina,* and in gender with the masculine *rex,* because "the Masculine gendre is more worthy then the Feminine, and the Feminine more worthy then the Neuter" (C v recto). Some English grammarians attempt to apply the Latin adjective agreement rule directly to English:

> Where the substantive or substantives include different genders, the most worthy is to be taken, the masculin before the feminin, the feminin before the neuter; as *both my parents, father and mother, are kind,* the Adjective *kind,* though it varies not it self, let the gender be what it will, yet ought to be understood of the masculin; and, if it was to be expressed in a language, where the ending is varied, the ending would be masculin. [Maittaire 1712, 40]

Robert Lowth, in his *Short Introduction to English Grammar* (1762), is perhaps the first writer to point out that gender agreement in English occurs not between adjective and noun but in the pronoun system, specifically the third person pronoun, "which must agree . . . with the Noun for which it stands" (30). The doctrine of worthiness is therefore transferred from adjective–noun concord, where gender in the adjective is an accidental category, to questions of agreement between the pronoun and its antecedent, where gender is intrinsic to both noun and pronoun. The concept of worthiness is no longer a rule of thumb to resolve the syntactic puzzle of what to do when an adjective refers to nouns of differing genders, but a reflection of a natural order that places man at the head of creation, with woman in a subordinate, subservient, and frequently invisible second place.

In his encyclopedic *Grammar of English Grammars* ([1851] 1880), the nineteenth-century Quaker grammarian Goold Brown carries the notion of grammatical masculine supremacy to an absurd extreme. Although Lindley Murray ([1795] 1968) considers the plural *parents* as a common-gender noun, expressing both the masculine and feminine, and the singular *parent* (if the particular parent is not specified) as a noun of the masculine or the feminine gender, Brown finds *parents* always to be masculine, "for the gender of a word is a property indivisible, and that which refers to the male sex, always takes the lead in such cases" (255). Brown goes on to illustrate his claim using a sentence involving all three genders:

> If one say, "Joseph took *the young child and his mother* by night, and fled with *them* into Egypt," the pronoun *them* will be masculine; but let *"his"* be changed to *its,* and the plural pronoun that follows, will be feminine. For the feminine gender takes precedence of the neuter, but not of the masculine. [255]

According to Brown, although an individual parent may be a woman, *parents* are always men.

If the masculine gender is more worthy for sublunary nouns, it therefore follows, according to the grammarians, that supernatural deities must also be grammatically masculine. James Harris writes in *Hermes* ([1751] 1765) that God is "in all languages *Masculine,* in as much as the masculine Sex is the superior and more excellent; and as He is the Creator of all, the Father of Gods and Men" (50). And James Beattie ([1788] 1968) considers any attempt to overthrow the generic masculine, to upset this natural order of the sexes in gods or grammar, to be not just heterodox but pagan:

> Beings superiour to man, though we conceive them to be of no sex, are spoken of as masculine in most of the modern tongues of Europe, on account of their dignity; the male being, according to our ideas, the nobler sex. But idolatrous nations acknowledge both male and female deities; and some of them have given even to the Supreme Being a name of the feminine gender. [137]

Silencing Women

Elizabeth Sklar (1983, 357) notes that the term *customary gender* or one of its synonyms has replaced *most worthy gender* in the vocabularies of more recent grammarians and usage commentators, though there has been little change either in the basic presentation of the rule of gender agreement or in the intent to ignore the feminine gender and silence the female sex. George O. Curme, in his grammar of English (1931), says that the masculine pronoun is *usually* employed with nouns of indefinite gender, and that the more precise *he or she* is not common because "the idea of the oneness of man and woman is present to our feeling" (552). Fowler's *Modern English Usage* (1965) speaks of the "*convention* (statutory in the interpretation of documents) that where the matter of sex is not conspicuous or important the masculine form shall be allowed to represent a person instead of a man" (404). And Wilson Follett writes in *Modern American Usage* (1966) that, "by a long-standing *convention* the masculine pronouns serve to denote both sexes after a genderless word" (68). Of course the most prescriptive language commentators do not rely either on custom or worthiness. They regard the use of the masculine as inevitable and incontrovertible, and feel no need to explain the absence of the feminine. Thus Eric Partridge proclaims, "The pronoun following [the indefinites *anyone, anybody, nobody, somebody*] is *he* or *him* or *his* or *himself*, not *they* or *theirs* or *their own* ([1947] 1974, 40). Even the dispassionate descriptive grammarian may find himself—the pronoun is used advisedly—ignoring the gender question to concentrate on the more controversial problem of number agreement between a pronoun and its indefinite antecedent. Unlike Partridge, Quirk et al. admit the plural *they* as well as the masculine singular *he* as acceptable pronouns for *someone, everyone,* and *anyone,* but are silent on the fate of the missing feminine singular *she* (1972, 219).

The modern paraphrases of the doctrine of worthiness are but thin masks for the underlying assumption of male superiority in life as well as language; despite the attempts of the wary language commentators to include women under masculine terms, the effect is to render women both invisible and silent. Language reformers have attempted for the past two hundred years or more to revise the generic masculine into a system that is more balanced with respect to gender. The history of these attempts merits its own discussion, and will be sketched in chapters nine and ten below. But, though questions of gender neutrality have surfaced at the present time as a primary linguistic concern, the grammarians who gave us the doctrine of worthiness considered that the most important, or at least the most interesting, aspect of English gender lay not in agreement, which seemed fairly cut and dried to them, but in the personification of abstract and inanimate nouns.

METAPHORICAL GENDER

In English, gender is often extended from humans to animals and inanimates by means of personification, the endowment of nonhumans with human features and behavior. The dominant metaphor in such extension has been one of human sexual behavior that is physiologically descriptive and that reflects the theory of the worthiness of the genders. Commentators on personification regard the masculine gender as more important than the feminine; thus, when the feminine occurs with great frequency, as it does for example in the nonliterary written and spoken English of American males, theorists feel compelled to come up with an explanation of this apparent violation of the natural order of things.

The grammarian James Harris ([1751] 1765) views the personification of inanimates as the act of recognizing in them those traits which most closely parallel the stereotypical notions of male and female physical characteristics and sexual behavior. According to Harris, males are active and physically strong, and their sexual function involves inpregnation or any analogous act of giving:

> We may conceive such Substantives to have been considered, as Masculine, which were 'conspicuous for the Attributes of imparting or communicating; or which were by nature active, strong, and efficacious, and that indiscriminately whether to good or to ill; which had claim to Eminence, either laudable or otherwise.' [44]

Females, on the other hand, are passive and physically attractive, and their sexual function involves an act of receiving, of being impregnated and bearing fruit:

> The Feminine on the contrary were 'such, as were conspicuous for the Attributes either of receiving, or containing, or of producing and bringing forth; or which had more of the passive in their nature, than of the active; or which were peculiarly beautiful and amiable; or which had respect to such Excesses, as were rather Feminine than Masculine.' [45]

Harris personifies the sun and the moon as a stereotypical human couple, the female existing not as an independent creature but as a passive reflection of the male. The sun is regarded as masculine, "from communicating Light, which was native and original, as well as from the vigorous warmth and the efficacy of his Rays; the Moon . . . as *Feminine,* from being the Receptacle only of another's Light, and from shining with Rays more delicate and soft" (45). The heavens are masculine because they are the source of the rain that impregnates the earth, which in turn is feminine in all languages "from being the grand *Receiver,* the grand *Container,* but above all from being the *Mother* . . . of every sublunary Substance" (46–47). Ships are feminine because they are receivers and containers; cities are feminine because they contain, mother, and nurse their inhabitants. One might think, Harris says, that the ocean would be feminine, because it receives rivers and is the container and "productress of so many Vegetables and Animals," but in fact "its *deep Voice* and *boisterous Nature*" make it masculine (49–50).

Time is masculine, as is death, because of its "irresistible Power." According to Harris, the idea of a female death would be ridiculous. *Virtue* and its like are feminine, "perhaps from their Beauty and amiable Appearance." *Vice* is also classed as feminine, although it is the opposite of virtue. Harris's notions of female behavior lead him to state that "the Fancies, Caprices, and fickle Changes of Fortune . . . make a very natural *Female,*" and he explains that the *Furies* were personified as women by the ancients because "female Passions of all kinds were considered as susceptible of greater excess, than male Passions" (56–57).

While Harris's view of gender was accepted for well over a century, a few grammarians insisted that chance and idiosyncrasy played as great a role in metaphorical gender as did sex stereotyping. James Beattie ([1788] 1968) challenges the notion that masculine things are necessarily powerful, and feminine ones receptive. Pointing to death and the sun as undoubtedly strong forces, he notes that while Greek *thanatos,* 'death,' is masculine, Latin *mors* is feminine, as are its French, Spanish, and Italian offshoots. Furthermore, Beattie reminds his readers that the sun, though masculine in Latin, is feminine in the northern languages, whereas the feminine Latin moon is masculine in German (138–39). More recently, Mario Pei (1949) has sought to explain this north–south reversal of celestial gender assignments "as due to the sun's strength in southern lands and its weakness in the north, and to the gentleness of the southern moon as contrasted with the icy moon of cold northern nights" (122).

Beattie considers a number of other variable gender personifications: Catullus and Ovid represent the deep-voiced, boisterous, masculine sea of Harris as feminine; ships, which are natural containers, are feminine in Greek, Latin, and English, yet masculine in French. *Love* may be feminine, as is its goddess, Venus, yet *Amor* and *Cupid* are male. And Phoebus is the charioteer of the sun, but Beattie hazards a guess that "no doubt the Saxons would have put a woman in that role" (140–41). He concludes that inanimates cannot be easily pigeonholed:

> Allegories and the idols of heathens, appear in so many different lights we *cannot* predict their gender assignment, which varies from country to country. There are both gods and goddesses of war. Strength, one would think, must be male and therefore Hercules is a man; yet Necessity, who must be even stronger, is personified by Horace as female for no other reason, that I can guess, but because her name in Latin happens to have a feminine termination. [141]

Taking a stronger position, William S. Cardell (1825) rejects any personification of inanimates as a deviation from truth and nature which can only lead to inconsistency:

> If *virtue* is *feminine* from its *beauty,* why were all the *crimes* of *Babylon* personified in the character of a *woman?* why are *vice, slander,* and deceitful *fortune* also *feminine;* and why have mortals been so much afflicted by *sorceresses, witches,* and midnight *hags?* [49–50]

Despite such judicious objections, commentators, supported by a long tradition of assigning such human traits as curiosity, vanity, and lust to animals, continue to insist that personifications reflect particular sexual qualities. Alexander Crombie ([1802] 1830) classifies the *horse* as masculine because of its usefulness and its generous nature, while the *hare* is feminine because of its timidity. The elephant is masculine because of its great strength and size, as well as its sagacity, fortitude, and docility, and the *cat,* Crombie notes without comment, is female, while the *dog* is male (40–41). Simon Kerl (1861) is more general in his claim that *he* is "preferred for what is large, bold, or pre-eminent; *she,* for what is effeminate or dependent; and *it,* for what is small, unimportant, or imperfectly known" (104).

Sex Objects

Lorenz Morsbach, in *Grammatisches und Psychologisches Geschlecht im Englische* (1913), adds a modern touch of psychology to support the traditional view of commentators like Harris: he finds that it is "a psychologically natural thing to assign the feminine gender to what is mild, gentle, and weak, and the masculine to all that is violent and forceful. . . . The needle is made feminine, the sword, masculine" (cited in Svartengren 1927, 108). But in other recent treatments, the feminization of inanimates is held to be an emotional phenomenon rather than an attempt at gender-stereotyped personification. The emotion in question, however, is usually assumed to be the desire of the male for the female, and while the male is depicted by the grammarians as a creator or user, the female is relegated to the role of tool or object.

The desires and activities of women, including their use of personification, do not seem to interest the commentators. For example, Eduard Maetzner (1874), commenting on the nonliterary personification of inanimates by English speakers, who for Maetzner are apparently all men, writes: "The people apprehend inanimate things which they handle, and with which they are familiar as objects of their predilection, as feminine beings, for instance, the miller his mill" (1:256). Henry Sweet ([1891] 1931) agrees that in ordinary language the tradesman, who is invariably represented as a male, employs a conjugal metaphor in feminizing the objects with which he works, for example *ship, boat, balloon,* and *steam-engine:* "This personification seems to have arisen from a fanciful comparison with *wife*" (2:43). Drawing from an extensive list of examples collected from American popular fiction—written chiefly by men—in which such inanimates as warts, guns, screws, houses, and teeth are personified as feminine by male narrators and characters, T. Hilding Svartengren (1927) concludes that the use of the feminine pronoun for inanimates is not so much a personification as a process that reduces woman's role from the already subservient wife and companion to one of objet trouvé: "It is a kind of sublimated and attenuated sexuality, which is not confined only to what is womanlike, but open to anything that takes a man's fancy" (84). Charles Ferguson adds that "*she* is a normal pronominalization for an object implicitly or explicitly being compared as to how well it works, or in contexts involving attitudes about fixing or operating upon objects" (cited in N. Baron 1971, 115).

The doctrine of worthiness submerged and silenced the feminine, and Harris's theory of personification stressed the amiable, passive, and dependent nature of the womanly. Twentieth-century studies that treat feminized inanimates—called by Svartengren the "emotional she"—as sublimated male sex objects do little to improve on the status of the feminine in earlier theories. Gösta Langenfelt (1951) denies women any linguistic role when he claims that the source of this feminization is merely a grammatical mistake of Gaelic- and French-speaking immigrants who often used *she* incorrectly for *he* or *it* when speaking English (95).

Returning once again to the doctrine of the worthiness of the genders, though clothing it in the respectability of linguistic terminology, André Joly (1975) claims that "the feminine is literally seen to be 'dominated' by the masculine, just as the species is subordinated to the genus" (257). Although in the animal kingdom the human tradition of masculine domination is often reversed, Joly defines males as major powers, and so any animal, regardless of size, is treated as masculine when it is "presented as an active power and a possible danger to the speaker," while the feminine pronoun, representative of minor power, is employed when the animal "is regarded as a potential prey, a power that has to be destroyed—for sport or food—, hence a dominated power. More generally, *she* will be said of any animal, big or small, that is in some way subordinated to the speaker" (271–72). Since Joly does not specify the sex of the speaker, we may assume he is *not* discussing the language of women.

For Joly, the masculine is the normal state for a noun that exhibits sex. Animates, he tells us, are masculine unless otherwise marked. If the neuter pronoun *it* is not used to refer to an animal, the speaker must choose "the animate referring pronoun that neutralizes the opposition between masculine and feminine: this pronoun is *he*" (276). In other words, the masculine is superior to the feminine.

THEORIES OF GENDER

The earlier attempts to explain the origins of linguistic gender—and some of the more recent ones as well—are based on distinctions of physiological sex that somehow become represented in language; most of these presuppose the separation of the feminine out of the masculine, both mythologically and grammatically. In the *Grammaire générale et raisonnée* ([1660] 1969), commonly known as the *Port-Royal Grammar*, Arnauld and Lancelot attribute the rise of gender to the preexisting division of human nouns into the categories male and female, a division which began with words for men and women but was extended to include words indicating the function or office that each sex could hold. For example, Latin *rex,* 'king,' *judex,* 'judge,' and *philosophus,* 'philosopher,' were masculine because the word *man* was understood when each was mentioned, while *woman* was understood for *mater,* 'mother,' *uxor,* 'wife,' and *regina,* 'queen.' But according to the Port-Royal grammarians, true linguistic gender arises only with the requirement of concord, or agreement between a noun and its adjective. The motivation for this requirement is somewhat vague, yet many subsequent theorists agree that gender does not exist within nouns themselves as an isolated word class, but is a function of some kind of concord between a noun and another word, whether adjective, pronoun, or article. What Arnauld and Lancelot say is, "Noting that humans are basically distinguished by sex, people decided to vary adjectives, giving them different endings when they applied to men or women ... and they called these masculine and feminine genders" (31).

For Samuel Ramsey ([1892] 1968), gender is more closely tied to Genesis: the feminine term is separated from the masculine, usually by derivation, and is marked by the addition of a suffix. Ramsey claims that in primitive times "an additional vowel sound was often added to female names, and in some way became attached to other words used in speaking of [women]" (229). Again, the motivation for the first gender distinctions is not spelled out, but it is clear that for Ramsey gender has become a precarious category in the grammar of Modern English, and that of the three genders it is the masculine which was created first and which will outlast the newer feminine and neuter. Ramsey reminds his readers that in English, gender exists only in the pronoun system, and he suggests that even there it is not entirely necessary: "If two little words and their variant forms—five monosyllables in all—*she, her, hers, it, its*—were dropped, gender would be thereby wiped from the language" (228). In Ramsey's opinion the

106

masculine pronouns are sufficient for our needs; Adam needs no linguistic helpmeet.

More recently, the French linguist Antoine Meillet (1948) expresses essentially the same sentiment. Meillet comments that the Indo-European masculine is the more inclusive gender, serving as generic and, in the case of an adjective agreeing with two nouns, one masculine, one feminine, as the more worthy. The feminine, in contrast, is more limited in its range and importance, being *only* a variant [*une différenciation*] of the masculine that is derived by means of the addition of a suffix, either -*a*- or -*ya*- (219). Thus the grammatical feminine initially carries the meaning 'female,' and this notion is then extended to nonliving things which are considered as animate: the earth (f.) in contrast to the heavens (m.), the tree (f.) as opposed to its fruit (n.). An active organ is animate: the *hand,* which receives, is feminine, in opposition to the masculine *foot,* though Meillet does not account for the fact that hands can give as well as receive. Nor does he explain why *foot* is masculine, though this notion has been a grammatical commonplace for some time. The Modists imagined the foot to be active when it wears down a stone, and Jakob Grimm regards the hand as feminine because, like a woman, it is smaller and daintier, while the foot is masculine because, like a man, it is larger and stronger (cited in Brugmann 1897, 7–8).

GENDER IN INDO-EUROPEAN

In Indo-European languages, gender does not originate in a reflection of natural sex distinctions. Instead, as Istvan Fodor (1959) sees it, the system of assonance-based concord followed the division of nouns into animate and inanimate types, or genders, and the differentiation of nominative and accusative noun forms (196). The third Indo-European gender division does reflect sexual difference, however: it arose through the analogical force of the suffix of nouns ending in -*a,* which eventually became associated with the referential feminine. Once in place, grammatical gender can acquire secondary, though important, functions: it can express, if imperfectly, the distinctions of natural gender; it can become productive as well, giving rise to new sex-specific words; and it can be used for personification in literature. But gender is also a fragile category: not only can its functions change, it can disappear entirely from a language (206–13). In this relatively enlightened view, the feminine is a subset not of the masculine but of the more general category *animate,* with the implication that the masculine cannot exist until the feminine has been created. However, most theorists insist that the origins of gender mirror the formation of Eve from Adam's rib.

J. Madvig, who like Lepsius believed that the first language was framed exclusively by men, and who generally opposed sound symbolism (the idea that sounds reflect particular meanings), argues that the Indo-European -*a* stems are feminine in part because their final vowel *symbolizes* the female, who, like the sound that represents her, is open, soft, and lingering (see Jespersen 1894, 59–60). And the Norwegian philologist A. Torp "fancies" that the Indo-European feminine nouns derive from what he "supposes" to be a feminine pronoun, -*a,* that was attached directly to the masculine stems to feminize them (Jespersen 1894, 62–63). Antoine Meillet's analysis is almost identical to Fodor's, with one important difference. According to Meillet, after the initial separation of animates from inanimates, the second division of the animate nouns involves the birth of the feminine from the masculine; although he does not specifically say so, this creation parallels that of Eve in Genesis: "Most of the feminine forms originated in masculine forms. Thus out of the masculine -*ont-/-nt-* of the present participle came the -*nti/-ntja* form" (Fodor 1959, 19–21).

The anthropologist Sir James Frazer (1900) offers the opinion, not favored by other speculators, that linguistic gender may originally have been subjective, "indicative only of the sex of the speaker, and not at all intended to imply, as it was afterwards understood to imply, any sex in the thing spoken of" (89). According to Frazer, a man might have said *equus* for 'horse,' a woman *equa.* Men might have called a woman *feminus,* but since women called themselves *femina,* that form survived, and its gender reference eventually changed from subjective to objective, denoting the sex of the thing spoken of. In Frazer's account, unlikely as it is, the masculine and feminine genders are at least linguistically coordinate structures, and women are allowed to define themselves.

Which theory of gender is ultimately correct is not a question to be resolved here. What is important is that although linguistic gender may originally have had very little to do with sex, three nominal categories did arise in the Indo-European languages, and they were assigned names that do reflect natural gender by Greek grammarians who saw language as a transcription of life. The assignment of these names, masculine, feminine, and neuter, calls up the sexual division of the natural world. In particular it has called up in the minds of language speculators our too-often unquestioned assumptions about the qualities of masculinity and femininity, and this in turn has greatly influenced the study of linguistic gender. Such influence extends not just to the study of natural languages, but to the creation of artificial ones as well, which, though they claim to be based on logic, treat the feminine gender as one that is derived from and dominated by the masculine. The study of linguistic gender invariably calls up the metaphor of Eve and the metaphor of sex. As the American grammarian Josephine Turck Baker put it in her defense of the generic masculine in the first issue of her journal *Correct English* (1899), "The 'masculine' embraces the 'feminine' even in grammar" (20).

NATURAL VS. GRAMMATICAL GENDER

Many English linguists, claiming objectivity, have seen the loss of grammatical gender by their language during the Middle Ages as an improvement, a step forward in the development of speech. For them, loss of gender simplifies grammar, making English easier to learn for native and foreigner alike than a language such as French, where all nouns, animate or not, are masculine or feminine, or German, where they are masculine, feminine, or neuter. In addition, so-called natural gender languages like English permit the metaphorical assignment of gender to such words as *sun, moon, earth, river,* even *English* itself, in order to achieve a stylistic effect. According to Robert Lowth (1762), the inability to personify reduces the poetic capacity of a language: in Greek, Latin, French, Italian, and German, "in which Hill, Heaven, Cloud, Religion, are constantly Masculine, or Feminine, or Neuter, respectively, you make the images obscure and doubtful, and in proportion diminish their beauty" (30n).

A more objective look at language use reveals that gender in English is not entirely natural, and that gender in such languages as Latin, French, and German is not entirely grammatical. Richard Johnson's Latin grammar of 1706 contains a long list of nouns whose gender is disputed by classical authors, and grammatical gender in modern languages may be equally variable. L. C. Harmer (1954) has pointed out a number of inconsistencies in French gender, and Marguerite Durand (1936) has observed a weakening of gender markers in spoken French. It has long been known that Old English, which possessed a system of grammatical gender, also allowed natural gender concord between animate nouns and pronouns. An override mechanism may exist in other languages as well; according to E. Moravcsik, "every language having grammatical gender may optionally pronominalize according to natural gender" (N. Baron 1971, 115).

Although gender in English is now primarily natural, the rule of the generic masculine shows that nonreferential gender still exists. Many authorities insist that an agreeing pronoun be masculine when the gender of an animate noun is indeterminate, or even when the referent of the noun may be feminine. Likewise, the word *man* and its numerous compounds (*mailman, policeman,* and so forth) are often regarded as common-gender nouns despite their overt masculine reference. As a result, in sentences like *Everyone loves his mother* and *The chairman adjourned the meeting,* the masculine pronoun or noun is forced to refer "unnaturally" to a person who may be male or female, with the result that many feminine nouns, together with their female referents, are rendered invisible.

Just as English gender is not entirely natural, the metaphorical assignment of gender in English is not entirely flexible. As early as 1712 Michael Maittaire observes that the personifications of the usually neuter inanimate nouns of English are influenced by the languages from which we borrow our ideas: *sea* and *sword* are treated as masculine, *city, ship,* and *tree* as feminine, not because we see them as reflecting the characteristics of one sex or the other but because these are the genders assigned to them in Latin, Greek, or French. Furthermore, the literary personification of inanimates in English is bound by poetic convention. James Beattie ([1788] 1968) argues that in English we cannot reverse personifications that have been fixed by custom: we cannot say of the sun, *she is set,* or of the moon, *he is changed* (143). Paul Erades (1956) goes so far as to argue that *he* and *she* have become so vague that they may be used to refer to nouns of any gender or of no gender at all. In "Deviation in English Gender" (1973), Dell Marcoux finds some evidence to indicate that English speakers do not always assign pronoun gender according to the natural gender of an antecedent noun or according to traditional patterns of personification, and dialect evidence from Britain suggests that the use of an undifferentiated personal pronoun such as *a* or *un* is still to be found among certain groups of speakers (see below, chapter ten).

Another factor that complicates the English natural gender system still further is the frequent sex-marking of English human nouns through the addition of feminine suffixes such as *-ess, -ette,* and *-ine,* or through the creation of sex-specific phrases such as *lady doctor* and *male prostitute.* Since this marking involves women more often than men, it has led to the charge that English is a sexually biased tongue which singles women out, making them as a rule invisible through the use of the generic masculine, yet sometimes forcing visibility on them through such as words as *authoress, suffragette,* and *chorine* in order to belittle or repress them. The claim has been made that in languages with grammatical gender, such specific sex-marking is more limited, and sex stereotyping is less likely to occur, because speakers of these languages are used to a linguistic system in which gender has no direct connection with sex. For example, Casey Miller and Kate Swift (1977) contend, "For people who speak languages in which the assignment of gender is frequently unrelated to sex, the impact is much less sexist than are the blatant generic uses of *man* and *he* in English" (41). But such a claim can be disputed, for as we have seen, the argument that the grammatical gender of nouns both reveals and limits the natural abilities of men and women has been put forth all too often. The French satirist Sylvain Maréchal (1801) was not entirely serious in his claim that a woman may not be an *auteur* without renouncing her sex because that word is a masculine noun (37). However, some eighteenth- and nineteenth-century English grammarians asserted that the *-or* suffix marked the English noun *author* as masculine, so that the feminine-suffixed form *authoress* was required when referring to women writers. Taking this linguistic absurdity even further, Wilhelm H. Riehl claims to prove in *Die Familie* (1882) that a woman's place is in the home, not in the world of affairs, because the German word for *state* is masculine and the word for *family* is feminine. In the next chapter we will examine the various ways in which women's words are marked in English and the attitudes that have arisen in response to such marking.

CHAPTER 7

Marked Women

She shall be called man-ess,
because she was taken out of man.
Augustin Calmet

Whether or not grammatical gender in Indo-European originated in a birth, or separation, of the feminine from the masculine, one major function of referential gender in Modern English is the marking of feminine nouns as derivatives of either masculine or common-gender nouns. The marking of nouns as referentially masculine, common enough in Old English, now occurs only in cases where role stereotyping is blatantly violated, for example, in the nineteenth-century terms *man milliner* and *man-midwife* and the more recent *male model* and *househusband*. While gender markers frequently disappear from English words, feminine markers are far more likely to be retained than are their masculine equivalents. Also, feminine English nouns tend to acquire negative connotations at a much faster rate than masculine or neuter ones, creating semantic imbalances in originally parallel masculine/feminine gender pairs like *fox, vixen* and *governor, governess*. Efforts on the part of feminists and usage critics to eliminate feminine nouns like *authoress* in favor of unmarked equivalents on the grounds that the marked terms are demeaning have been only partially successful. It is exceedingly difficult to remove the mark of Eve from women's words.

MARKING REFERENTIAL GENDER

There are two principal ways of marking the referential gender of English nouns: visibly, by means of compounding or suffixation, and invisibly, by the very meaning of the word, for example, *mother/father, boy/girl,* and *stallion/mare,* words with unrelated roots that belong to one gender or the other not because of their form, but because of their inherent though morphologically invisible meaning.

Compounds may be formed by using the personal pronouns, for example *he-lion* and *she-ass,* as well as by prepositive sex-specific nouns, as in *gentleman cow* (a euphemism for the taboo *bull*) and *girl child*. Personal names are also used in sex-specific compounding—usually but not always in reference to animals: *billy-goat, nanny-goat, tomcat,* and *jackass*. In some cases, the prefix may be used to reverse the implied sex of the noun, for example, *tomboy, male nurse, lady doctor. Tomboy,* referring originally to a high-spirited male, was used for both sexes, then exclusively for girls. The absence of *female nurse* and *man doctor* indicates that the apparently common-gender *nurse* and *doctor* are taken to be sex-specific by speakers of English.

Many compound terms, particularly in earlier forms of English, are used simply for the purposes of gender differentiation: for example, *hyse-child, knave-child, knave-gerlys* (*girl* being originally sex-neutral), and *knight-child* are used for boy children, and *wifchild, maidechild,* and *women-children* for girls. Two sixteenth-century citations from the *Oxford English Dictionary* (*OED*) also serve to illustrate the early parallel treatment of males and females: *he sayntes* is paired with *she sayntes* (1537) and a *Hee Foyst,* or 'male pickpocket,' is the partner in crime of a *Shee Foyst* (1592).

Despite such parallels, many of the *he-* and *she-* human compounds have acquired a negative—the *OED* labels it contemptuous—connotation, perhaps because they are frequently used to indicate that a sex stereotype has been violated. More often we find *she-* or some other preposed feminine (*lady, woman, female, girl, maid*) applied to a noun which usually denotes a male: *she Apostle, she-David, she Mercury, she-Macchiavel, she-preacher, she bishop, she pope, she captain,* even *she-Priapus* and *she-man. She* may form part of an unflattering attributive compound meaning 'woman' (*she handfull, she-baggage, she-malady*) or it may single out something as belonging to women, for example, the pejorative *she-poetry. She* may also indicate inferior quality (for example, of timber: *shee-beech, she-pine*), and it is used of men to indicate effeminacy or weakness: *she-king, she-he*. Although there are far fewer examples, *he-* parallels *she-* in its distribution. It too has become pejorative in reference to humans, with the possible exception of *he-man,* and it may indicate inappropriate sex role behavior, as in *he-*

frump and _he-whore_. According to the _OED, he-she_ can denote both a masculine woman and an effeminate man.

Like _she-, lady_ serves in attributive compounds to indicate women in roles thought to be unusual if not unfortunate: _lady-actor, lady ambassador, lady-bullfighter, lady-citizen, lady-critic, lady-doctor, lady farmer, lady president, lady clerk, lady secretary, lady typewriter_ (these last three coined at a time when men customarily performed such office tasks as typing and filing), and _lady tyrant. Girl_ also appears in these compounds: _girl clerk, girl graduate, girl miser, girl mute, girl pilgrim, girl typewriter, girl warrior, girl water carrier,_ and _girl worker. Woman, lady,_ and _girl_ in addition appear as the second element in compounds indicating job classification or function (_saleswoman, saleslady, salesgirl_). These employment terms will be discussed in chapter nine.

Female, in a sense which the _OED_ labels obsolete, is used in attributive compounds to indicate that which is womanish, effeminate, or weak: _female drudgery, female fear, female discord._ In addition it marks simplicity, inferiority, or weakness (_female truth, a female improvement_), and in reference to precious stones it denotes a pale or otherwise poor color. On the other hand, _male_ as an attributive indicates superiority, strength, or greatness. Like _female,_ it may be used cross-sexually, though it does not occur as frequently: _male aunt, male bawd_ ('pander'), _male hustler, male whore,_ and _male widowhood_ ('the state of being a widower').

In twentieth-century American slang (generally speaking, only the slang of males has been recorded), the related prefix _fem-_ (or _femme,_ which occurs unmodified as a negative synonym for 'woman') is relatively productive. We find it used in unflattering references to women in traditionally male roles: _femarines,_ 'women marines'; _femme newsie,_ 'woman newspaper vendor'; _fempire_ (_fem- + vampire_), 'flirtatious young woman'; _femme students;_ and _femme sem_ (from _female seminary_), 'women's college.' The entertainment business gives us _juve femme,_ 'female juvenile actor,' and _femcee,_ a blend of _female_ and _emcee._ Lately we find variations on the theme _fem lib,_ a contemptuous reference to the women's liberation movement.

By and large, human gender-specific compounds are used in Modern English to mark women, and many of these supply a negative connotation. Some, such as the gender pair _the weaker sex/the stronger_

114

sex, distinctly label women as inferior to men; others intimate this sexual disparity instead: women are called *the fair* or *gentler sex;* men, *the superior sex* (imputing inferior status to women, though the correlative phrase *the inferior sex* does not seem to occur). In some cases double gender marking occurs, perhaps to underline the inappropriateness or rarity of the feminine noun, or to emphasize its negativity. We find the double-feminines *lady patroness, womman synneresse* ('woman sinner'), and *womman strumpet.* Some feminine compounds exist alongside synonymous suffixed forms. As a suffixed form like *actress* becomes familiar, the force of its marking is diminished; the coining of *she-actor, actoress* or *actorine* may stress the femininity of the noun, a further indication of the continued need to mark the feminine noun as unusual or aberrant.

The most popular method of gender differentiation in Modern English involves the use of suffixes. In the vast majority of cases feminine suffixes—all of them borrowed from other languages because the native English gender suffixes were either lost or neutralized—are added to masculine or common-gender nouns, producing such forms as *duchess, coquette, executrix, heroine, comedienne, chanteuse,* and *ballerina.* As with compounding, the marking provided by the suffixes often goes beyond the simple recording of gender; the pejorative connotations that have attached themselves to feminine nouns form the basis for the debates over the past 150 years as to the appropriateness of the continued use of these words.

For aristocratic titles such as *duke/duchess* and *count/countess,* the feminine term essentially balances the masculine. But in other cases, there is a definite imbalance between the male and female members of the pair. Although *governor* and *governess* are used through the nineteenth century as a balanced pair with the meaning 'ruler, monarch,' in the sixteenth century they both developed the additional meaning 'teacher.' Only *governess* retained this sense past the 1700s, and it has since widened to cover women charged with the general care of young children. In the late seventeenth century the word acquired the additional, dependent sense, 'wife of the governor.' Today the masculine and feminine terms are so far apart in meaning that they are no longer a gender pair in anything but form.

In effect, the act of suffixation serves not to create a balanced gender pair but an unbalanced one, since it implies the derivation of one of the terms from the other. Although the masculine is occasionally the marked term, most often it is the feminine which receives the suffix. In some cases there is no gender pair because no masculine equivalent exists: English has borrowed *ballerina* from the Italian and *chanteuse* from the French, but we eschew the masculine *ballerino,* and *chanter,* our equivalent of the French masculine *chanteur,* is not our usual word for a male singer. However, in most instances the use of the feminine suffix implies that the feminine noun derives from the masculine and that it is of secondary or inferior status. Most of the native English suffixes do not involve this type of lopsided derivation, but it is always evident in their replacements, the borrowed form *-ess,* which was the most productive feminine suffix from the fourteenth to the nineteenth centuries, and the forms *-ine* and *-ette,* two common twentieth-century suffixes whose earlier use in English was not gender-related.

NATIVE SUFFIXES

Old English employed the agentive suffix *-a* to indicate a person performing a particular act, function, or profession. This suffix may have functioned in the common gender, as Knutson (1905) suggests, for example, *cuma,* 'one who comes,' and *bana,* 'murderer,' but it also clearly marked nouns as grammatically masculine. A small number of these agentives, or words that indicate the performer of an action, as well as nonagentives of similar pattern, formed gender pairs in which the masculines in *-a* had corresponding feminine forms suffixed in *-e.* These pairs mark the semantic gender of nouns: *husbonda, husbonde,* 'male and female householder'; *webba, webbe,* 'male and female weaver'; *wicca, wicce,* 'male and female witch'; and *widuwa, widuwe,* 'male and female widow' (although this last pair exists in Old English, most citations concern the feminine form). It should be noted that in such cases the feminine noun is not necessarily derived from the masculine, nor the masculine from the feminine. Instead, both masculine and feminine suffixes appear to be attached to a common root, usually a noun or verbal stem.

The gradual leveling of Old English final *-a, -o,* and *-u* to *-e* obliterates this grammatical and semantic gender distinction, and, as a result, some gender pairs were altered. *Wicca* and *wicce* fell together to form the common-gender *witch,* which later shifted its semantic

116

field once again to become primarily though not exclusively feminine. *Husband* became restricted to 'male householder,' and *wife,* which existed as one of several correlatives for *husband* in Old English, assumed the position of its sole correlative.

Widow, on the other hand, after serving as a common-gender word (a suffixed feminine *widowess* occurs as late as the sixteenth century, and the gender pair *widow men* and *widow women* is found ca. 1700), came generally to be marked feminine, and a new masculine in *-er, widower,* came into being in the fourteenth century to restore the gender pair. Whether or not *widower* derives from a distinctly feminine *widow* is not easy to resolve, though it is clear that in Modern English the masculine and not the feminine is the marked term. As we noted in chapter three, a similar situation exists with the gender pair *bride* and *bridegroom.* Were the situation reversed, with the feminine as the marked term, commentators would not hesitate to argue that masculines freely double as sex-neutral nouns, but they are less willing to admit that feminines may function as generics. We are so accustomed to thinking that the linguistic feminine, like the biblical one, must derive from the masculine that any reversal of the process brings forth a special philological justification. Samuel Ramsey ([1892] 1968) remarks that *"widower* from *widow* is entirely anomalous" (234). Leonard Bloomfield ([1933] 1965) finds such a reversal of sex roles so unusual that it merits its own name: he calls gender pairs in which the male derives from the female, such as *gander* from *goose* and *drake* from *duck,* examples of "inverse derivation" (238). Otto Jespersen refuses to admit that inverse derivation can occur with human nouns, and the etymologists Weekley, Skeat, Partridge, and Onions all shy away from an explicit acknowledgment that the basic order of the universe may be so rudely overturned as to allow male terms to be born from female ones. They either find that *widower* comes directly from the Old English masculine, or that *widow* never lost its masculine significance at all.

The one Old English feminine agentive suffix that survives in any significant number of words is *-ster,* though it has lost its feminine signification in all but one modern example, *spinster.* According to the *Oxford English Dictionary,* a *spinster* is originally a "woman (or, rarely, a man) who spins." The word occurs as an occupational title as early as 1362, and is used as such, with increasing rarity, down to the present century. The *OED* suggests that *spinster* in this sense may refer to men as well as women, just as *carder* and *spinner* could refer to women as well as men, and Knutson (1905, 22) notes that both *spinner* and *spinster* are clearly masculine in Howell's *Vocabulary* (1659), where they are distinguished from the feminine *spinstress,* which arose after *-ster* had ceased to function as a feminine suffix. Jespersen (1927, 135) argues unconvincingly that *spinster* was originally a common-gender word which came to refer to women, particularly the old yet still unmarried ones, because they were the chief spinners.

As an occupational title, *spinster* could form part of a woman's name. A number of occupational words with the *-ster* suffix survive in Modern English only as proper nouns, for example, *Baxter, Brewster,* and *Webster,* 'baker, brewer, and weaver.' But while *spinster* is the only English word to retain the original feminine significance of this suffix, its seventeenth-century use as "the proper legal title of one still unmarried" (*OED* s.v.)—derived no doubt through the same metaphorical association of women with the needle trades that derives *wife* from *weaver*—prevented it from functioning as a surname to be passed on to succeeding generations. In the eighteenth century *spinster* acquired the pejorative meaning it holds for most people today, "a woman still unmarried; *esp.* one beyond the usual age for marriage, an old maid" (*OED,* s.v.) though in Britain it remains the legal designation of an unmarried and unemployed woman.

There is some disagreement over the original meaning of *-ster.* Jespersen (1927) cites Schroeder's fanciful derivation, reminiscent of the absurd etymologies that we examined in chapter three, tracing the English *-ster* to the Latin feminine suffix *-trix.* Schroeder claimed that it first entered the language through the word *miltestre,* 'prostitute,' from the Latin *meretrix,* and spread by association to agent nouns referring to other feminine occupations, then to masculine words as well. Jespersen rejects this theory as unlikely: "A loan-word meaning 'prostitute' was hardly the kind of word from which a massproduction of analogical words would spring up to denote women (and men) occupied in a more decent way" (135–36).

But Jespersen too proposes an unlikely explanation for *-ster,* contending that it is a gender-neutral suffix, not a true feminine. His strongest evidence is a feeling that "the transition of a special feminine ending to one used of men also is . . . totally unexampled in all languages." Furthermore, Jespersen rejects the common explanation that -*ster* was transformed from a feminine to a masculine term as women's work was transferred to men. He is reluctant to admit that men, even if they wanted to perform women's work, "would then submit to having the feminine name applied to them, least of all if there was by the side of it a male form." Jespersen claims that the Middle English *demestre*, a general term for 'judge' labeled by the *OED* as the feminine form of *deemer*, could not possibly refer to a woman, nor does he think it likely that men would willingly adopt such surnames as *Baxter* if they had the taint of feminine reference (129–30).

Jespersen argues that Old English words in -*estre* which clearly refer to males—for example, *plegestre*, 'athlete, more specifically a boxer or wrestler'—cannot be considered feminine, though he readily allows masculines with -*er* suffixes to refer to women. Knutson, on the other hand, describes a balanced gender system which allows both sexes to cross lexicographical gender boundaries, citing both masculines in -*ster* and feminines in -*er* (for example, the Modern English *housekeeper* and *dressmaker*).

In derivation with -*ere* and -*estre*, the feminine is not taken from the masculine. Rather, both masculine and feminine terminations are appended to a common root, the present-stems of verbs or certain monosyllabic nouns of action, to produce such pairs as *laerestre, lareow,* 'female and male teacher'; *hoppestre, hoppere,* 'female and male dancer'; *sangestre, sangere* 'female and male singer'; and *seamestre, seamere,* 'female and male tailor.'

In the *Anglo-Saxon Dictionary* (1898), Bosworth and Toller explain the one instance where the referents of *baecestre*, 'baker,' are masculine rather than feminine, by arguing that the men in question are eunuchs, and the *OED* justifies masculine references for Old English words in -*ster* as cases of "men exercising functions which among the English were peculiar to women." Jespersen questions such explanations, but they cannot be dismissed outright. It is difficult to determine whether these masculine uses of the feminine suffix are in any way pejorative, but we might explain this sort of sexual marking in Old English as the equivalent of the Modern English practice of marking gender when an occupational sex boundary is being crossed or sexual identity is somehow being compromised.

The sexual identity of -*estre* eventually does become compromised.

Although in the fourteenth century it was still a productive suffix, it began generally to be replaced by the French feminine *-esse*. Thus we find *daunster* occurring alongside *daunceresse,* 'woman dancer,' and *dwelster* alongside *dwelleresse,* 'female resident.' By the sixteenth century the older forms in *-ster* had come to be considered masculine, or common gender, and new feminines in *-ess* were formed using the old feminine suffix as a stem on which to build: *backstress,* 'woman baker,' *seamstress,* 'woman tailor,' *songstress,* 'woman singer,' and *huckstress,* 'woman salesman.' For the suffix to lose femininity as its primary significance and become available as a general occupational term, if not an exclusively masculine one, *-ster* cannot have been exclusively pejorative. Unlike the major native feminine markers, *-e* and *-ster, -ess* is used to derive the feminine from the masculine noun, and although the negative associations of *-ster* cannot easily be traced to its original feminine signification, the negative associations of *-ess* can.

ALIEN SUFFIXES

In the translation of Augustin Calmet's *Great Dictionary of the Holy Bible* (1812), the creation of Eve presents the clearest illustration of the derivative nature of the *-ess* suffix: "And of the rib (or piece from his side) thus taken from man, he made a woman (womb-man, Saxon), or *man-ess*." And seeing Eve for the first time, Adam names her after himself: "She shall be called *man-ess,* because she was taken out of man" (s.v. "Adam").

The suffix *-ess,* which comes originally from Greek, through Latin, was the customary indicator of feminine derivatives in Old French. After the Norman Conquest, a number of French words in *-ess* were borrowed into English, including *countess, hostess, lioness, mistress,* and *sorceress.* From the fourteenth century, the suffix was attached to native English agent nouns in *-er,* producing *danceress, dwelleress, teacheress,* and *sleeress* ('female slayer'), and to other native words as well, creating such new feminines as *goddess.* The popularity of *-ess* increased in the fifteenth century, when it was appended to words in *-ster,* and since the sixteenth century it has produced many literary or hyperliterary forms, including the unlikely *operatress, heroickess, husbandess, interlocutress,* and *teetotaleress.* Of the 550 *-ess* words found by Edwin Dike (1937) in the *OED,* the feminine antedates the masculine in only twenty-three instances, the most extreme case being *waileress* (1388), which occurs over two centuries before *wailer* (1647).

There has been a noticeable decrease in the coining of new *-ess* forms since the mid nineteenth century. However, the history of the English lexicon, literary as well as nonliterary, clearly shows a continual cycle of marking, unmarking, and remarking for feminine nouns. Sometimes several feminines correspond to a single masculine. In one extreme case cited by Dike, *ambassador* is paralleled by five feminines, *ambassadress, ambassadrice, ambassadrix, ambassatrice,* and *ambassatrix.* As late as 1911 Henry Bradley states that we still freely add *-ess* to native English words, and the suffix remains active in twentieth-century slang, though it is not as productive today as *-ette* or *-ine.* The following list shows the various types of derivation in *-ess.*

Masculine nouns: *bishopess, coxcombess, fellowess, knavess.*
Masculine or common-gender nouns in *-er* or *-or: avengeress, censoress, drinkeress, playeress, writeress.*
Unsuffixed nouns: *doggess, druidess, goddess, pilgrimess, umpiress.*
Nouns whose *-er* suffix has been deleted: *adulteress, cateress, governess* (for *governoress*), *interpretess, murderess, sorceress.*
Verbal stems: *confectioness, entertainess, instructess.*
Irregular constructions: *clergess,* 'female clerk, or scholar,' *coloness* (? for *coloneless*), *tyraness,* 'female tyrant.'

As early as the eighteenth century forms in *-ess* were being declared moribund, and nineteenth-century usage books frequently opposed them. While Samuel Johnson includes *poetess* in his dictionary of 1755, defining the word as 'she poet,' Joseph Priestley only a few years later, in 1761, announced the approaching death of the word: "We do not call a female author an *authoress;* and if a lady writes poems, she is, now-a-days, called a *poet,* rather than a *poetess,* which is almost obsolete" (Dike 1933, 213). The 1860 edition of Worcester's dictionary includes both *poetess* and *poetress* as current, calls the fifteenth-century *authoress* "well-established," and suggests it is a relatively recent coinage: "heretofore *author* was commonly applied to writers of both sexes; and some still so use it." But Henry Alford (1864) frowns on the suffix: "Very many, indeed most names of occupations and offices, are common to both sexes, and it savours of pedantry to attempt by adding the feminine termination to make a difference." Alford fears the creation of such additional monstrosities as *groceress, tea dealeress,* and *vendress of stamps* (89).

Priestley's judgment was premature, however, and Alford's advice to his readers did not take. *Authoress* and *poetess* persist, though their death is still repeatedly announced. Dike, for example, celebrates the loss of the "Victorian" *authoress,* and is relieved that *poetess,* if not also dead, "is at least waning." But Philip Howard finds *authoress* still current in 1977, and casts a vote for its retention, a tacit admission that the existence of the word is still imperiled (94). Dike's assessment of *poetess* is apparently also premature. The *OED* considers *poetess* current, along with the following coinages in *-ess* that today's readers will recognize as now relatively rare: *giantess, Jewess, patroness, priest-ess, quakeress,* and *tailoress.* According to Gowers, *instructress, poet-ess,* and *proprietress* "are more tenacious of life than most of the old *-ess* words," and *conductress,* 'woman driver,' has been legitimately revived (Fowler 1965, 195).

Though a few words in *-ess* persist in twentieth-century English, the variety of such words has declined markedly in the standard language. While *poetess* is occasionally employed in American English, the most frequent example to be met with is *actress.* Much rarer, in the edited prose that has been subjected to frequency analysis, are *hostess, waitress, governess,* and *stewardess* (Francis and Kučera 1982). British English also recognizes *authoress, manageress,* and *proprietress* (Hofland and Johansson 1982). The suffix produces some, but not many, new terms intended for the standard language, for example, *juroress* (Mencken 1937), the pair *homestress* and *house-stress* to replace *housewife* (Forbes 1947; Wheelock 1947), and the recent *crimestress,* apparently an analogue for masculine *gangster* (Shapiro 1985). New slang terms include *actoress, bankeress, bewitch-tress, eagless* ('female pilot'), *emotress, emotion-picturess* ('movie ac-tress'), *fascinatress, funstress, Heebess, spyess,* and *sarongstress,* this last a reference to Dorothy Lamour (Berrey and Van den Bark 1942). Despite their documented rarity (forms in *-ette* and *-ine* are even rarer in edited prose), feminine suffixed forms have maintained a high de-gree of visibility.

With the decline of *-ess* in both slang and standard English, a gap has occurred that is being filled in a number of ways. Some notional masculines, like *doctor,* are reinterpreted as common gender, but in many cases, the need to specify sex is still felt, and composition has replaced suffixation as a means of indicating sex in the standard language: we find *woman doctor* rather than *doctress* (the frequency of such composed forms in edited prose is not noted by Francis and Kučera [1982] or by Hofland and Johansson [1982]). But suffixation is still productive in English, particularly in slang, and while *-ess* has declined in coinages, two suffixes, *-ine* and *-ette,* whose earlier use in English did not primarily involve the marking of gender, have been drafted as replacements.

According to the *OED, -ine* is primarily used as a suffix meaning 'having the quality of,' a sense that is evident in the words *masculine* and *feminine* themselves. It is also common in the naming of chemicals, for example *chlorine* and *morphine.* Its feminine sense is historically restricted to a very few words: *heroine* (from the French feminine suffix *-ine*) and *landgravine, margravine* (from the Dutch and German feminine suffix *-in). -Ine* may also be used for derivative products, for example, *dentine, nectarine,* and *grenadine,* and for feminine personal names, most deriving from masculines: *Caroline, Ernestine,* and *Josephine.*

With the exception of personal names, there were few early coinages in *-ine.* In 1605 the language historian Richard Verstegan created *freundine* or *freundina,* "a woman-friend, a shee-friend," as a sex-specific alternative to the ambiguous, common-gender *friend.* In his fourteenth-century Bible translation the reformer Wycliffe had used another form of the feminine, *frendesse.* As a feminine suffix, however, *-ine* has been most productive in twentieth-century slang, where we find it in show business and in the military, as well as in more general use, either to emphasize sex or to refer derivatively as well as derisively to women in men's roles. The following examples, taken from Berrey and Van den Bark's *American Thesaurus of Slang* and from miscellanies appearing in the journal *American Speech,* show that while *-ine* is productive in the coining of feminine nouns, individual new words in *-ine* are short-lived: *actorine,* 'actress,' *booberine,* 'a stupid or scatterbrained young woman,' *chorine,* 'chorus girl,' *curvarine,* 'curvacious chorine,' *doctorine,* 'female doctor or medical student,' *dudine* (also *dudene, dudette, Mrs. Dude*), *knitterine,* 'female knitter,' *motorine,* 'female driver,' *peacherine,* 'attractive female,' *sailorine, soldierine,* and *starine,* 'female star.'

The other productive feminine suffix in present-day English is *-ette,* borrowed from the Old French feminine corresponding to the masculine diminutive *-et*. Although *-ette* is gender-specific in French, it does not acquire a gender distinction in English until the twentieth century. *-Ette* was a popular diminutive suffix in the nineteenth century, though coinages like *sermonette* were frowned on by some usage critics. A new use of the suffix to mean 'artificial,' as in *leatherette*, drew less censure. Along with the earlier sense of smallness and the more recent one of artificiality, twentieth-century slang has revived *-ette* as a gender marker. World War II saw a dramatic increase in *-ette* words as women entered traditionally male jobs and became more prominent in American society in general.

Many words in *-ette* carry a negative connotation. As Louise Pound says in her foreword to *The American Thesaurus of Slang*, one of the most popular categories of slang has been the creation of "derisive terms for women and girls" (1942, vii). *Suffragette*, for example, is a word coined in 1906 by a British newspaperman [*sic*] who did not approve of the activities of the men and women known more neutrally as *suffragists*. The list below illustrates by topic just some of the large number of words in *-ette*. Most come from *The Thesaurus of American Slang* (Berrey and Van den Bark 1942), the miscellanies of *American Speech*, and Mamie Meredith's "Be a Cabette" (1952). As with feminine words in *-ine*, most feminines in *-ette* do not survive very long (*majorette, starlet*, and possibly *bachelorette* are exceptions).

Work: *astronette, cosmonette, aviatrette; farmerette, spuderette, tractorette,* 'woman farmer'; *pickette,* 'woman striker.' Also *welderette, guidette, porterette, firette,* 'woman firefighter,' and *copette,* 'woman police officer.' Women drivers include *cabettes, chauffeurettes* (also *chauffrettes*), and *conductorettes,* 'women bus drivers.'

Show business: *starlet* (found in Francis and Kučera 1982; first Hollywood use, 1941; literal reference to a small star, 1830). Also, *usherette, croonette,* 'female crooner,' *flickerette* (along with *flickerine*), *oomphlet,* and *screenette,* 'movie actress,' *glamorette,* 'glamor girl,' *sex-tette,* 'female sextet,' and the further derivation *saxtette,* 'a sextette of saxophones.'

Sports: *batherette* (also, *batherine*), *tankerette* and *tanksterette,* 'female swimmer'; *champette,* 'female champion,' *jockette,* 'female jock or jockey,' *(drum) majorette*.

Military: *kaydette,* 'female cadet'; *yeomanette* and *yeoette,* 'female employees in the U.S. Naval Reserve.'

Male college slang: *flapperette, giglette (giggle + ette),* 'giddy girl,' *chickenette,* 'young woman,' *heiferette, undergraduette,* 'college woman.' *Borette, lemonette, washoutette,* 'unpopular or unattractive woman'; *neckette, beastette, devilette* (also, *speedster*), 'woman of easy morals.' Feminine derivatives of masculine negative terms include *heelette,* 'female heel,' *chiselette,* 'female chiseler,' and *gigolette,* 'female gigolo.'

Names of social, athletic, and professional women's groups: *socialette,* 'society woman'; also *Blondettes, Barberettes, Rockettes, Roxyettes* for groups of singers or dancers; *Defenserettes,* a women's patriotic sewing group; *Bachelorettes, Matronettes, Veteranettes,* for social clubs; *Keglerettes, Jackettes* for sports teams. A recent United States Supreme Court ruling may result in the acceptance of the *Jaycee-ettes* as regular members of the *Jaycees* service organization.

Related Words in *-euse:* this French feminine suffix produces *jitneuse* (from *jitney*), 'woman bus or cab driver,' *scripteuse,* 'woman writer, or script girl' and two synonyms for H. L. Mencken's coinage, *ecdysiast: strippeuse* and *stripteuse.*

Related Words in *-trix:* this Latin suffix produces the pseudolearned *aviatrix, educatrix,* and *juratrix.*

Miscellaneous: *bachelette, bachelorette,* 'unmarried young woman'; *brownette, brunette; hay feverette,* 'female hay fever sufferer'; *hoboette* (also the clipped form *boette*), 'female tramp.' Presumably a *bachelorette* would attend a *stagette (stag + ette),* or 'women-only party,' on the eve of her wedding.

Like the diminutive suffixes *-ee, -ie* and *-y, -ette* has been popular in the names of products designed for women. In the 1930s a woman's undergarment was marketed with the trade name *Maculette,* derived from *immaculate + -ette,* though the coiners of the name were unaware that by removing the negative prefix *im-* in the interest of brevity, they had created a product whose name to any Latinist would mean 'stained or spotted,' just the opposite of what was intended. Other garments include the *Moc-inette,* a sport shoe; underwear called *Flatterettes, Puckerettes,* and *Holly-ettes;* and girls' pajamas named *Jamarettes.* Manufacturers have found though that it is not always profitable to give a product a name with feminine connotations. *Women and Language News* (1983) reports that the Charter Arms Corporation, which in 1971 introduced a woman's pistol called the *Undercoverette,* a smaller version of the *Undercover,* dropped the new name as men began to show interest in buying the new gun.

WOMEN'S WORK

The meaning of the suffix *-ess* or of its newer counterparts, *-ine* and *-ette,* has never been the subject of much debate. It is the use of the suffix, rather than its signification, that has provoked controversy. But the meaning of the correlative suffix *-er* is another matter: while some commentators treat it as common gender, others see it as exclusively masculine. For example, Lindley Murray ([1795] 1968) assumes that the nominal suffix *-er* refers only to males:

> When we say of a woman, she is a philosopher, an astronomer, a builder, a weaver, we perceive an impropriety in the termination, which we cannot avoid; but we can say that she is an architect, a botanist, a student, because these terminations have not annexed to them the notion of sex. [25]

Sylvain Maréchal pretended to exclude French women from professions ending in the masculine suffix *-eur,* but Murray, who wrote the most popular English grammar before 1850, indicates that women should not be anything that ends in *-er.* According to Alexander Crombie, Samuel Johnson, influenced by similar sentiments, resists calling a woman a *philosopher,* preferring *philosophress* instead ([1802] 1830, 42–43*n*); Casey Miller and Kate Swift go so far as to argue that in the nineteenth century, such *-er* words as *seamer* could refer to women if *only* women performed the type of work involved (1977, 44).

Lindley Murray readily admits that women have the ability to write; for one thing, his grammar was originally written to teach youngsters in a nearby girls school the correct forms of English. A revised version of Murray's comment in the third edition of his *Grammar* shows that the author is more troubled by women entering traditionally male professions than he is by the meaning of the troublesome *-er* suffix. Murray still finds it awkward to call a woman a philosopher, an astronomer, a builder, or a weaver (this last is doubly ironic since, as we saw in chapter three, the etymologists of Murray's day, who derived *wife* from *weaver,* assumed that weaving was woman's work), but he removes *architect* from the sex-neutral category, replacing it with *writer.* Apparently Murray thinks it is more appropriate for women to write than to design buildings. He may have been influenced in this change by Latin grammars that classified *architectus* as masculine because of its presumed association with the male nature as well as its masculine ending. At any rate, Murray momentarily forgets that *writer* ends in what he views as the exclusively masculine *-er:* "We can say [a woman] is a writer, a botanist, a student, because these terminations have not annexed to them the notion of sex" (1797, 35).

Not everyone accepted Murray's strictures. Walter Savage Landor, describing an imaginary conversation between Samuel Johnson and John Horne Tooke, has the lexicographer ask the etymologist whether the *-or* in *author* is masculine. Horne Tooke replies that since English words do *not* distinguish masculine or feminine by "declension," the same practice should be extended to borrowings. A queen, he tells Johnson, may be a governor; a godmother may be a sponsor. But while he accepts *-er* and *-or* as common-gender suffixes, Horne Tooke regrets that he can find no linguistic justification for words in *-ess* (Landor [1824–26] 1927, 55).

Three quarters of a century after Murray, the meaning of the agentive suffixes was still discussed in English grammars. Peter Bullions, in his *Practical Grammar of the English Language* (1868), notes that the masculine *-er* and its feminine counterpart, *-ess,* do not always pattern symmetrically, and that there are more masculine-only than feminine-only agents: "Many masculine nouns have no corresponding feminine; as, *baker, brewer,* etc.: and some feminine nouns have no corresponding masculine; as, *laundress, seamstress,* etc." (30). But Bullions makes it clear that when both members of the pair exist, the masculine is always the more general term, taking precedence over the feminine as well as including it.

Simon Kerl, in *A Comprehensive Grammar of the English Language* (1861), bends the worthiness doctrine slightly, allowing both masculine and feminine agent nouns to function generically in certain cases: "When, for either sex, the appropriate term is so seldom used as to be uncouth, the other term may be preferred; and whenever there is a term for but one of the sexes, it may be used for the other, if necessary." Despite this liberal attribution of generic function to agent nouns of *either* gender, Kerl implies that masculine terms referring to women are more common than feminine ones referring to men. Echoing Murray, Kerl takes the referent rather than the suffix as the more important indicator of gender: "Some descriptive terms are so rarely needed to denote women, that they have no corresponding feminine terms. Ex.—Printer, carpenter, robber, baker, brewer, hostler, lawyer, fop, drummer, colonel" (103). Kerl also lists feminine terms for which he finds no corresponding masculines, including *laundress* and *seamstress,* as well as *brunette, coquet, jilt, dowdy, vixen, termagant,* and *hag,* but there is no indication that he would approve of *laundress* in reference to a male clotheswasher or *seamstress* for a male tailor.

James C. Fernald, an editor of the Funk and Wagnalls *Standard Dictionary,* considers it a blessing that in English, nouns denoting living beings are "utterly indeterminate in gender." Fernald finds no more than 150 nouns in ordinary use that are distinctly masculine or feminine, and he argues that the active tendency of the English language is to minimize nominal gender. Among the common-gender personal nouns, Fernald cites quite a few in *-er:—writer, author, editor, instructor, teacher,* and *doctor*—as well as *nurse, physician, friend,* and *secretary* (1919, 11–12). Fernald's argument for gender neutrality would have more force had he resisted the temptation to call a female prophet, albeit a biblical one, a *prophetess.*

As recently as 1926, H. W. Fowler, in his still-popular *Modern English Usage,* argues for the men-only interpretation of the *-er* and *-or* suffixes, advising his readers that *author* is a masculine term and that women who write should properly be called *authoresses.* And contemporary French feminist writer Monique Wittig ([1973] 1975) politicizes Maréchal's comment on *auteur* by claiming that she "cannot be '*un écrivain*'" because the noun is grammatically, and therefore referentially, masculine (11). In contrast Bobbye Sorrels (1983), who insists on the gender neutrality of the *-or* and *-er* suffixes, suggests that, if we cannot give up such words as *authoress,* we might create a new male-specific suffix to balance it, for example, *-epp,* as in *authorepp,* 'male author' (25). Although Fowler's call for additional *-ess* words is retracted by Gowers in his 1965 revision of the work, and Sorrels does not think her proposal likely to succeed, the practice of marking the gender of nouns in standard English and in slang continues, as does the debate over the appropriateness of such marking.

THE USAGE DEBATE

In an 1834 article entitled "Man-Assimilation (Something Not to Be Read by the Ladies)," one C. P., who objects that women's long curls look like whiskers and fears that the radical new dance known as the waltz threatens American manhood, complains not only that masculine nouns like *postmaster, supervisor,* or *selectman* are used to refer to women, but also that words in *-ess* are applied to "our fair young fellow citizenesses," who are usurping men's roles. C. P. decries the admission of *studentesses* to "our female colleges," and though he opposes the title *doctress,* he urges that if women must be educated, they be given their own degrees, not *bachelors* or *masters,* but *maidens* or *mistresses of art.*

The British clergyman and usage commentator Henry Alford (1864) writes a more balanced opinion on the use of words with an *-ess* suffix:

> Certain names of occupations and offices seem to require them, and others to forbid them. We say *'emperor'* and *'empress';* but we do not in the same sense say *'governor'* and *'governess.'* In this latter case the feminine form has acquired a meaning of its own, and refuses to part with it. [88]

Alford notes that *king* has been used both for male and female monarchs, though he is reluctant to press this point. The title of Alford's book, *The Queen's English,* bears this out, as does his cautious assessment of the current gender neutrality of *king* in the Victorian era: "Perhaps *sovereign* would be the better word now."

As early as 1855, Richard C. Trench comments that words in *-ess* "are daily becoming fewer" (118). Some writers were happy to bid them farewell, though others fought for their retention. When he was editor of the *New York Evening Post,* William Cullen Bryant banished *authoress* and *poetess,* along with a number of other controversial usage items that were acquiring the taint of journalese. Some of the opinions of the language critic Edward S. Gould were first published in Bryant's newspaper. Gould (1867) finds *authoress* and *poetess* not just superfluous words but "philological absurdities, because they are fabricated on the false assumption that their primaries indicate *men*." Gould, who insists that *journal* can refer only to a *daily* publication and that *paraphernalia* may be used only as a reference to the possessions of a bride, excluding her dowry, charges that words in *-ess* smack of affectation and "pedantic pretension to accuracy," and he warns that our future dictionaries will contain such monsters as *writeress, officeress, manageress* (now a common word in England), *superintendentess, secretaryess, treasureress, singeress, walkeress,* and *talkeress* (21–23). Yet Gould's colleague, Richard Grant White, a critic of art as well as usage, approves of *authoress, poetess,* even *paintress* and *sculptress.* Forgetting that *-ess* is a borrowed suffix, he writes, "The distinction of the female from the male by the termination *-ess* is one of the oldest and best-established usages of English speech" ([1870] 1891, 205).

Perhaps the firmest nineteenth-century advocate of words in *-ess* is Mrs. Sarah Josepha Hale, a leader in the movement for the education of women and the self-described *editress* of *Godey's Lady's Book,* a popular American women's magazine. Like White, Hale considers feminine agent nouns to be part of our linguistic heritage, and hopes to revive the *-ess* suffix "whenever the two sexes are, to any considerable extent, employed in the same pursuit," for example, *arbitress, huntress, janitress, monitress, portress, preceptress, scholaress, songstress, tailoress,* and *traitress* (1865, 464). She also favors such innovations as *Americaness* and *Presidentess* (for the *wife* of the president) and, with women entering the formerly all-male domain of teaching, some of them even teaching in the same schools as men, Hale suggests the creation of a separate but equal *teacheress* and *professoress* to improve the language and to acknowledge women's progress.

Twentieth-century Usage

In *Modern English Usage* (1926), Henry Fowler disputes the feminist claim that such words as *authoress* are derogatory and imply the inequality of the sexes (s.v. "feminine designations"). According to Fowler, who assumes that feminines should always be marked in the vocabulary, a well-formed word in *-ess* is better than a compound like *woman author* because it does the work of two words. (H. L. Mencken, discussing *-ette* in the second edition of *The American Language* [1921], disapproves of this "effort to make one word do the

work of two." The comment is omitted from the fourth edition [1937],
an indication that the suffix was not easily resisted.)

Fowler argues that, "with the coming extension of women's voca-
tions, feminines for vocation-words are a special need of the future,"
and he faults the ambiguity of common-gender nouns: "Everyone
knows the inconvenience of being uncertain whether a doctor is a man
or a woman; hesitation in establishing the word *doctress* is amazing in
a people regarded as nothing if not practical." One senses that the
convenience of *doctress* is primarily to allow Fowler to avoid women
doctors, though he insists that a feminine termination does not imply
inferior professional status, and he lists a number of recently im-
pugned feminine nouns which he would like to rehabilitate: *authoress,
chairwoman, conductress, directress, draughtswoman, editress, inspectress, jurywoman, manageress, paintress, patroness, poetess, police-
woman, protectress,* and *tailoress.* Fowler also prints a list of "words
unfortunately not provided with feminines," including *artist, aurist,
clerk, cook, councillor, cyclist, lecturer, legatee, martyr, motorist, oculist,
palmist, president, pupil, singer, teacher,* and *typist.*

In 1928 Maurice H. Weseen comments that "the tendency toward
an excessive use of feminine endings, especially *-ess,* is condemned by
most authorities" (s.v. "feminization"). More recent comments support Weseen's stand, not that of Fowler. Frank Colby ([1944] 1947)
advises his readers that such nouns as *poet, writer, author,* and *play-
wright* have no hint of masculinity. Stretching linguistic history, Colby
blames the popularity of words in *-ess* on the nineteenth century, when
such "plushy titles as doctoress, clerkess, judgess, janitress, wizardess,
huntress, laboress, songstress, yes, and even teacheress and professoress" were de rigueur (s.v. "feminine nouns").

Actually, while *-ess* reached its height long before the nineteenth
century, most words in *-ess* did not achieve much currency, and none
were ever obligatory. Colby's excursion into pseudohistory camou-
flages the fact that the real words he objects to are the feminines of his
own day. Colby wrote his book on usage during World War II, when
the presence of women in formerly all-male areas of the work force led
to the coining of many words in *-ette.* Colby maintains that there is no
place for such gender-specific nouns in the modern, unisex world at
war: "To feminize the words seems pretty silly in this lusty era of
women shipbuilders, taxi drivers, transport flyers, top sergeants, and

petticoated naval officers who must be addressed as 'sir.'" Though he permits *waitress, actress, hostess, enchantress, divorcée, fiancée, congresswoman, saleswoman,* and *executrix,* Colby insists on *postmaster* and *chairman* for women as well as men, adding, "Do we not say of a woman grammarian that she is a master of English?"

In *A Dictionary of Contemporary American Usage* (1957), written by language expert and television personality Bergen Evans in collaboration with his sister, Cornelia Evans, the use of *female* as a synonym for *woman* is labeled "contemptuous" (s.v. "woman"), and a restrained statement about the feminine suffix appears: "No one could have foreseen, fifty years ago, that women were soon to do so much that men had thought they alone could do that to attempt to call attention to it would burden the language" (s.v. "author"). Writing alone two years later, however, Bergen Evans is blunter in his view of feminized nouns, if not of women: "Since some female [*sic*] has, at one time or another, done almost everything men can do, the language was cluttered with agent nouns with female suffixes" (Evans 1959, 18). In this work, *actress* is the only uncluttered form allowed.

Sir Ernest Gowers, who revised Fowler's *Modern English Usage* in 1965, accepts more words in *-ess* than Evans does, though he notes that suffixation has been replaced by compounds using *woman* in the creation of new sex-definite words such as *airwoman* and *horsewoman.* While Fowler approved of *chairwoman,* Gowers objects that it sounds too much like *charwoman,* recommending *chairman* instead. But the American journalist and lecturer Roy Copperud (1980) sees a decline both in feminine nouns and such composed phrases as *woman lawyer* and *lady physicist,* which he notes are often considered objectionable. Convinced that changes in language follow changes in society, Copperud is overly optimistic in suggesting that "equality of the sexes is finally here" (s.v. "feminine forms").

Alive and Ill

Writing in 1930, Mamie Meredith is the first language authority to trace gender suffixation not to the women who were entering roles formerly occupied only by men, but to the masculine *reaction* against this increase in the sphere of women's activity: "As soon as woman got out of her rightful place as mistress of a home she began to make trouble for the writers and speakers who had to mention her unwonted doings" (476). Meredith links the creation of feminized nouns with opposition to the early women's rights movement which, by 1865, had become "a hackneyed and much abused subject" in American magazines: "the ultra-chivalrous American gentleman not only persisted in speaking of *Ladies'* Rights, but stigmatized women workers, wherever he could, with the suffix *-ess*." She concludes that the use of the suffix decreased as the novelty of women entering the professions wore off.

The decline of *-ess,* first noted by Trench, has become a recurrent theme. Jacques Barzun (1974) is only one of many authors who over the past two centuries have announced the death of words that refuse to die. Barzun writes, "We have laudably got rid of *poetess* and *authoress,* as well as of the short-lived *doctress* and *paintress,* which some early feminists demanded as their right" (18). And feminist Norma Wilson defines *-ess* in "A Woman's New World Dictionary" (1973) as "an archaic word-ending which denotes female." But in a search of current dictionaries the authors of *An Intelligent Woman's Guide to Dirty Words* (Ruth Todasco et al. 1973) come up with a long list of words in *-ess,* and a short one for *-trix* and *-ette* suffixes, to demonstrate that the feminine agent nouns are all too alive and well in our modern lexicons.

Despite the death certificate issued by Barzun, the 1983 *Webster's Ninth New Collegiate Dictionary* lists both *authoress* and *poetess,* with no indication that either is obsolete. The absence of labels will signal to any reader that not only *authoress* and *poetess,* but such terms as *farmerette, mediatrix,* and *tutoress,* all of which are included in the dictionary, are part of the current vocabulary, as are *governess* (in the sense 'one who governs' as well as its later sense of 'tutor') and *ambassadress* (both 'female ambassador' and 'wife of the ambassador'). Furthermore, there is no indication that any of these words may have pejorative connotations.

There are a number of indications that, while *-ess* is still alive, it is not particularly well. Julia Penelope Stanley (1977a) has claimed that occupations with less social prestige are marked with *-ess* or *-ette,* and she generalizes that a noun acquires negative connotations when it is explicitly marked for sex. Unfortunately, this has always been true for *women writers* in English. Usage data for *authoress* and *poetess* clearly indicate the negativity with which these terms are charged. According to Charyl Kneevers (1984), the reviewers of Sylvia Plath's poetry downplay the work of this *poetess* (the label occurs frequently) in comparison to that of men. Some reviewers deny that Plath is writing poetry at all, calling her work instead the unformed emotional outpourings one can only expect from a woman. Others insist that Plath is not responsible for any brilliance her poems may have: they see her not as a writer at all, but as a vehicle—not even a person—through which the poems write themselves. And Carol Ohmann has shown that when Emily Brontë published *Wuthering Heights* under the name of Ellis Bell, critics assumed she was a man and reviewed her work as bold, strong, masculine stuff, a powerful and original representation of human cruelty, bestiality, and violence. When her identity as a woman was revealed, the tone of criticism shifted abruptly, and *Wuthering Heights* became just another female novel, a love story written with the kind of gentility that was reserved for the ladies. The negative power of feminine nouns forced the three Brontë sisters to write under pseudonyms. As Charlotte Brontë explains with some restraint, "We had a vague impression that authoresses are liable to be looked on with prejudice" (Ohmann 1971, 913).

Although we may wonder why a dictionary does not record the pejorative connotations of feminine derivatives—both *Webster's Ninth* and the unabridged *Webster's Third* define the suffix *-ess* simply as 'female,'—we cannot fault it for including feminine agent nouns. Several sources record an increase in their use in the past fifteen years. Laurie Bower states in *English Word-Formation* (1983) that *-ess* is still a productive suffix, though it suffers from competition with *-ette* and with composed forms using *woman*. Bower cites only two examples, *astronautess* (according to the *Barnhart Dictionary of New English Since 1963* [1973] this comes from the mouth of a male NASA official; the form is in competition with *astronette*, cited earlier) and *seeress*, 'female clairvoyant.'

Most of the recent increase in feminine agent nouns is the result of negative reaction to the new woman's movement, but, as was the case in the nineteenth century, some of it is directly sponsored by feminists. Casey Miller and Kate Swift report in *The Handbook of Nonsexist Writing* (1980) that *Goddess* and *Creatrix* have recently been revived to call attention to the female nature of the supreme being (111–12). Una Stannard (1977) observes the trend toward feminine nouns:

[Feminists] also force their femaleness into language, insisting a female representative to Congress must be called a Congresswoman, a female head of a committee a chairwoman, even a female orchestra conductor a maestra. . . . Feminists themselves have resurrected the feminine suffix, deliberately using poetess, aviatrix, murderess. The rationale is that women must be verbally integrated into the English language. [349]

In explanation of this phenomenon, Julia Penelope Stanley (1977a) argues that "the use of neutralized terms perpetuates the invisibility of women in positions outside their traditionally defined roles," and like Sarah Hale she recommends the use of explicitly marked gender pairs, using words already present in the language rather than coining new ones, to remedy the situation (74).

It is not unusual for words with negative connotations to reverse themselves and become positive, and vice versa: the interchangeability of *bad* and *good* in English slang is only one of many examples. Whether this can happen with feminine agent nouns is not certain, though, and feminist support for these nouns has always been sporadic. Stanley's solution seems intended as a temporary measure to ensure the quicker recognition and acceptance of women in nontraditional roles, yet Stannard (1977) cautions that "women will have to acquire the self-confidence to present themselves to the public primarily as human beings, not as females" (349). Miller and Swift, who feel that words in *-er* lost their masculine significance when English lost grammatical gender (1977, 41), advise their readers to avoid feminine endings and to choose gender-neutral terminology instead. They note that *Negress, Jewess,* and *Quakeress* are almost defunct, and, as an indication of the separatist, pejorative connotations of such terms they remind us that "no one ever came up with *Whitess, WASP-ess,* or *Protestantess.*"

Even the entrenched *actress* and *waitress* may eventually be replaced. Miller and Swift argue that the terms are neither separate nor equal: "The distinction between *actor* and *actress* is not a distinction between male and female; it is the difference between the standard and a deviation" (1977, 46). They point out that for the first half century after women were allowed on the British stage, *actor* was used for both sexes. *Actress,* coined a few decades after the initial appearance of women actors in the late seventeenth century, only gradually took over as the primary word and, we are told, the situation is now starting to reverse itself: "Many women in the theater and films are beginning to take back the term actor," which is recommended by the authors as an appropriate generic word (1980, 110).

The resolution of the *waiter/waitress* pair is handled differently. Rather than advocating a common-gender *waiter,* Miller and Swift seem to favor the introduction of a new word. They record the gender-neutral *waitron* (*waiter* + *on* or *one*) as the option adopted by one Boston restaurant. The false-Latin plural *waitri,* noted by Lawrence Poston, III, (1965), has been adopted as a sex-neutral job descriptor by at least one newspaper, though the *-i* is actually a masculine plural doubling as a generic masculine. Some restaurants now use the term *server* to avoid charges of sex discrimination. Bobbye Sorrels (1983) doubts that *waitress, hostess,* and *actress* can successfully be replaced. She advises her readers that if they must use the feminine term, they should at least refrain from employing *waiter, host,* and *actor* in any generic sense (26).

It is not possible to predict with any certainty what will happen to masculine or feminine agent nouns in the future. The English language has a long if not honorable history of gender marking. When a feminine gender-specific suffix has been lost, another suffix or a compound phrase has always come along to replace it. On the other hand, gender marking has often functioned pejoratively, and individual words that are marked for gender tend to fall into disuse once that marking becomes useless or excessively objectionable. As long as men and women are perceived to have traditional roles, and as long as some of us reject these roles and cross traditional boundaries, it is probable that such terms as *househusband* and *astronette* will continue to be coined. But it is also possible that such words, like most of their predecessors, will be short-lived, and that a world of common-gender occupations, a paradise renamed, awaits us. At present, however, what concerns us is the vexed notion of just what constitutes a common-gender word, and the meaning of the word *man* lies at the heart of this problem.

CHAPTER 8

Marked Men

At first both sexes were in Man combinde,
Man, She-Man did with his body breed.
Thomas Overbury

When the gender of a particular human noun is not contextually significant—and with due respect to Fowler it seldom matters whether
a doctor or a nurse is a man or a woman—speakers and writers of
English are usually content to use nouns not marked for gender. But
these generics, like the feminine agent nouns discussed in the previous
chapter, are not without controversy, for many of those that already
exist in English are ambiguous, having both a gender-neutral as well
as a masculine or, more rarely, a feminine significance, and suggestions
for new, unambiguously sex-neutral terms are usually met with stiff
opposition. Perhaps most troublesome to linguists, feminists, and
usage critics alike has been the use of the word *man* itself, in phrases
such as *the man in the street* and compounds like *mankind* and *chairman*. Some authorities argue that *man,* at first a word in which both
genders were combined, now refers primarily to males, while others
claim that the neutral sense of *man* is not dead and that the word still
retains the primary meaning 'human being.' In any case, one must
admit that in actual use it is often unclear whether *man* refers to
people in general or to men only.

MAN EMBRACING *WOMAN*

While it is generally agreed that the original sense of *man* in Proto-
Germanic or Indo-European was simply 'human being,' by historical
times the word had developed a masculine marking that eventually
supplanted the primary, unmarked meaning. According to the *Oxford*

English Dictionary, in all of the Germanic languages *man* has the two-
fold sense of 'human being' and 'adult male human being,' a situation
which creates the potential for ambiguity. All the Germanic languages
except English have transferred the original, generic sense of *man* to
a new, derivative word—for example, German and Dutch *mensch,*
Swedish *menniska,* and Danish *menneska*—thereby freeing *man* to
mean 'adult male human being.' (The fact that the original generic
and not the later masculine meaning of *man* is shunted to a new word
indicates the dominance of the sense 'adult male.') Such a transfer,
however, is not always completely successful. Otto Jespersen (1924b)
notes that because *mensch* is grammatically masculine, "Germans in
some connexions hesitate to use it about a woman" (231).

There can be no doubt that *man* served as a gender-neutral noun
during earlier stages of English, but there is some disagreement as to
whether or not the meaning of *man* in Modern English, which failed
to develop a derived generic, has been in any way restricted to minimize ambiguous reference. The *OED* claims that *man* in the sense
'human being' had become obsolete by the nineteenth century; other
authorities limit its present use to proverbial or literary language; but
Jespersen and most recent dictionaries find it current. Usage guides
are also divided on the appropriateness of gender-neutral *man,* and
the word has become a political issue in the discussion of linguistic
sexism and language reform.

Early *Man*

During the Old English period, *man* functioned both as a generic and
a sex-specific noun, as well as an indefinite pronoun. As a pronoun it
meant 'one, anyone, they, or people': Wudewanhad is þæt man wunige
on clænnysse æfter his gemacan, ægðer ge weras ge wif, 'Widowhood
is when one lives in celibacy after [the death of] his mate, either the
men or the women.'

As a 'noun *mann* (or *man*) is used in Old English in the sense 'human being,' while *wer* and *wif* are the common terms for 'adult male'
and 'adult female.' It frequently translates Latin *homo: hic et haec homo*
is rendered by Ælfric as *ægþer is mann ge wer ge wif,* 'a human being
is either a man or a woman.' As a gender-neutral noun, *man* may also
refer exclusively to females, for example, Ercongota hali femne and
wundorlic man, 'Ercongota, a holy woman and wondrous person.'

However, with males alone _man_ generally means 'adult male': For ðam forlæt se man fæder and modor and geþeot hine to his wife, 'Therefore a man shall leave his father and mother and join himself to his wife' (Old English citations are taken from Bosworth and Toller [1898], _An Ango-Saxon Dictionary;_ Toller's _Supplement_ [1921]; and the _OED_).

With the loss of _wer_ in Middle English (it survives today only in the compound _werewolf_, 'man-wolf'), _man_ emerged as the noun of choice in reference to males. It continued to be used in a generic sense as well, though with increasing rarity. In the sixteenth century one could still call Adam and Eve the sole "paire of men in Paradise," but by the eighteenth century _man_ was likely to be interpreted as a masculine without an explicit stipulation including women: "There is in all men, both male and female, a desire and power of generation" (Hume); "Such a deplorable havoc is made in the minds of men (both sexes) in France" (Burke).

The Generic Masculine as Law

The literary historian Charlotte Stopes (1908) sees the ambiguity of _man_ as an imperfection in the English language that is "the efficient cause of the present disabilities of women" (5). Examining the legal meanings of _man_, she demonstrates that nineteenth-century English lawyers were willing to admit _man_ as a gender-neutral term only under conditions that were favorable to males. According to Stopes, legal opinion held that "the word 'man' always includes 'woman' when there is a penalty to be incurred, and never includes 'woman' when there is a privilege to be conferred" (12).

The likelihood of _man_ excluding women both semantically and legally had become so great by the mid nineteenth century that it was felt necessary to redefine the word. In 1850 the British Parliament passed the Acts of Parliament Abbreviation Bill, designed not so much to restore women's rights but, as its name indicates, to shorten the language of the statutes. Section 4 of the Abbreviation Bill defines the inclusiveness of various terms commonly found in parliamentary acts. The word _month_, for example, is to mean calendar, not lunar month, unless otherwise specified. Similarly, _county_ is to include any towns or cities located therein. The bill also provides that, in general, _man_ is to include _woman_:

> Be it enacted, That in all Acts to be hereafter made Words importing the Masculine Gender shall be deemed and taken to include Females, and the Singular to include the Plural, and the Plural the Singular, unless the contrary as to Gender or Number is expressly provided. [*British Sessions Papers* (1850) 338.I.5]

Gender and number are here treated together, as they commonly are in grammars, but it is noteworthy that they are not treated in identical fashion, for though the inclusiveness of number is reciprocal—singular implies plural, and plural, singular—that of gender is not: the feminine does not imply the masculine. Eve does not speak for Adam.

On June 16, 1851, just one year after its passage, an attempt was made in the House of Commons to repeal the Abbreviation Act because, according to John Stuart, "the wording of Acts during the present Session was as long as on any former occasion." More important, Stuart is concerned that it may inadvertently give women rights which they should not have. He points out that the Reform Bill of 1832 provides that "every male person paying rent, and occupying a house of a certain value, should be entitled to a vote," and he warns, "that clause should mean every female person also, and the consequence would be that females would be entitled to vote." Furthermore, Stuart fears that private parliamentary bills settling estates upon the male issue of a person will have to include all female issue as well, and he asks, "Could a more monstrous absurdity be palmed off on the House?" The Abbreviation Act was defended against these claims by the attorney general, who noted that its force was not retroactive, and that it would not allow women to vote, though were it to do so he would not be at all disturbed. Because of the late hour (several speakers expressed a desire to go to lunch) and evident lack of support for repeal, voting was postponed for six months; the Repeal Bill quietly died, and the generic masculine was given the force of law (*Hansard's Parliamentary Debates* ser. 3 v. 117 [1851]: 843).

Despite the Abbreviation Bill's attempt to legislate the inclusive masculine, the *Oxford English Dictionary* notes that when *man* refers to women it does so only indirectly, not inclusively: "In modern apprehension *man* as thus used primarily denotes the male sex, though by implication referring also to women." In addition, the use of *man* has become restricted to proverbial or literary language, where it "occurs only in general or indefinite applications (e.g. with adjs. like *every, any, no,* and often in the plural, esp. with *all, any, some, many, few,* etc.)." The *OED* editors find that in ordinary or colloquial language, the gender-neutral function of *man* has shifted to such words as *body, person, one, folk(s),* and *people.*

Although Jespersen assumes generic *man* to be current in twentieth-century English, all his examples are literary, not colloquial (1922, 132), and he agrees with the *OED* editors that instead of *man,* "the tendency recently has been to use unambiguous, if clumsy expressions like *a human being . . .* or the shorter *human,* pl. *humans*" (1924b, 231). We might add to this list of alternatives the word *individual,* used increasingly as a synonym for *person* in the nineteenth century and still popular today.

DEFINING *MAN* AND *SHE-MAN*

Despite the demonstrable shift in meaning from the unmarked generic to the marked masculine sense, lexicographers almost universally record 'human being' as the primary current definition of *man.* Only when *man* is placed in opposition to *woman* does an imbalance appear in their definitions—an imbalance that is sometimes slight but that often involves a polarization of the two terms into positive and negative. In treating the masculine sense of the word *man* or one of its derivatives, such as *manly,* dictionaries frequently cite the supposed masculine qualities of strength, bravery, and firmness, while definitions of *woman* and *womanly* either are vaguely neutral, for example, 'having the qualities of a woman,' or they reflect complementary negative views of the sex as weak, timorous, and changeable. Some of these positive and negative meanings are a function of the general cultural approbation or aggrandizement of the masculine, and derogation or trivialization of the feminine, and while their existence is unfortunate, their appearance records a fact of linguistic and social history. But one also senses that in some cases, the antifeminism of the linguistic tradition, or of an individual lexicographer, produces a lack of parallelism in the treatment of *man* and *woman* as male and female human beings and puts an inappropriate emphasis on the portrayal of woman as a derivative and inferior being, a variant or *she-man* who is not a full and equal participant in *mankind.*

Nathan Bailey, in his *Dictionarium Britannicum* (1736), defines

141

man as "a creature endowed with reason," completely ignoring the sense of the word as 'adult male human being.' Perhaps Bailey assumed that his readers were men and did not need to be told who they were. He does, however, find it necessary to specify sex in defining *woman* as "the Female of the Human Race," and Bailey devotes considerable space to a list of proverbs in English and other languages that illustrate woman's supposed fickleness, deception, and ability to cause woe.

Unlike Bailey, Samuel Johnson includes an entry for gender-specific *man* in his *Dictionary of the English Language* (1755), though he defines the word by negation: "Not a woman." In fact Johnson records fourteen different senses for *man,* while he allows *woman* only two: Bailey's "the female of the human race," together with "a female attendant on a person of rank." Johnson represents *manly* using the positive terms 'firm, brave, stout, undaunted, and undismayed,' while *womanly* is glossed as the more neutral 'becoming a woman; suiting a woman; feminine; not masculine, not childish, not girlish.'

Noah Webster does not hesitate to call a male a male in his *American Dictionary of the English Language* (1828), labeling the marked sense of *man* as "a male individual of the human race, of adult growth or years." Webster also expands the definition of *woman* to read "the female of the human race, grown to adult years," making it for the first time almost exactly parallel to the corresponding sense of *man.* His treatment of *manly* and *womanly,* however, reflects the imbalance found in Johnson. Charles Richardson goes beyond Webster in *A New Dictionary of the English Language* (1836), specifying that *man* in the sense of 'human being' "is a general term to include each sex," though Richardson does not note this under *man,* where we might expect to find it, but under the entry for *woman,* who is called "the female of man or human kind."

The Century Dictionary (1891) begins its definition of *man* with the zoological "featherless plantigrade biped mammal of the genus *Homo*" that is in keeping with the dictionary's scientific approach to language. There is a less scientific imbalance in the *Century*'s treatment of the qualities associated with the sexes: although the characteristics that make a *man* are not specified, we are told that those of *woman* include tenderness and gentleness in reference to women, and effeminacy and weakness in reference to men. Funk and Wagnalls's *Standard Diction-*

ary (1895) similarly neglects to specify what is in question when it defines *man* as "a male person who possesses the qualities or virtues appropriate to the stronger sex," though it assumes the quality of strength, while *woman,* though not characterized as the weaker sex, is said to possess the virtues of gentleness, tenderness, compassion, and modesty.

While *Webster's Second New International Dictionary* (1950) and the *Random House Dictionary* (1967) do not specify either masculine or feminine qualities in their definitions of *man* and *woman, Webster's Third* (1961) treats *woman* in terms of a positive–negative contrast: "gentleness, affection, and domesticity or on the other hand fickleness, superficiality, and folly." However, *man* is discussed only in the positive terms of courage, strength, and vigor, even though a saying like *Isn't that just like a man?* readily admits a negative interpretation, imputing to *man* such traits as selfishness, brutishness, stubbornness, and insensitivity.

The Thesaurus

Collections of English synonyms and antonyms, which first appear in the late eighteenth century, tend like dictionaries to emphasize the differences between men and women, and to present an unbalanced view of the vocabulary that stresses the semantic primacy of *man* and the secondary status of *woman.* The *British Synonymy* ([1794] 1968) of Hester Lynch Thrale Piozzi, the first major work of its kind, does not discuss *man* and *woman,* though Mrs. Thrale, as she is most commonly known, justifies her own work by alluding to the stereotype of women as accomplished talkers: "While men teach to write with propriety, a woman may at worst be qualified—through long practice—to direct the choice of phrases in familiar talk."

George Crabb's *English Synonymes* (1816), which claims to be the first "scientific" treatment of the subject, contains only one relevant entry, a discussion of the differences between *female, feminine,* and *effeminate:* "Beauty and delicacy are *feminine* properties; robustness and vigor are masculine properties; the former, therefore, when discovered in a man entitle him to the epithet *effeminate.*" Even more scientific in its intent is Peter Mark Roget's *Thesaurus of English Words and Phrases* ([1852] 1858), conceived not as a synonymy but as a system for classifying every concept known to the human mind.

Like John Wilkins in the seventeenth century, Roget intended his treasury of words to serve as the basis for the development of a "strictly *Philosophical Language*" (xxiv). Roget therefore arranges his concepts into one thousand grouped categories; *man* and *woman* appear in categories 372, *Mankind;* 373, *Man;* and 374, *Woman* (under Class III, Matter; group 3, Organic; division 1, Vitality; subgroup 2, Special).

Mankind, the head word for Roget's general, neutral category, is exemplified by "the human race or species; man, human nature, humanity, mortality, flesh, generation." Other synonyms include *human being, person, individual, creature, one, people, folk,* and *society.* The two subdivisions of the general category, *man* and *woman,* are presented as visually parallel: they appear on the page as separate but equal in two columns arranged beneath *mankind.* Their treatment, however, is not quite parallel.

Roget's synonyms for *man* include *manhood, virility,* and *he,* as well as a number of words referring to political rights or social status, some of which are today considered gender-neutral: *citizen, denizen, burgess,* and *cosmopolite.* Synonyms for *woman* include *womankind,* whose reference, unlike that of *mankind,* is gender-specific. There are several other words for *woman* not paralleled in the section on *man,* including a number that focus on gender: *female, the sex, the fair, the fair sex, the softer sex, the weaker vessel.* Roget omits the obvious correlative *male* as a noun, and there is no corresponding reference to *man* as the stronger sex. The category *woman* also contains one reference to clothing, *a petticoat;* and a number of diminutives or terms suggestive of youth: *damsel, girl, lass, lassie, maid, maiden, demoiselle, nymph, wench,* and *grisette,* none of which are matched under *man.* Roget even omits the common parallel masculine terms *boy, lad,* and *laddie.*

In the revision of Roget's work by C. O. Sylvester Mawson (1911), some additions to the category *woman—bachelor girl, new woman, suffragist, suffragette*—suggest her changing role in society, while other new entries, such as *spinster* and *old maid,* do not. No corresponding changes occur under *man,* where there is no mention of the term *bachelor,* the source of *bachelor girl*—despite the existence of a perfectly ordinary term for an unmarried man, Mawson is more interested in uncommon words referring to the marital status of women. A new subcategory is added under *woman* containing synonyms for *effeminacy,* all labeled as contemptuous, though no category appears for *man* to contain the corresponding terms that indicate masculinity in women. Mawson improves on Roget by adding some literary citations to illustrate each category, but as with the proverbs in Bailey's dictionary, such illustrations tend to portray women unfavorably. Mawson's citations for *woman* conclude with Tennyson's "woman is the lesser man."

More recent versions of Roget correct some but not all of the gender imbalance of the original. Robert A. Dutch, editor of *The St. Martin's Roget's Thesaurus of English Words and Phrases* (1965), offers *womankind* as a synonym for *mankind,* and *everywoman* as a parallel to *everyman,* though there are many who would question whether the feminine compounds may function as common gender. The latest revision of *Roget's Thesaurus,* by Susan M. Lloyd (1982), closely parallels Dutch's edition, though there are even further attempts to equalize the treatment of the sexes. Lloyd renames Dutch's general category *Mankind* as *Humankind;* she adds to his masculine-generic synonyms *Adam* and *fellow* two feminine parallels, *Eve* and *girl,* as well as some words referring to the male role in marriage, *spouse* and *family man;* and—for the first time in any major reference work—she introduces a distinctly negative masculine term, *weakling.* Lloyd also includes a category for male sexual variance which contains *homosexual, eunuch,* and *castrato. Ms.* appears in the series of titles for women, and perhaps to balance this radical Americanism, Lloyd includes *trouble and strife,* Cockney rhyming slang for 'wife.' *Lesbian* parallels *homosexual,* and a number of terms referring to the woman's movement appear: *women's rights, Women's Lib* or *Liberation, feminist,* and *sister.* Deleted from Dutch's entries for *Female* are *coed, undergraduette,* and *girlie.*

Other collections of synonyms preserve the general imbalance so far as the sexes are concerned. J. I. Rodale's *Synonym Finder* (1961) lists the nouns that express the qualities of *man,* including *hero, man of courage, lion, paladin,* and *brick,* but instead of a corresponding set of positive terms for *woman* we find *paramour, doxy, broad, tart, strumpet, chippy,* and *piece. Webster's Collegiate Thesaurus* (1976), edited by Mairé Weir Kay, presents synonyms for *woman* as *wife* and *mistress,* but none for *woman* simply as person. However, one of the most unbalanced treatments of the sexes occurs in *Roget's II: The New Thesau-*

rus, "by the editors of the *American Heritage Dictionary*" (1980), which in its laudable effort to defeat the lopsided vocabulary of sexism renders males and females, and the legitimate words that refer to them, more or less invisible. *Roget's II* includes synonyms for *man* as a member of the human race and, more generally, as the human race itself, though neither of these senses is as current or common as the sex-specific one. The work even includes a category for *the man* (inclusive of both sexes) as a slang term meaning 'the police.' But there are no synonyms for *man* as an adult male human being, and no entry whatsoever for *woman.*

USING *MAN*

The ambiguity of *man* poses problems for usage critics as well as lexicographers. James Anderson, who hoped to make language as gender-specific as possible, complains in 1792 that such words as *man* and *horse* "are often forced to denote the whole genus instead of the male only, which is their proper meaning" (197). And while Richard Grant White (1881) accepts generic *man* as a collective noun, as in *Man proposes, God disposes,* he notices a tendency to avoid the word in reference to single human beings, for example, *Every man should obey the law* (390). White is concerned with the increasing use of the substitutes *person* and, more particularly, *individual,* a term that is still held in disfavor by many authorities. *Individual* was labeled as colloquial by the *Century Dictionary,* and the *OED* calls it a vulgarism or term of disparagement, although J. Lesslie Hall (1917) finds numerous occurrences of *individual* in reputable eighteenth- and nineteenth-century literary sources (134–36).

The historian Mary Beard (1946) is perhaps the first writer to condemn the generic use of *man* not only because it is used imprecisely at times when precision is critical (for example, in legal documents) but also because it is unfair to women. Beard complains that such terms as *primitive man* allow male anthropologists and historians to ignore women or to portray them as a subject sex, and that men use the ambiguity of *man* as a convenient shield to hide behind:

> Men who discuss human affairs frequently do so with an ambiguity amounting to double talk or half talk or talk so vague that one cannot be sure in every case whether they are referring to men only or to both

men and women. This gives them a peculiar advantage of self-defense if the charge is made that they are not remembering women at all when they speak or write of "man" or "men," for they can claim that they are using these words in their generic sense. [47]

The first recognition and detailed discussion of ambiguous *man* in a work on English usage occurs in Bergen and Cornelia Evans's *Dictionary of Contemporary American Usage* (1957): "The singular *man* is used more often to mean the [human] race, and the plural *men* to mean the males. But this rule is not followed consistently." The Evanses are more concerned with the formation of proper plurals for *man* and the phrases and compounds in which it appears than they are with its ambiguity, which does not, for them, pose much of a problem: "When the context does not show that only the male is meant, it will generally be assumed that *men* includes *women,* regardless of what the author may have had in mind, as when Milton undertook to *justify the ways of God to men.*"

Only in the 1970s did the controversy over the use of *man* as a generic erupt, fueled by the new woman's movement, the attention being paid to sexism in language, and the creation of such gender-neutral words as *chairperson.* Clear lines were drawn between those who insisted on the currency of the double meaning of *man* and those who rejected it. Writing in the *Columbia Forum,* Jacques Barzun (1974) opposes the use of *-person* as a substitute for *-man* in compounds—he remarks that "person is not a word to cherish and ubiquitize"—and maintains that *man* still retains its generic sense. However, Barzun considers the problem of the double meaning of *man* separately from that of the generic *he* prescribed by the doctrine of the worthiness of the genders, and he expresses the regret that English never developed a common-gender possessive pronoun (17–19).

Anthony Burgess replaced English *man* with a Russian equivalent in his novel *A Clockwork Orange* and argued as a panelist for the *Harper Dictionary of Contemporary Usage* that a word cannot have two meanings. However, like Barzun, Burgess (1976) accepts the ambiguity of *man* and objects to any linguistic innovation that involves the replacement of this native English word by one like *person,* which comes originally from another language. In the same year Casey Miller and Kate Swift ([1976] 1977, 48) proclaim the demise of the common-gender sense of *man,* which had seemed so vital and trouble-

147

some to them only a few years earlier that they urged the adoption of a new word, *gen,* to replace it and relieve the strain of its ambiguity (*New York Times Magazine,* 16 April 1972, 106).

Only lately have a few usage books and language commentators begun advising readers against the use of *man* as a generic. Roy Copperud (1980) insists that "*man* [is] first of all . . . 'a member of the human race; a human being'" (s.v. "feminism"). But, assuming once again that masculine-gender words can function generically, Casey Miller and Kate Swift (1980) argue that they should not be so used. Miller and Swift justly complain that "conventional English usage . . . often obscures the actions, the contributions, and sometimes the very presence of women," a situation that could be reversed more easily were the generic masculine avoided (7–8). Bobbye Sorrels (1983) takes a similar position. Referring to experiments which indicate that the words *man* and *mankind,* when used in clearly generic contexts, evoke masculine images in the minds of male and female test subjects, Sorrels argues that the employment of *man*-words as generic terms stereotypes the sexes and places males in dominant roles, and she recommends that "the egalitarian communicator . . . not use male words to include females" (25).

The Reader's Digest guide, *Success with Words* (1983), which traces the history of *man* in detail, acknowledges the continued existence of both the general and specific senses of the word but offers citations in which the generic use of *man* is compromised through careless phrasing: "As for man, he is no different from the rest. His back aches, he ruptures easily, his women have difficulty in childbirth." In addition, the reader is warned that "the *man* . . . *he* style of writing carries with it strong male connotations" (s.v. "man"). Such writing may indeed exclude women, or at least render them invisible; the guide suggests that writers use such alternatives as *men and women, human beings,* and *people* in order to avoid ambiguity.

A New *Man*

In 1605 Richard Verstegan addressed the need for a gender-free term to denote "a humaine creature in general." In his example, Verstegan restricts the word *man* to its masculine sense, and he recommends *mensca* (plural *menscan*) to fill the lexical gap:

This woord *mensca* or *menesca* & somtymes *mensce* was with our ance-
ters asmuch to say as *a humaine creature* in general, to wit, either man
woman or chyld, the high and low duitsh haue it stil, though a litle
different in pronountiation. It is a woord of necessarie vse as for example,
a man beholding some lyuing thing a farr of in the feild, not wel decern-
ing what it is, wil say it is either a man or a beast, now it may be a
woman or a chyld, and so not a man, and therefore hee should speak
more properly in saying it is either a *mensce* or a *beast,* &c. [228]

Recognizing that *man* no longer refers primarily to human beings
in the abstract, a number of word coiners have proposed new words
to carry the generalized sense of *man.* Among the substitutes offered
are the following:

man, stuman, uman, 'human being, man, woman.' Leon Bollack
(1899)
manu, mana, mano, 'man, woman, both sexes'; also a set of picto-
graphs: "a straight line for a man, a circle for a woman, and when
we wanted to express both, our pictograph would show a circle
with a line bisecting it." Eve Merriam (1964, 209–10)
gen, from *genesis* and *generic;* suggesting continuity (as in *progeny*),
warmth (*gentle*), and sexuality (*genital*); suitable for gender-neutral
compounds such as *genhood* and *genkind.* Casey Miller and Kate
Swift, *New York Times Magazine,* 16 April 1972, 106
human, for example, *the Family of Human.* Mary Orovan ([1972]
1976)
wo/man (includes both *woman* and *man*). "A Woman's New World
Dictionary" (1973)
emman. David H. Stern, *Los Angeles Times,* 19 January 1974, sec. 2,
p. 4
maman, 'man-woman'; *birl,* 'boy-girl' (facetious). Paul B. Horton
(1976)
womyn (pl. *wimyn*). Theresa Pellow-McCauley, *The Peacemaker* 32
(January, 1979) 2–3
mann (from Old English). Irene B. Keller, *New York Times,* 4 February 1979, sec. 4, p. 18

These alternatives have not proved popular. We will see as we consider other gender-neutral neologisms that it is difficult to legislate

the adoption of new English words. For that matter, it is difficult to legislate any reform of the English language because no mechanism exists to promulgate reform, and more important, because we are unable to agree on what reforms, if any, are necessary.

The Myth of *Man*

The debate over the meaning of *man* has led some writers to question the very existence of sex-neutral words. The novelist and literary scholar Dorothy Sayers (1969) holds that Latin *homo*, often cited as an example of a word that is truly gender-blind, is not neutral at all, but primarily masculine, "because Man is always dealt with as both *Homo* and *Vir*, but Woman only as *Femina*" (117). Similarly the feminist writer Mary Daly (1978) argues that the so-called gender-neutral words of English (for example, *people, persons, individuals, children, workers, officers*) are most often used in reference to males and have consequently developed masculine connotations (18). Julia Penelope Stanley (1977a) adds that the apparently gender-neutral pronouns *we* and *you*, used by writers to refer to themselves and to their readers, are frequently covert masculines. We have had occasion to observe this phenomenon in the comments of men writing on the language of women.

Lacking a comprehensive frequency study, we cannot assess with any accuracy just what the present state of the use of *man* may be. Since many people sought an alternative like *people* or *human being* long before generic *man* became a feminist issue, it might not be too hazardous to agree with the *OED* that for most of us it has been some time since there was a pair of men in paradise. Despite pronouncements to the contrary, the range of generic *man* seems to be shrinking, even within the literary/proverbial registers where it is most likely to occur. And in ordinary language its range is even more limited, as speakers continue to avoid generic *man* in favor of *person* (which, as we will see, also serves as a substitute for the taboo *woman*), *human, individual,* indefinite *you,* even *guy* and *fellow,* which are used more and more to refer to either sex (and are therefore as ambiguous as *man*).

Avoidance of ambiguity may not be the only reason for the shift away from gender-neutral *man*. The degree of formality is also an important factor in word choice, and it is likely that the history of *man* has been influenced as much by ideas of style as it has by a conscious or unconscious fear of double meaning. The ornate alternatives to gender-specific *man* (*individual, human being, genus homo*) may be triggered by a sense that *man* is too ordinary or unimpressive, while the informal alternatives to generic *man* (*you, folks, people*) may occur because generic *man* is felt to be too high-toned, too forceful, or even too inclusive, certainly inappropriate in informal conversational style. More common than generic *man,* though, and more controversial today in both formal and informal use are the compounds involving *man,* which we will examine in chapter nine. But since the history and use of *woman* in many senses parallels that of *man,* it is only appropriate that we first consider the issue of *woman* and its synonyms.

THE *HERSTORY* OF *WOMAN*

As we saw in chapter three, *woman* comes from Old English *wifmann*. In its discussion of the etymology of the word, the *Century Dictionary* (1891) raises an intriguing point: "It is notable that it was thought necessary to join *wif,* a neuter noun representing a female person, to *man,* a masc[uline] noun representing either a male or female person, to form a word denoting a female person exclusively." The compound *woman* is curious in that a linguistic whole is formed that is somewhat less than the sum of its parts: *woman,* a semantic feminine, is created through the combination of a word already feminine in reference and a sex-neutral word. It is a lexical case of *woman* born from 'woman.'

We may never know just why the word *woman* was formed when the synonymous *wif* already existed, but three factors seem to be involved: analogy, disambiguation, and euphemism. The creation of *wifmann* may have been motivated in part by analogy. Although we cannot be sure which member of the gender pair was coined first, *wifmann* is paralleled in Old English by *wæpmann,* literally 'weaponed person,' a common synonym for gender-specific *wer,* 'man.' But analogy alone does not explain why the compound is formed from *wif* rather than from some term which might more closely match the literal or metaphoric meaning of *wæpen,* or why *wæpmann* was adopted instead of **wermann* (*wer* appears as an element in other Old English compounds), as the correlative pair *wer/wif* would predict.

The existence of a number of competing terms for _man_ and _woman_ is not unusual. We can generally, but not always, find slight differences in meaning that distinguish the synonyms. For example, in addition to Old English _wer_ and _wæpmann_ we find _esne,_ a word often used in reference to servants, retainers, or males of lower status; _guma,_ which like _mann_ corresponds both to Latin _vir_ and _homo;_ and two words, _secg_ and _beorn,_ whose use is restricted to poetry. Besides _wif_ there are _fæmne, meowle,_ and the poetic _ides._ But distinctions between _wif_ and _wifmann_ are particularly interesting, since of the two feminine terms that survive, one word is built on the other.

In Old English, _woman_ and _wife_ are to some extent synonymous. However, the increased use of _woman_ in the generalized sense 'adult female human being' is accompanied by and must in all likelihood be related to the narrowing of _wife_ to mean 'married woman,' and one reasonable explanation for the change involves the separation of the semantic overlap shared by the two words. Old English _wif_ referred exclusively to female persons, either single or married, or to supernatural creatures in the form of women, for example, Grendel's mother in the _Beowulf_ saga. It was used to translate Latin _mulier_ and _femina,_ 'woman, female,' as well as _uxor,_ 'wife'; to form compounds like _wifcild_ and _wiffreond,_ specifying a child or a friend as female; and, in grammatical texts, to indicate the grammatical feminine, just as _wer_ indicated the masculine and _naðrum_ the neuter. _Wifmann_ in turn could be used to indicate the gender of plants and to refer to a servant, two senses not attested for _wif._ But most important, _wifmann_ does not occur in Old English in the sense 'spouse.'

Wife continues to be used both for 'spouse' and 'woman' through the nineteenth century, though according to the _OED_ the sense 'woman' becomes restricted "to a woman of humble rank . . . esp. one engaged in the sale of some commodity," for example, _ale-wife._ _Woman,_ on the other hand, does not acquire the additional, narrowed sense of 'wife, spouse,' until the fifteenth century, long after the etymological connection between _woman_ and _wife_ had become obscure.

We may conclude then that one basic distinction between the competing terms _wife_ and _woman_ in Old English involves the labeling of marital status. _Wifmann_ is semantically neutral with respect to marriage: it does not specify whether a woman is married. _Wif,_ however, is an ambiguous term that may specify such status in certain contexts.

The adoption of *woman* as a generalized term may have paved the way for the eventual narrowing and disambiguation of *wife,* or it may have been the *result* of such narrowing, but more interesting is the fact that, like the marriage-neutral Modern English title *Ms., woman* offers a way of referring to adult female humans, at least during the Old English period, without referring to marital status. Modern German distributes the two senses 'woman' and 'wife' to two different words. *Weib,* which is cognate with Old English *wif* and which like *wif* originally carried both meanings, has become the generalized term for 'woman,' while *Frau* functions both as the standard word for 'spouse' and the equivalent of the English honorific title, *Mrs.* It is also used for a mature woman regardless of marital status. *Weib* does survive in the narrower sense 'wife,' but as such it is always marked as dialectal or poetic. In French no lexical differentiation occurs: *femme* serves for both 'woman' and 'wife' in the standard language.

The masculine correlatives show a similar pattern of development. Just as *wif* in Old English was used to mean both 'woman' and 'wife,' *wer* served to refer to a 'male adult,' and to a 'husband.' Both the masculine and feminine terms were ambiguous, and both were eventually disambiguated. As a further complication, the masculine term *wer* disappears and is replaced by two words, *man* and *husband,* to represent its generalized and specialized meanings. The process of disambiguation took place over several centuries, as we see from the persistence of *wife* in the generalized sense 'woman' in Modern English, and it may still be incomplete, since both *man* and *woman* can now be used in certain contexts to mean 'spouse.' There may well have been a social motivation—something to do with the changing role of marriage—behind this disambiguation. After all, the masculine and feminine lexical systems were refined in a similar fashion to isolate references to persons by marital status from references to persons by sex in general. And both disambiguations involve the narrowing of one term and the adoption (through borrowing in one case and compounding in another) of a new term. *Husband,* imported from Old Norse, is employed for *wer* in the narrowed sense 'spouse,' while *man* narrows to replace *wer* in its generalized sense 'adult male.' Similarly *wif* narrows to 'spouse,' and *woman* is created for the generalized 'adult female.' The systemic nature of the disambiguation suggests that it was perceived as useful and necessary, that it represents a parallel and symmetrical refinement of the ways of referring to men and women. However, disambiguation in and of itself does not explain why *wifmann* is built on *wif*.

The rise of *man* and *woman* may well represent an early semantic shift in favor of marriage-neutral terms, but before we claim that this shift reflects an embryonic Anglo-Saxon feminism—and we have no reason to think that such a position is correct—we must consider another, rather more negative explanation of the relationship between *wifmann* and *wif*. Though this explanation is also unsupported by evidence, it seems to fit better with the later history of the word *woman*.

As Wilfred Funk has shown, many terms for 'woman' originate as neutral or positive in connotation, only to become degraded over the years (1950, 247–48). *Lady,* an aristocratic designation, became in the seventeenth century a synonym for *prostitute*. While it has since recovered from such extreme derogation, *lady* has lost the elevated status it once enjoyed. *Courtesan,* a word which now means 'prostitute,' originally denoted a female member of court. *Wench* at first meant 'child'; *tart* originated as a term of endearment; and etymologists seem to agree that *whore* came from an Indo-European root meaning 'dear.' The term *woman* is itself today held in mixed esteem, and *wife,* the word it replaced as a generalized reference to 'adult females,' has developed pejorative meanings in many of its survivals in the generalized sense: *fishwife, old wives' tale.* Even in its specialized sense of 'spouse,' *wife* is not as positive as its masculine correlatives; the idiom *man and wife,* for example, lacks the parallelism of *husband and wife:* it places the female spouse a notch lower than the male by defining her in terms of her relationship to the male. *Wife* may also be used as a label to depersonalize a woman and to mark her as property.

The avoidance of Modern English *man* to some extent parallels the avoidance of *woman,* though it seems largely a stylistic affair, not directly attributable to pejoration. In any case, it is clear that euphemism has played a part in the fortunes of *man* and *woman*. We can suggest—although it must be stressed again that there is no evidence to support this speculation—that if *man* functioned as a prestige term in Old English, it could have replaced *wer* in the same way that *individual* has been displacing *man*. Similarly, adding the prestige term to *wif* to form the compound *wifmann* could create a more polite, more neutral, somehow less tainted alternative to *wif* which, like other English words referring to women, might have undergone some degree of pejoration that it is now difficult to trace. *Woman,* and perhaps the sex-specific sense of *man* as well, may later have become taboo through association with the words they replaced—such has been the fate of many euphemisms, for example, *toilet,* originally 'a piece of cloth'—and this could explain the modern avoidance of the words as common or impolite.

AVOIDING *WOMAN* AND *WIFE*

English speakers avoid the use of *man* in its generic sense, but many of them also shun *woman* in any of its senses, preferring instead the alternatives *lady* and *girl,* and in earlier times, *female, person,* and *young person.* Apparently many people sense that *woman* is too blunt, too sexual, too demeaning, too clinical, or too common, so that conversational politeness calls for a euphemism, and proper writing style calls for a fancier word. This was not always the case, and it does not have to be the case now. For some two hundred years, two groups who do not usually agree on matters of language have been advising us that *woman* is the word of choice for 'adult female human being.' Feminists see the synonym *female* as animalistic in its reference, and they regard *lady* and *girl* as trivializing or derogatory words that bar women from equality with men. Usage critics find these same words *lady, female,* and *girl* to be insulting, pretentious, journalistic, or prudishly euphemistic. But despite a bombardment of advice and protest, many people still regard *woman* as taboo and avoid it if they can.

As early as the eighteenth century writers lament the disappearance of the words *woman* and *wife* from the speech of the more respectable elements of English society. According to the anonymous author of a satirical article in *The Connoisseur* (1754), an unmarried woman must be referred to as a *miss,* and one with a husband as a *married lady,* for "the plain old English word wife has long been discarded in our conversation, as being only fit for the broad mouths of the vulgar." *Lady,* we are told, has replaced *woman* as well as *wife* in fashionable speech. In addition to *married ladies* the author complains of *maiden* or *young ladies*—expressions which are "indifferently applied to females of the age of fourteen or threescore"—*fine ladies,* and *ladies of pleasure,* who

155

openly profess a trade which the *fine ladies* "carry on by smuggling" (222–23).

Evidence from the *OED* shows that *lady* has been a synonym for *woman* since the thirteenth century, though especially in its earlier use it referred more narrowly to 'a woman of superior position in society.' By the nineteenth century it had become the general though more polite equivalent of *woman,* while its masculine correlative, *lord,* retained its narrowness. As we see from the article in the *Connoisseur,* however, the widening of the scope of *lady* was not universally welcomed. The corresponding widening of *gentleman* was also criticized on the grounds that it was not polite, but pretentious. In her study of eighteenth-century vocabulary, Susie Tucker (1967) reports Hugh Kelly's ironic remark on the spread of *lady* and *gentleman:* "It would be unpardonably vulgar to call a milk-woman by any other appellation than that of a lady; and the meanest artisan . . . if he happens to want an apprentice, will publicly advertise for a young gentleman" (50). In the nineteenth and twentieth centuries the use of *lady* as a euphemism for *woman,* and *gentleman* for *man,* was even more vigorously opposed. K. C. Phillipps (1984) comments that by the mid nineteenth century, *lady* and *gentleman* had become heavy with moral overtones (for example, "Act like a lady," "A gentleman would never do that"), thus making their use objectionable in upper-class British speech (7-8).

Another synonym for *woman,* the noun *female,* enters English during the fourteenth century, at about the same time as the adjective *female.* By the eighteenth century we find some opposition to the noun, although most writers treat it as standard. According to Tucker, the *Critical Review* in 1756 calls the noun *female* ludicrous, and "seldom or perhaps never used by genteel people" (1967, 57). However, Samuel Johnson accepts *female* in his *Dictionary* (1755) as a noun meaning "a She; one of the sex which brings young" (his illustrative quotations make it clear that Johnson is thinking not of animals in general but specifically of 'woman'). The author of the article in the *Connoisseur,* who objects to *lady,* does not hesitate to use *female* as a noun in his writing, but by the nineteenth century, *female* comes under attack from usage critics and feminists alike. The *OED,* tacitly admitting that *female* still appears in less reputable publications, says that the noun is "now commonly avoided by good writers, exc[ept] with contemptuous implication," and _Webster's Third New International Dictionary,_ which employs usage labels sparingly, marks the word as disparaging when used for women.

Usage Critics and Feminists

Almost every nineteenth- and twentieth-century usage guide comments on the misuse of _lady_ and _female,_ an indication that the objectionable words had become firmly entrenched in the language as euphemisms and that _woman_ and, to a lesser extent, _wife_ had become highly stigmatized words. In his _Dictionary_ of 1828 Noah Webster specifies that the noun _female_ is appropriate in reference to animals and plants; _lady_ is defined as a courtesy title used of women just as _gentleman_ is of men. Webster implies that only _woman_ should function as the general term for "the female of the human race," though he was not indisposed toward euphemism in his own writing. In the bowdlerized version of the Bible that he published in 1833, Webster justifies his emendation of scriptural vulgarity while using the noun _female,_ as well as _young person,_ a frequently criticized alternative to _girl:_ "Many [biblical] words and phrases are so offensive, especially to females, as to create a reluctance in young persons to attend Bible classes and schools" (cited in Read 1934, 386).

For James Fenimore Cooper the avoidance of _wife, woman,_ and _man_ is evidence of pretension and social climbing. According to Cooper (1838), a man of high breeding "calls a spade, 'a spade.' . . . He never calls his wife, 'his lady,' but 'his wife,' and he is not afraid of lessening the dignity of the human race, by styling the most elevated and refined of his fellow creatures, 'men and women'" (122–23). The use of _lady_ to mean _wife,_ acceptable in the eighteenth century and found in the writings of Austen and Disraeli, had come to be considered pretentious in England as well (Phillipps 1984, 123). And Henry Alford (1864) complains,

> Why should a _woman_ be degraded from her position as a rational being, and be expressed by a word which might belong to any animal tribe, and which, in our version of the Bible, is never used except of animals, or of the abstract, the sex in general? [227]

While Alford implies that it is men who are guilty of this semantic degradation, Richard Grant White (1870) blames the avoidance of _woman_ on "every one of the softer and more ambitious sex who is dissatisfied with her social position, or uncertain of it." White rejects three centuries of authoritative usage of _female_ as a noun because he feels that no amount of evidence can deny the fact that "a cow, or a sow, or any she brute is a female, just as a woman is." He labels the British preference for _female_ over _woman,_ "one of the most unpleasant and inexcusable of the common perversions of language," and he terms the American penchant for the euphemism _lady_ "nauseous" (180).

Like White, usage critic Alfred Ayres (1882) advised his readers that the substitution of _lady_ for _woman_ represents a kind of "pin-feather gentility" that is avoided by "persons of refinement." In Ayres's view, "Ladies say 'we _women,_'" while "_vulgar_ women talk about 'us _ladies._'" Despite his defense of _woman,_ Ayres considers the phrase _men and women_ "too advanced" and the equivalent _ladies and gentle-men_ "too vulgar," recommending in their stead a compromise, _ladies and men,_ that has attracted few converts (s.v. "lady").

Sarah Josepha Hale, who as we have seen tried to popularize feminine nouns, agrees with Dean Alford that _female_ is an animal epithet. Although her ardent defense of woman's right to linguistic dignity is characterized in _Notable American Women_ (1971) as "safe but trivial," Hale carried her campaign against _female_ beyond the pages of _Godey's Lady's Book._ A supporter of women's education, Hale in 1865 urged Matthew Vassar to remove the word _female_ from the name of the newly opened _Vassar Female College._ Vassar agreed and in turn requested that the trustees of the college abandon the word as degrading, unscriptural, and ungrammatical. In 1867, when the name change was approved, Vassar proudly wrote to Hale that "the central marble slab on the front of the Edifice containing the word 'Female' was removed, relieving the Institution from the odium which has so long disgraced it" (Taylor and Haight 1915, 30–31).

Another supporter of _lady,_ anonymous and apparently male, writes to the _Atlantic Monthly_ in 1895 to lament the disappearance of the only word which can signify "that mysterious combination of character, temperament, education, and experience into one beautiful whole, which sex, nor birth, nor position, nor any single advantage, outward or inward, can assure." The writer, who admits that such terms as _saleslady_ and _gentlemen and ladies_ are objectionable, observes that it is ladies themselves who are condemning and avoiding the word *lady*—a sharp contrast to the opinion of White and Ayres—and he sounds his warning "lest the idea itself should be losing credit among the feminine half of creation" (76: 431–32).

The Return of *Woman*

Reports of the relative status of *woman* and *lady* frequently conflict. Albert F. Moe (1963) finds evidence that in the 1880s *woman* was considered a negative or low-status term, while *lady* was held to be positive and socially obligatory (295). But in their turn-of-the-century study of the English vocabulary, James B. Greenough and George Lyman Kittredge ([1901] 1920) claim that the use of *lady* is decreasing and that *woman* is making a well-deserved comeback. Greenough and Kittredge also observe that although things are changing, they are to some extent remaining the same, for the negative connotation of *woman* has been transferred—by women—to a new word:

> *Person* has suffered an amusing deterioration. It has been more or less employed as a substitute for *woman* by those who did not wish to countenance the vulgar abuse of *lady* and yet shrank from giving offence. The result has been to give a comically slighting connotation to one of the most innocent words imaginable. [326]

In 1919 H. L. Mencken also asserts that *lady,* particularly in compounds, is becoming less popular, at least in the United States. Mencken observes that what the British call *ladies' singles,* American tennis players refer to as *women's singles;* that Americans say *women's wear* for the British *ladies' wear;* and that the occupational terms *saleswoman* and *salesgirl* are replacing *saleslady* (121).

The optimism of Mencken, Greenough, and Kittredge over the return of *woman* was somewhat premature. Fowler remarks in 1926 that *lady* and *female* are still being misused, and he notes that the stigma attached to the noun *female* has been picked up by the adjective as well, with the result that the unobjectionable *female suffrage* is avoided in favor of the "clumsy" *woman suffrage.* Fowler also opposes the tendency to use *lady* in phrases denoting occupations: *lady doctor,* according to him, would be better phrased as *woman* or *female* doctor, though he prefers the even less cumbersome *doctress* (s.v. "female"; "lady").

Fowler wrote for a British audience, but twentieth-century American usage commentators continue the tradition of recommending *woman* and condemning *lady*. Their comments are at best only an indirect indicator of actual usage, for as John Algeo (1977) has shown, usage books tend to "address themselves mainly to an inherited list of problems rather than to real issues in contemporary English" (67). But they do indicate that interest in the problem of *lady* and *woman* has remained strong on both sides of the Atlantic. Maurice Weseen (1928), for example, says of *lady*, "This euphemism has become so perverted in use as to nauseate most grammarians and critics." Frank Colby advises, "No lady should ever resent being called a woman, for all ladies are women, as all gentlemen are men" ([1944] 1947, 99). Bergen and Cornelia Evans (1957), who note that *woman* is a general term worthy of dignity whereas *female,* once an elegant euphemism, is now contemptuous, are virtually alone in accepting the persistence of *lady*, particularly in the United States, as a more formal term for almost any woman. Harry Shaw (1975) says that there is normally no justification for the use of *lady* (100). And as recently as 1980 Roy Copperud feels obligated to remind his readers that "*woman* is the workaday word, and the idea that it contains a hint of disparagement is mistaken and generally held by the uneducated" (s.v. "woman").

Are All Ladies Women?

In 1962 Louise M. Ackerman affirmed in the pages of *American Speech* the opinion of newspaper columnist Ann Landers that *lady* and *woman* are synonymous in American English. Yet according to Cicely Raysor Hancock (1963), many women use *lady* but not *woman* to refer to an adult female. A second, larger group reverses this pattern, using *woman* for the speaker and her female friends or relatives, for other social equals, and for social superiors, reserving *lady* for inferiors (with a conscious sense of politeness, for example, *cleaning lady*) or for strangers whose social status is not evident. A third group uses *woman* or *girl* regardless of social class or degree of familiarity.

Two recent feminist usage handbooks join their predecessors in preferring *woman* to *lady*. Casey Miller and Kate Swift (1980) find that *lady* can convey esteem in certain contexts, for example, *first lady* and *leading lady*. But, citing *saleslady*, Miller and Swift warn that as an occupational indicator *lady* implies a lesser valuation. They note that there is still some taboo associated with *woman*—according to them because it connotes competence and sexual maturity—and they recommend *woman* as "the most useful all-around word for referring to adult female people" (74–77). Bobbye Sorrels simply urges the complete elimination of *lady* as a noun or adjective (1983, 139).

Despite the long tradition of commentary and advice on the terms *lady* and *woman*, there has been only one empirical study of the use of the words. In 1984 Linda Bebout tested a number of assumptions about *lady, woman, girl, gentleman, man,* and *boy* through a questionnaire administered to a group of Canadian college students. Bebout found instances where actual usage contradicts the predictions of the usage manuals. For example, her responses indicate a slight preference for *lady* in the occupational pairs *cleaning lady/woman* and *saleslady/ -woman*, though *woman* is preferred as a prenominal modifier for both *bus driver* and *doctor*. In addition, men seem to prefer *lady,* and the word tends to occur in more formal or polite contexts.

For some two hundred years the taboo against using *woman* has conflicted with its official status as the standard word for 'adult female human being.' It is not surprising then that speakers and writers exhibit ambivalence toward *woman* and alternatives such as *lady,* making decisions about these words on a case by case or context by context basis. The persistence of *lady* does not mean that the advice of feminists or usage critics has gone unnoticed. Some speakers and writers try to follow it, others to go against it. Many times the advice complicates actual usage, rather than reforming or simplifying it. Noting that female respondents showed a greater tendency than males to use sex-neutral words, Bebout remarks that the choice of *woman, lady,* or *girl,* "always dependent to a large extent upon social factors, is probably now confounded by ideological ones for many speakers" (26).

We have seen a similar ambivalence toward generic *man* and the alternatives that have been developed to replace it. The use or the avoidance of *man,* though not affected by the stigma of taboo, is also subject to ideological pressures. Concern with the proper way to refer to women as well as men—linguistically, socially, and ideologically— has resulted in a number of lexical innovations, some of them recent, others the product of earlier times.

CHAPTER 9

New Words and Women

The women . . . busied themselves in inventing new words.
Victor Renault

Finding the right word to express or suppress a gender distinction is not always easy. Daniel Cook (1959) reports that in 1913 a man was arrested for accosting a woman with the greeting "Hello, chicken." At his trial the accused contended that he meant no insult, pleaded Webster in his defense, and got off on a lexical technicality. The judge, consulting a dictionary, found for the defense and released the prisoner.

Despite this legal precedent, the status of *chicken* in reference to women is not entirely clear. Webster himself notes in his *Dictionary* of 1828 that *chicken* may be "a term of tenderness," and several lexicographers cite Swift's line, "Stella is no chicken," that is, 'Stella is no longer young,' to illustrate the sense of youth that may be conveyed by the word. Over the years, however, the word acquired a feminine, and ultimately a pejorative, connotation. *Webster's New International Dictionary* (1907), the most likely source for the judge's ruling, defines *chicken* as 'a young person, child, especially a young woman.' By 1930 *Webster's Second New International* marks the word as slang for 'a young woman of easy familiarity,' but the plaintiff's outrage and the prisoner's contrived defense suggest that in this earlier instance *chicken* had already become disrespectful, if not blatantly insulting.

The anecdote is an extreme example of the problems inherent in addressing women and, to a lesser extent, men, in English, which contains few formal honorific status markers in its lexicon compared to other languages. Although some honorifics are prescribed by context (*your honor,* for a judge), the choice of less formal vocatives depends largely on the amount of positive (*sir, madam*) or negative (*boy, girlie*) status accorded the addressee. Usage books agree, for example, that a woman is not to be addressed as *lady* (Lady, you dropped your glove); many suggest *Miss* or *Madam,* depending on the apparent age of the woman, as proper alternatives when a vocative is needed.

Perhaps the most controversial honorifics of late have not been vocatives, but the gender-specific titles *Mister, Miss,* and *Mrs.* prefixed to the names of men and women. These titles pose a problem for Modern English speakers: they generally reveal the marital status of women but not that of men. Furthermore, when a woman is referred to exclusively by her husband's name, for example *Mrs. John Smith*—a practice frowned on by twentieth-century usage critics and feminists alike—she is deprived of her name and her individuality, and rendered both subordinate and invisible.

The asymmetry of our titles may be merely inconvenient: a woman who prefers *Miss* may take offense when addressed as *Mrs.,* and vice versa. Yet it may also be evidence of male control both of language and society. The feminine title, it is claimed, tells a man whether a woman is sexually available, but a woman is given no such information about a man. Actually *Miss* and *Mrs.* do not necessarily convey accurate information on marital status, since *Miss* is frequently used as a professional title by women who are married, and *Mrs.* may be retained by women who are widowed or divorced.

Several remedies have been offered for restructuring both the male and female title paradigms, and unlike many proposed language reforms, one innovation, marriage-neutral *Ms.,* has achieved some success. A look at the history of the title paradigm shows its flexibility: it has undergone significant changes over the past five hundred years.

MASTER AND MISTRESS

Mr. derives from *master,* which appears in English in the ninth century, and first occurs as a masculine title prefixed to a name in the late thirteenth century. By the eighteenth century *Master* had been completely superseded by the derived form *Mister,* which developed its own pronunciation and generally appeared in written texts as the abbreviated *Mr.* As early as 1563 the title *Master* comes to mean 'young gentleman,' in contrast to *Mr.,* which is reserved for older men. Originally indicative of rank or compliment, the social range of *Mr.* has continually widened, reaching the point where it can be used to refer to any adult male. The title _Master,_ when it occurs, is now limited to boys of unspecified age who are considered too young to warrant the use of _Mr. Mr._ has always been neutral, or unmarked, with respect to marital status, but the _Master/Mr._ age distinction is shared in some sense by the _Miss/Mrs._ feminine title pair.

Both _Miss_ and _Mrs._ derive from _mistress,_ the feminine form of _master._ As with many gender pairs, _master_ and _mistress_ develop along somewhat different lines, and _mistress_ acquires some pejorative meanings that _master_ does not. _Mistress_ enters English from French in the early fourteenth century, with the meaning 'governess.' Other senses, dating from the late fourteenth or early fifteenth century, include 'female head of household; a woman who rules or has control; a female instructor; a concubine.' In addition, _Mistress_ serves as a prefixed feminine title, which is neutral with regard to marital status, from the fifteenth to the later nineteenth century.

The _Oxford English Dictionary_ suggests that _Miss_ may originally have been a spelling pronunciation of _Mis_ or _M^is_, the written abbreviations for _Mistress_ that were common in the sixteenth and seventeenth centuries. _Miss_ first appears as a title for an unmarried woman around 1666. It can refer to a concubine in the seventeenth century, though it is also found in reference to an unmarried girl of the ages ten to seventeen. The conflict between these meanings is resolved as _Miss_ develops connotations of youthfulness and begins to serve as a correlative of _Master._ Like _Mistress,_ however, _Miss_ did not originally indicate marital status, referring in the eighteenth and nineteenth centuries to married women as well as single ones.

Paralleling the development of _Mr.,_ the title _Mrs._ eventually becomes a distinct word. Like _Mr.,_ it is rarely written out in full, and it too develops its own pronunciation [mɪsɪz] by the nineteenth century. _Mrs._ occurs as early as 1615 as a title for a married woman, but during the seventeenth and eighteenth centuries it can also be prefixed to the name of an unmarried girl or woman.

Miss and _Mrs._ have been interchangeable to some extent for much of their history, though they begin to sort themselves out as indicators of age and marital status during the latter part of the eighteenth century. In 1781 the _Gentleman's Magazine_ mentions the recent use of _Miss_ to refer to unmarried women, although the _Monthly Review_ in

1775 had labeled this new style injudicious, recommending *Mrs.* as a more appropriate term for single women (Tucker 1967, 159). By 1790, however, Noah Webster is found complaining that the American tendency to use *Miss* for *Mistress* is a gross impropriety: "The word Mistress (or Madam to an old lady) should always be applied to a married lady, and *Miss* to one who has never been married" (Thornton [1912] 1962, 2:583–84). Despite Webster's formulation of the rule, *Miss* continued to be used in America and in parts of England throughout the nineteenth century to refer to married women as well as single ones (Wright 1898–1905, s.v.). In 1801 we find a defense of the broad use of *Miss* that may be the earliest rationale for a marriage-neutral female title: "*Miss,* applied equally to married and single ladies, may sometimes lead foreigners into an error, but then by simplifying the language it facilitates its acquisition" (*Restorator,* 1).

REVISING THE PARADIGM

Even as the titles *Miss* and *Mrs.* were beginning to differentiate with respect to marital status, discontent with the developing paradigm was apparent. An anonymous eighteenth-century writer expressed the wish "that some middle term was invented between Miss and Mrs. to be adopted, at a certain age, by all females not inclined to matrimony" (*Connoisseur* 1754, 223–24).

Describing another kind of discontent, Una Stannard (1977) complains that the use of *Mrs.* forced wives to assume the status of their husbands and discouraged them from achievements of their own. For example, in the 1840s the wife of John Tyler called herself *Mrs. Presidentess,* and later *Mrs. Ex-President Tyler* (17). The anthropologist Elsie Clews Parsons (1913) notes that *Mrs.* prevents married women from being treated as persons in their own right, the independent equals of men:

> There are married women, of course, to whom the historical symbolism of the wedding-ring does not appeal, or to whom all labels . . . are snobbishness, or who, like married men, do not feel called upon to give themselves away. These ladies may go ringless, but as yet no woman has found any escape from being addressed, at least by servants and shopkeepers, as 'Mrs.' [50]

Stannard finds that one way to escape the yoke of *Mrs.,* which allows a married woman to exist only in terms of her spouse, is to eschew titles altogether. This approach was recommended by Elizabeth Cady Stanton at the Women's Rights Convention held at Seneca Falls in 1848, and the convention adopted a policy that women use "their own female names and with no Miss or Mrs to indicate marital status" (3).

Another solution, advocated by the actress Fola La Follette at a feminist rally in 1914, lay not in the abandonment of titles, or for that matter in the creation of a new one, but in the formal extension of *Miss* to serve as the general female title both before and after marriage (Stannard 1977, 177). La Follette may have known that only a century or so earlier this generalized reference had been a standard function of *Miss;* that only lately had the word disappeared as a title for married women in colloquial American English writing; and that such use was still current in dialectal British and American speech.

New Words

The first new words proposed to remedy the deficiencies of the English system of titles are masculine, not feminine terms, designed to round out rather than truncate the paradigm. The earliest is the jocular creation of the American satirist Ambrose Bierce ([1911] 1943), who alleges that titles themselves are somehow un-American, and prefers that they be done away with altogether:

> [*Miss* is] a title with which we brand unmarried women to indicate that they are in the market. Miss, Missis (Mrs.) and Mister (Mr.) are the three most distinctly disagreeable words in the language, in sound and sense. Two are corruptions of Mistress, the other of Master. In the general abolition of social titles in this country they miraculously escaped to plague us. If we must have them let us be consistent and give one to the unmarried man. I venture to suggest Mush, abbreviated to Mh. [*Devil's Dictionary,* s.v. "Miss"]

Perhaps the best way to round out the paradigm would be to draft *Master,* the historical correlate of *Miss,* to indicate an unmarried man, but such a suggestion was never made, possibly because it was both logical and linguistically justifiable, and therefore might be taken seriously. The following list typifies proposals for a new male title, most of which were not intended for actual adoption:

Mk., for *Mark,* that is, 'a mark worth shooting at by single women.'
  Baltimore Evening Sun (1941), cited by Hench
Br. or *Bch,* 'bachelor'; also *Wd.,* 'widow,' and *Wr.,* 'widower.' Atcheson
  L. Hench (1941)
Bar, 'bachelor'; *Wow,* 'widower,' Theodore Bernstein, and
Murm, 'married man'; *Smur,* 'single man,' Russell Baker. Cited by
  Miller and Swift (1977, 93)
Mrd., 'married man'; *Mngl.,* 'single man.' Bobbye Sorrels (1983)

Other proposals offered a sex- and marriage-neutral title to replace
rather than complete the present paradigm of *Mr., Miss, Mrs.;* for
example:

Pn., 'person.' Varda (Murell) One, cited by Israel Shenker, *New York
  Times,* 29 August 1971, 58
Pr., 'person.' John Clark, *Newsletter of the American Anthropological
  Association* 13 (1972): 117–18
Msf., 'myself,' and *Citizen.* Cited in Hecht et al. (1973, 59)
Masir (*madam* + *sir;* suggestive of *master*). David H. Stern, *Los An-
  geles Times,* 19 January 1974, sec. 2, p. 4
Em. Jeffrey J. Smith, *Em Institute Newsletter* (June 1977)
M. Bobbye Sorrels (1983)

Ms.

The title *Ms* appears on the tombstone of Sarah Spooner, who died in
1767 in Plymouth, Massachusetts, but it is certainly an abbreviation
of *Miss* or *Mistress,* and not an example of colonial language reform
or a slip of the chisel, as some have suggested. The modern marriage-
neutral title *Ms.,* however, is well over fifty years old. It appears as
early as the 1930s, though it does not receive much public discussion
until it is picked up briefly by the business community in the 1950s,
and later by the new woman's movement in the 1970s, when the popularity of the title increases dramatically.

The earliest account of *Ms.* to turn up so far appears in a letter from
M. J. Hirshtein to the *New York Times* in May, 1932. Hirshtein cites
a debate in the business community over the use of *Miss* or *M's.* for a
woman whose marital status is in doubt:

> One school of thought argues that should we address a married woman
> as "Miss," no harm is done, for if anything she feels flattered; whereas

should an unmarried woman be addressed as "Miss," then most certainly no harm has been done.

In arguing against the use of "M's," this school says that it is too indefinite and that if it is used before the name of a single woman, it makes her extremely conscious of her "bachelor-girl" state and thus creates within her a real feeling of antagonism. [24 May 1932, sec. 3]

Hirshtein's letter implies that readers would be familiar with the usage question, and indicates that *Ms.* was a commercial rather than a feminist issue at the time. His use of the form *M's.* suggests that the term may have been perceived as an abbreviation of *Miss.* Although Hirshtein calls upon the readers of the *Times* for advice, no discussion of the issue is forthcoming.

In *The Story of Language* (1949), Mario Pei treats *Ms.* as a creation of the women's rights movement rather than the world of business. Pei links the abbreviation directly to *Miss:*

Feminists, who object to the distinction between Mrs. and Miss and its concomitant revelatory features, have often proposed that the two present-day titles be merged into a single one, "Miss" (to be written "Ms."), with a plural "Misses" (written "Mss."), even at the cost of confusion with the abbreviation for "manuscripts." [79; this passage is deleted from subsequent editions of the book]

The pronunciation indicated by Pei, [mɪs], suggests that the term may have been at first nothing more radical than a new abbreviation for the marriage-neutral sense of *Miss,* a sense which, though frequently labeled as dialectal or nonstandard, had never entirely disappeared. *6,000 Words* (1976), a supplement to *Webster's Third New International Dictionary,* confirms the pronunciation "mis" as well as the more familiar "miz," and early twentieth-century secretarial and etiquette handbooks as well as feminists recommended using *Miss* when a woman's marital status was unknown.

Most lexicographers assume that *Ms.* derives not from *Miss* but from a blend of *Miss* and *Mrs.,* the two words it is intended to replace. But if Pei's statement is correct, we must account for the pronunciation shift of *Ms.* from [mɪs] to the present form, [mɪz]. Two interrelated possibilities suggest themselves: [mɪz] may come from the generalized Southern pronunciation that makes homophones of *Miss* and *Mrs.* Or it might be a pronunciation that arose to differentiate the

new, abbreviated title from its source, *Miss*. As an honorific, *Miss* had
become ambiguous, remaining marriage-neutral for some speakers
while indicating an unmarried woman for most. Developing a new
pronunciation for the marriage-neutral sense of *Miss* would resolve
this ambiguity, and would be in keeping with the tradition of titles
developing their own distinct pronunciations ([mɪstər] from [mæs-
tər]; [mɪs] and [mɪsɪz] from [mɪstrɪs]). With the new pronunciation,
which could have been reinforced by the Southern pronunciation of
Miss and *Mrs.*, *Ms.* might then come to be reinterpreted as a blend of
Miss and *Mrs.*

We cannot be certain about the origins of *Ms.* until more early citations come to light. In the meantime, this interpretation is attractive
because it provides *Ms.* with a history it does not at present have,
connecting the title to the woman's movement of the nineteenth and
early twentieth centuries, and showing it to be an integral and logical
development of the feminine title paradigm of *Mistress, Miss,* and its
abbreviations *Mis* and *Mrs.*, from the sixteenth century to the present.
Furthermore, *Ms.* has always been closely identified with *Miss,* and
there are some indications that this identification persists. For example, the *Prentice-Hall Complete Secretarial Letter Book* (1978) treats
Ms. as an abbreviation of either the general or the restricted sense of
Miss, recommending the use of *Miss* or *Ms.* for single women or
women whose marital status is unknown, but *Mrs.* for married ones.
In addition, in an informal survey of undergraduate women students
at the University of Illinois, many younger unmarried women expressed a preference for *Ms.* while they are single, but indicated their
intention to adopt *Mrs.* when they marry. If such women do switch to
Mrs., then *Ms.* will have replaced *Miss* in the traditional *Miss/Mrs.*
title pair, at least for these speakers and writers, and its use as a marriage-neutral term will be compromised. As we will see below, a similar compromise of semantic neutrality is noticeable in the use of such
new sex-neutral nouns as *chairperson.*

The Use of *Ms.*

Early citations indicate that *Ms.* was discussed in the 1950s not in
terms of feminism, as Pei suggests, but in the context of business
writing. The term is not mentioned in Frailey's *Handbook of Business
Letters* (1948) or in Saunders's *Effective Business English* (1949),

which advises omission of any title if a woman's marital status is not known. But shortly thereafter, interest in *Ms.* revives. In 1950 the Merriam-Webster company received three queries about the new title, and in 1951 readers of the *Dartnell Better Letters Bulletin,* edited by Lester E. Frailey, and the *Bulletin of the American Business Writing Association,* edited by Chester R. Anderson, were invited to discuss the "current movement to use *Ms.* for all women" (Anderson 1951, 8). Anderson, who recalls the initial interest in the term in the 1930s, points out that *Ms.* is the logical equivalent of *Mr.,* but he is compelled to wonder aloud whether "the women [are] interested in being logical to this extent." Anderson's own resistance to logic leads him to frown on *Ms.,* at least until it gains wider acceptance.

Frailey is apparently more open to innovation, for *Ms.* is cited in Frailey and Schnell's *Practical Business Writing* (1952) as a title "that saves debating between *Miss* and *Mrs.*" (151). *Ms.* is also recommended in *The Simplified Letter* (1952), issued by the National Office Management Association (*OED* Supplement H–N [1976], s.v.). Brown and Doris's *Business Executive's Handbook* (1954) notes without elaboration, "A few business concerns now use *Ms.*" (627). And in the seventh edition of her *Standard Handbook for Secretaries* (1956), Lois Irene Hutchinson formally includes *Ms.* in her list of titles for men and women (the sixth edition in 1950 makes no reference to the term). Hutchinson advises her readers, "Always use 'Mr.,' 'Mrs.,' 'Miss,' or 'Ms.' before a personal name, unless another title is applicable, as 'Dr.' . . . If in doubt about 'Miss' or 'Mrs.,' use 'Miss' or Ms.' (meaning either 'Miss' or 'Mrs.')." Hutchinson does not indicate a pronunciation for *Ms.,* but she apparently treats it as separate from, though an alternative to, *Miss.* Hutchinson resorts to the traditional generic masculine in the most troublesome case: "If unable to tell whether the addressee is a man or woman, use 'Mr.'" (310). Though *Ms.* was new enough to warrant definition for readers who might not have come across the term, Hutchinson would not have recommended its use if she had considered it to be at all controversial. Other writers were slower to endorse the term. By 1968 Hanna, Pophan, and Beamer, in *Secretarial Procedures and Administration,* express a reluctant acknowledgment that *Ms.* had become a common title in business letter writing. The authors advise women to identify their status as *Miss* or *Mrs.,* for "otherwise, correspondents are not sure how to address you and must use the indeterminate form *Ms.*" (196).

Whether *Ms.* was coined by a feminist, by a member of the business community, or by someone who was both, its appeal to the world of commerce was immediately apparent. It offered the writers of business letters a practical solution to the problem of addressing unknown female clients, leaving open the use of *Miss* or *Mrs.* once the addressee's preference was established.

The business community has never shied away from linguistic innovation, particularly when such innovation could be translated into good will and profits. Since the 1970s, when *Ms.* began to achieve wider notice, many corporations have prescribed its use in correspondence, and business writing textbooks such as the *Prentice-Hall Complete Secretarial Letter Book* (1978) and the *Katherine Gibbs Handbook of Business English* (Quinn 1982) recommend the adoption of *Ms.* when an addressee's title preference or marital status is unknown. But the general public and the literary establishment have been slower to accept the new term. *Ms.* achieved national recognition in a *Time* magazine article in 1970, an indication that the title had become common enough to make some waves. In 1972 it was given legal status when the California senate passed a law allowing women to use *Ms.* in registering to vote. In January of that same year *Ms.* magazine published its first issue. But the title also met with considerable opposition, and general usage books have not embraced the new title with the enthusiasm of their business counterparts.

Although William and Mary Morris, editors of the *Harper Dictionary of Contemporary Usage* (1975), advise their readers to use sexneutral language whenever possible, the usage panel of the *Harper Dictionary* votes more than two to one in favor of the traditional *Miss/ Mrs.* title paradigm. Some panelists compare the pronunciation of *Ms.*, [mɪz], to what they variously deem the stigmatized, incorrect, ignorant, lazy, rural, Black, or Southern pronunciation of *Mrs.* Others pretend to confuse *Ms.* with *ms.* the abbreviation for manuscript. They note that the title is not established and express resentment at being forced to use it. Several of the panelists prefer the less controversial and more egalitarian solution recommended at the Seneca Falls convention and endorsed by Ambrose Bierce: avoiding titles altogether.

Unlike business texts, recent general usage commentaries all express mixed feelings about *Ms.* Roy Copperud (1980) emphasizes the difficulties of the title and its "consequent loss of popularity" (254–

55). The *New York Times Magazine* labels *Ms.* a "useful business-letter coinage . . .[that] still sounds too contrived for news writing (5 August 1984, 10). In their *Handbook of Nonsexist Writing* (1980), Miller and Swift warn that the use of *Ms.* can be controversial, and they recommend using the addressee's preference, if it is known, or not using any title at all. Bobbye Sorrels prefers a sex-neutral honorific, such as *M.*, though she accepts *Mr.* and *Ms.* as a temporary measure (1983, 35).

Although frequently greeted with resentment and mockery, *Ms.* has become more and more common in professional correspondence. Many women have adopted it as the title of choice, though lately there have been contentions that the use of *Ms.* is declining. Unfortunately, no survey of actual usage has documented either the spread or the decline of the title. The English title paradigm, which has a history of instability, will probably continue to change. Titles, after all, are functions of social structure, and social structure is flexible. Even though some women may adopt *Mrs.* when they marry, others will retain *Ms.*, either as a statement of equality with men or simply as a convenience. As they did with *Miss,* many people may choose to adopt a dual set of titles, using either the new *Ms.* or the traditional *Miss* for business, and *Miss* or *Mrs.* (or even *Ms.* or *Mrs.*) for social occasions. In addition, men may not always employ the same feminine titles as women. In any case, it is likely that *Ms.*, whose origins remain to be uncovered, will be around for a while as an English honorific.

SEPARATE BUT EQUAL

One problem in gender-related honorifics arose in the second half of the nineteenth century, when women began graduating from American colleges and universities in considerable numbers. In certain cases, hiding behind Latin terminology forestalls controversy. For example, when soliciting donations, men's schools address their *alumni* and women's schools cajole their *alumnae* to open their purses. For coeducational institutions, the rule of the masculine generic is usually applied, and female graduates are embraced by the masculine *alumni* associations. The terms caused little stir in the past, partly because the generic masculine was less controversial than it is now and partly because many graduates had either forgotten their Latin declensions or had no classics to begin with. Vassar College dropped *female* from its name, though it produced only *alumnae* for some one hundred years. But when the school began graduating men, it switched to *alumni,* and many *alumnae* were outraged at their sudden defeminization.

The problem of degree names proved even more critical: many people considered it inappropriate to call women graduates *bachelors* or *masters*. For example, in 1888 Samuel Rockwell Reed, a columnist for the *Cincinnati Commercial Gazette,* criticizes Yale College for awarding a bachelor of laws degree to a woman. Reed advocates instead a *maid* of laws degree for women lawyers, arguing that if a woman is to be equal, independent, and committed to a career, she will have to remain unwed (270–71).

According to D. C. Gilman (1885), president of the Johns Hopkins University, hundreds of weak and inefficient colleges were actually manufacturing—"with an inventive skill that is truly American"—new degrees for their new clientele. In the same year, the *Pall Mall Gazette* satirizes the new feminine degrees:

> Silly fellows are constantly poking fun, for instance, at the insult it would be to an ungraduated husband to be married to a "master," and at the incongruity of giving clever but otherwise marriageable girls the title of "bachelor." The Americans have cut the knot in their usual practical fashion, and talk of Miss Bluestocking not as "Bachelor of Arts" or "Bachelor of Science," but as "Maid of Philosophy," "Maid of Science," "Maid of Arts," while a girl who has taken degrees in all the faculties is, we suppose, called a "Maid of All Work," what in this aristocratic country is a badge of servitude being in the free democracy of the West a prize of intellect. [5 March 1885, 3:2]

The earliest reference to a female degree may be apocryphal. In the *Knickerbocker* (1834), an author identified only as C. P. reports that Christian College in New Albany, Indiana, had "established the degrees of *Doctress* of Natural Science, of English Literature, Belles Letters [*sic*], the Fine Arts, and of Arts and Science" (12). It is not likely, though, that this school, which called itself the University of Indiana on its diplomas, ever issued any doctress degrees. Founded in 1833 by John Cook Bennett, who himself claimed the degrees of M.D. and LL.D., it was in fact nothing more than a diploma mill that closed down some time during its first year of operation, leaving no record of the degrees that were actually sold or awarded.

Some American schools, however, did award legitimate degrees specifically renamed to be appropriate for women, and the *OED* defines one sense of the noun *maid* thus: "In certain American universities used as a degree-title in correspondence to *Bachelor.*" According to reports of the United States Commissioner of Education, the following female degrees were awarded between 1873 and 1882 by such schools as Alfred College (New York), Wheaton College (Illinois), Independence Female College (Missouri), Boston University, and the College of Our Lady of Guadalupe (California): Graduate in Oratory, in Science, or in Theology; Laureate of Arts, or of Letters; Maid of Arts, or of Science; Mistress in Liberal Learning; Mistress of Arts, of the English Language, or of Liberal Arts, and S.A., or Sister of Arts. In addition, the Commissioner's Report for 1882 suggests the following degrees to replace *bachelor* for women students: Graduate in Liberal Arts, Laureate in Arts, Laureate of English Literature, Laureate of Science, Licentiate of Instruction, Maid of Philosophy, Proficient in Music. Alternatives to the master's degree all employ the correlative *mistress:* Mistress of English Literature, Liberal Arts, Music, Philosophy, Polite Literature, and Science.

Separate women's degrees, whether offered by women's colleges or by coeducational institutions, did not prove popular. While it may have seemed inappropriate to call a woman a bachelor or even a master, most degrees can be referred to by their abbreviations, B.A., M.A., and Ph.D., which suggest masculinity only to the hypercritic. The current woman's movement has proposed little change in educational terminology. Goddard College's pioneer graduate program in women's studies offered *ovulars* rather than *seminars,* and only a few new degree names present themselves. In 1975 Linda Franklin proposed the Spinster of Arts degree to replace the B.A. (Daly 1978, 394), and Bobbye Sorrels (1983) favors the establishment of gender-neutral rather than separate but equal, gender-specific degree titles: Undergraduate degree for the B.A., and First graduate degree for the M.A. (125; 143). Feminine or neuter alternatives to *doctor* do not seem to have survived much beyond Fowler's support of *doctress* half a century ago.

MANPOWER

We have seen that when women and men assume nontraditional roles in our society, the English lexicon changes to adapt to their presence. Not all women's or men's work is morphologically marked. According to Eduard Maetzner, in certain cases semantic association determines what we now refer to as covert gender, gender which becomes explicit only in the assignment of personal pronouns. Some jobs, offices, or functions are considered grammatically masculine or feminine simply because we assume they are held only by men or only by women. In his *English Grammar* (1874), Maetzner classifies as covert masculines the nouns *pope, knight, champion, general, corporal,* and *Cyclops,* and he labels as feminine the nouns *matron, virgin, concubine, muse, syren, Nymph,* and *Fury* (1:254). Were he writing later Maetzner might have included *doctor* and *lawyer* as masculines and *nurse, secretary, telephone operator,* and *teacher* as feminines. And today he would have to rethink his categorization once again.

As Maetzner suggests, the sex stereotyping of professions does have certain linguistic consequences. For example, when speaking of doctors in general it has been customary to use masculine pronouns: A *doctor* bills *his* patients even when *he* cannot cure them. We can interpret the choice of pronoun in two ways, either as a generic masculine, used for grammatical convenience but meant to include women, or what is probably more often the case, as a gender-specific pronoun which substitutes for the covert masculine noun.

Generic *She*

It has frequently been argued that masculine pronouns cannot function generically because they exclude women. This in turn is dismissed as nonsense by supporters of the generic masculine, who at the same time reject generic feminine pronouns because such pronouns implicitly exclude men.

For many years the pronoun *she* was used in educational circles to refer to all schoolteachers (a similar situation pertained in nursing and in secretarial studies). The pronoun choice was clearly motivated by the predominance at the time of women teachers, a situation which led the word *teacher* to be interpreted as a covert feminine noun. The generic masculine pronoun was invariably retained, however, in reference to pupils, school administrators, and the professoriate. Usage authorities supported the generic masculine for teachers as well: for the sentence *Every teacher should establish close personal relations with her pupils,* House and Harmon (1926) comment, "while the use of *his* does not exclude the idea of women teachers, the use of *her* clearly does exclude the idea of men teachers" (40).

In 1941 the editor of *School and Society* firmly opposes the use of the generic feminine for teachers on grammatical grounds: "It is good grammar to use the masculine pronoun when the gender of the antecedent is indeterminate, and the implication that teaching is exclusively a feminine occupation is a serious handicap to the profession" (*American Speech* 16:318). In the 1960s, a period when more and more men entered teaching in America (or reentered, for men once constituted the majority in this area), we again hear claims that the feminization of teaching—in particular the use of the generic *she* for teachers—is responsible for the low status and low salaries accorded the profession in the United States. One male teacher complained at a National Education Association (NEA) conference that the generic *she* constituted an "incorrect and improper use of the English language" which was detrimental to the image of the teacher. His grammatical attack on the feminine pronoun contained the underlying assumptions that teaching was not woman's work and that the predominance of women in the classroom had damaged the profession: "The interests of neither the women nor of the men in our profession are served by grammatical usage which conjures up an anachronistic image of the nineteenth century schoolmarm" (Fenner 1974, 110).

Today's Education, a publication of the NEA, claims to have been a leader in the shift from the generic feminine to the generic masculine teacher during the 1960s. Yet by the 1970s it reports discontent among women teachers over the use of a masculine pronoun which renders them invisible. Noting that men resent being included in generic feminines but expect women to accept the generic masculine as both fair and natural, the journal offers the possibility of a common-gender pronoun, *ne,* and calls upon its readers to suggest a solution to the problem of pronoun reference (Fenner 1974, 110). Although the use of the generic *she* has declined in education, the status and salaries of teachers have not improved significantly.

Lately there has been a trend toward sex neutrality in many occupational references. This has come about partly because of objections to linguistic sex stereotyping, and partly because men and women are more freely entering professions or performing industrial tasks that were once the exclusive domain of one or the other sex, for example, medicine, law, nursing, and teaching. One target of linguistic reform is the word *man,* a term whose gender neutrality has often been questioned, and which has freely formed compounds with occupational references: *mailman, policeman, salesman.* A few of the reforms involve the replacement of *man* by what is supposed to be a true gender-neutral synonym, *person.* But while the neutralization of some terms has gone relatively unnoticed, attempts to change others have proved extremely controversial. For example, *salesperson,* first used around 1901, is now welcomed as a useful word, while the analogous *chairperson* (1971) is much maligned. The neutrality of *person* itself has not gone unchallenged.

Salesperson and *Chairperson*

The word *salesman* appears in English as early as 1523, and unlike other compounds involving *-man* it seems always to have been taken as a masculine rather than a generic term. The sex-neutral *seller* is found some three centuries earlier, and the sex-specific *saleswoman* first appears around 1704, although according to the *Dictionary of American English (DAE)* it is not found in America until 1865, almost a decade after the appearance here of *saleslady. Salesgirl* dates from 1887; the sex-neutral plural *salespeople* appears in 1876, some time before the singular *salesperson,* first used at the turn of the century.

The sex specificity of *salesman* is so generally acknowledged that *saleswoman* has never troubled usage critics, although *saleslady* was frequently attacked as a pretentious and euphemistic example of the application of *lady* to those who do not merit the designation. According to Alfred Ayres (1882), a real lady is content to be called a *saleswoman,* whereas "your young woman who, being in a store, is in a better position than ever before . . . boils with indignation if she is not denominated a sales *lady*" (s.v. "lady").

The *DAE* cites one British critic who assumes in 1917 that the euphemistic *saleslady* is an Americanism, but at the same time H. L. Mencken (1919) contends that it is the British and not the Americans who are overly fond of words in *-lady* (121). In spite of Mencken's comment, Maurice Weseen (1928) sees the need a decade later to label *saleslady* as commercial cant that is not in good use, and though the word is not of great concern to usage critics at present, it is far from obsolete. Bebout (1984) finds in her survey of masculine and feminine word pairs a slight preference for *saleslady* over *saleswoman*.

Unlike *saleswoman,* which was well received from the start, the sex-neutral *salesperson* met with some initial opposition—Weseen calls the word recent commercial cant that is not recognized by dictionaries. But the eventual adoption of *salesperson* by the world of commerce indicates that the term meets a specific need, and no doubt paves the way for its eventual acceptance into Standard English. Roy Copperud (1980) argues that *salesperson* is free from stigma because it antedates the new feminism, and he claims that it would be incongruous to apply *salesman* to a woman.

Chairperson, however, is a different story altogether. The word first appears in 1971, according to the *Barnhart Dictionary of New English since 1963,* although the *OED* lists the earliest term for 'the person who runs a meeting' as the sex-neutral *chair* itself, which is first used in this sense in 1647, some seven years before the first recorded use of *chairman* in 1654. *Chairwoman* appears not long after, in 1699, though until recently it has not been held in much favor by language authorities. The *Dictionary of Americanisms* records a facetious *chairlady* in 1931. Other coinages proposed as alternatives to the unpopular *chairperson* include *chairone,* which has enjoyed very limited success, the feminist *chaircrone,* and *chairmember,* a nonce creation—appearing in *A Guide for the Media to Faculty at Tufts University* (1974)—whose lack of appeal can be traced to the unfortunate anatomical metaphor that it suggests.

Opposition to *chairperson* does not explain the initial negative reaction to *chairwoman.* The *OED* calls *chairwoman* "hardly a recognized name"; Weseen classifies it as a coined word not in good use for serious purposes; and George Philip Krapp (1927a) acknowledges its existence but maintains that in practice a woman is called a *chairman.*

Fowler (1926) lists _chairwoman_ as a word of recent coinage (though it was over two hundred years old at the time) that has met with opposition, and Gowers, in his revision of Fowler (1965), reaffirms that _chairwoman_ is not a popular word. Charles Barber (1964) assures his readers, without furnishing evidence, that women prefer such sex-neutral terms as _teacher_ to _woman teacher_ and _chairman_ to _chairwoman_ (105).

Language authorities have always insisted that, unlike _salesman,_ _chairman_ is sex-neutral, and both the sex-specific _chairwoman_ and the sex-neutral _chairperson_ had to fight for recognition. It would appear that the negative attention surrounding the introduction of _chairperson_ has relieved some of the stigma attached to _chairwoman,_ which has only recently become to some degree acceptable. But unlike _salesperson,_ neither word ever achieved the initial status of jargon that would indicate its acceptability within limited professional contexts.

The true neutrality of _chairperson_ has also been challenged. Both usage critics and feminists feel that such a word is often a pseudo-generic. Copperud disapproves of _chairperson_ because of its association with the feminist cause, but he objects to the word most strongly because it is not truly sex-neutral: "We know now that when it is used the chair is occupied by a _chairwoman_" (1980, 147). Mary Daly criticizes _chairperson_ as "inauthentic, obscuring women's existence and masking the conditions of our oppression" (1978, 24).

The current reaction to _-person_ compounds might well have been predicted from the history of the word, which for some time has had both feminine and pejorative connotations. Resentment toward these new words may also have something to do with the manner of their introduction. While _salesperson_ made its way into the language more or less unobtrusively, _chairperson,_ because it is an official title with legal or quasi-legal status, was often adopted by organizations through a majority vote or imposed by administrative fiat. The users of the English language are notoriously independent, if not rebellious. They are reluctant to change their linguistic habits when told to do so by reformers, even when such a change is logical, reasonable, or socially desirable. But just as demands for women's social and legal equality have historically been resisted, proposals for reform in the direction of sex neutrality seem to generate more violent opposition than other kinds of language reform, and the resistance to *-person* compounds must also be explained in part as a reluctance to allow women a legislative role in matters of language.

Personslaughter

The Second Barnhart Dictionary of New English (1980) records more than sixteen occupational coinages involving *-person*, including *adperson, anchorperson, businessperson,* and *councilperson.* The *OED* Supplement (1982, s.v. "person") contains a similar list. Many of these terms, for example, *freshperson* and *henchperson*, are humorous, though others are apparently serious and are actually enjoying some degree of currency. The suggestion that *man* be replaced by *person* in compounds has prompted ridicule in many quarters, and more than one writer has tried to demonstrate through the free but nonserious coinage of words in *-person* that unbridled neology may not be the answer to the problems of sexism in language. For example, in 1973 Russell Baker devised over forty outrageous examples of *nopersonclature,* including *policeperson, doorperson, milkperson, everyperson, personners* ('manners'), *persontle* ('mantle'), *personipulating* ('manipulating'), and *aperson* ('amen').

Taking a more dispassionate approach, Stuart Berg Flexner (1976) points out that some words involving *man* just do not neutralize well: *manhole, manslaughter,* and *man-at-arms* cannot become *personhole, personslaughter,* and *person-at-arms.* In such cases, we face three choices: to accept *man* as gender-neutral; to treat it as gender-specific and balance it with feminine correlatives (this will only work for words which refer to actual persons, for example, *woman-at-arms, womanslaughter*); or to seek an alternative neutral substitute like *murder* or *soldier* (399).

Separate, Not Always Equal

The "editress" Sarah Hale advocated separate but equal correlative terms to describe the various family relationships and occupational pursuits of men and women. Writing in 1865 she proposed over 150 pairs of terms, many of them utilizing words in *-ess* for the feminines, for example, *professor/professoress, scholar/scholaress,* and *tutor* (not *governor*)/*governess.*

While the gender pairs that Hale proposed were not generally adopted, Mamie Meredith (1952; 1955) has recorded a number of sex-specific terms that were actually used to indicate a woman's status or occupation. Many of the terms found by Meredith do not stress the equality of women with men in the work force. In addition to the familiar *Rosie the Riveter* and the parallel *Winnie the Welder* that appeared during World War II, she records several white-collar alliterative terms, including *Amanda the Administratress, Mimeo Minnie, Sadie the Office Secretary, Sally the Stenographer, Stella the Steno,* and the job category once common in want ads, *Girl Friday,* the not-quite parallel feminine of Defoe's *Man Friday.*

Meredith reports that in 1951 *Life Magazine* called a woman welder a *welderina* and that in 1950 Vera Green, writing in the *National Office Management Forum,* proposed *womanagement* as a term for business management by women executives. Green elaborates on her coinage, "Wo—abbreviation of woman—when joined with *man* could mean women and men work together, comparably and harmoniously." Meredith also records *Commandress-in-Chief,* used in reference to Eleanor Roosevelt; *Veepess* for the wife of the *Veep,* Truman's Vice-President Alben Barkley; and *Veepa,* for Eva Peron. Many of these terms were humorous, and most of them are not particularly flattering. Their use has no doubt added momentum to the search for a more neutral terminology.

Redefining Manpower

In 1975 a division of the United States Department of Labor called the Manpower Administration (now known more neutrally as the Education and Training Administration) issued a list of nearly 3,500 job titles revised to eliminate both sex and age references from the government's *Dictionary of Occupational Titles.* Gone are such allusions to age or sex as *man, woman, boy, girl, lady,* words in *-ess, junior, senior,* and *master.* Exceptions are made where sex is a bona fide occupational requirement, for example, *leading lady* or *leading man;* where "no meaningful neuter titles could be developed" (*host/hostess, waiter/waitress*); or where the job title is fixed by law (*masseur, masseuse, able seaman*). With the exception of the legally defined *master* of a ship, and the gender pair *ballet master/mistress, master* is to be eliminated from job designations: *yard master,* for instance, becomes _yard manager._ Despite such revisions, two sets of _master definitions_ appear in the Manpower Administration's list.

Since _chairman_ is not considered a job title, it does not figure among the terms revised, although _salesman_ is replaced not just by _salesperson_ (despite the fears of the language guardians, this is the only _-person_ compound in the government's revisions), but by _sales associate, sales representative, sales agent, driver,_ and _solicitor_ as well. _Man_ as a separate word or part of a compound is generally replaced by the agentive suffix _-er_ (whose neutrality in Modern English is now unchallenged): _servicer, repairer, flagger. -Ess_ is also replaced by words in _-er_ or _-or: seamstress_ becomes _sewer; laundress, launderer; inspectress, inspector;_ and _city hostess, goodwill ambassador_ (though _hostess_ itself is left unchanged). Where _-er_ seems awkward, alternative wording is sought. A _watchman_ is now a _guard,_ not a _watcher,_ and a _trail man_ is not a _trailer_ but the more colorful _trail cowpuncher._ The bucolic _swine herdsman,_ however, is a _swine herder,_ not a _swineherd. Bellman_ is changed to _bellhop; footman_ to _second butler; milkman_ and _iceman_ are now _driver, milk route_ and _driver, ice route,_ respectively. The _showman_ is a _show stager,_ and the _woodsman_ a _woods worker,_ less poetic, but also less discriminatory.

Man is also replaced by _worker, officer, mechanic, estimator, hand_ (as in _stagehand_), and _specialist_ (_bomb disposal specialist_). The few job titles that contain _-woman_ are similarly revised: a _charwoman_ becomes a _charworker,_ and a _policewoman,_ a _police officer. Forelady_ (there is no title _forewoman_) and _foreman_ (the commonest of all the job titles) are replaced by _supervisor. Maid,_ originally a word that applied to either sex, is defeminized to _general houseworker,_ or simply _cleaner,_ while _chambermaid_ is neutralized to _room cleaner._

There are a few curiosities among the job title revisions. Gender-neutral _comedian_ is changed to _comedian/comedienne_ for no apparent reason. Sometimes a sex reference is altered that involves not the person _performing_ a service, but the person for whom it is performed: _bridal consultant_ is renamed _wedding consultant._ Similarly, _lady attendant_ becomes the equally euphemistic _mortuary beautician,_ though _attendant_ is a popular neutralizing agent for other occupations: _children's matron_ is changed to _children's attendant; midwife_ to _birth attendant;_ and _matron_ to _restroom attendant._ Even ignoring the derivation of _mentor_ from the Greek masculine proper noun, the designation *child mentor* does not seem the proper sex-neutral alternative to *governess*. *Fisher*, for the earlier *fisherman*, while undoubtedly neuter sounds unnecessarily biblical, and *clergyman* is replaced by *clergy*, a noun that cannot refer to individuals.

Private persons have also tried their hand at job title revision. Robert Longwell, a professor at the University of Northern Colorado, proposed *-wan*, a pseudophonetic spelling of *one*, as a replacement for *-man* compounds (Dickson 1982, 113). Miller and Swift (1980) approve of *chairwoman*, though they also suggest the sex-indefinites *chairperson, chairer, presider, coordinator, president, convener,* and *chair*. For *Congressman* they offer *Congressional* and for *watchman* a revival of the earlier *watch*. Despite the Manpower Administration's edict, Miller and Swift find *master* a useful sex-neutral term. They consider *midwife* bisexual, and favor the use of the much-reviled *person*, favoring *personhood* (included in *Webster's Ninth New Collegiate Dictionary*) instead of *manhood* and *womanhood*. Miller and Swift prefer *people* to *persons* for the plural: *chairpeople, craftspeople, salespeople, spokespeople,* and *gentlepeople* (for *ladies and gentlemen*).

Bobbye Sorrels (1983) goes further than Miller and Swift in proposing linguistic renovations for English. Recognizing that there are difficulties inherent in ousting traditional vocabulary, Sorrels suggests an intermediate stage of reform in which *-person* compounds are used when sex is unknown or when reference is generic, while *-man* and *-woman* forms are to be retained for reference to specific individuals. Sorrels disapproves of *master* both as a noun and verb, recommending either *head* or *expert* as a nominal alternative and *conquer* as a replacement verb. She would also substitute *great* or *best work* for *masterpiece*, and *expert* for *maestro*. In her democratic zeal Sorrels deletes *king* as a game term (in chess, checkers, and cards), in favor of sex-neutral *president*, and she offers *humanslaughter, personslaughter,* and *wo/manslaughter*, as well as the fair but cumbersome phrase *manslaughter or womanslaughter*.

The confusion and controversy over occupational terminology will settle down as the present tendency to open up more employment opportunities to both sexes results in a decrease of sex stereotyping in the marketplace. Whether the increased pressure to use sex-neutral vocabulary will affect other aspects of life is not yet certain, but we should not be surprised if the vocabulary of work spills over into other registers, and into the so-called standard language as well. It always has. After comparing carefully edited American prose of the 1960s to more recent texts, Betty Lou Dubois and Isabel Crouch (1979) claim that "examples of generics found in the 1970s suggest that a significant language change may be in progress" (265–66). The intense response of opponents to sex-neutral terminology also provides indirect evidence that change is taking place.

It is still too early to tell which gender-neutral lexical items will survive the shakeout. While words in *-person* are controversial, some, like *salesperson,* may elude the stigma and survive. *Seller,* an older neutral term that is still in use, is not popular as a job title. The Manpower Administration, which prefers titles in *-er* when possible because they often involve the least radical restructuring of a word, avoids *seller* altogether in favor of a variety of synonymous terms.

Chairperson may succumb, as its critics hope, but it is more than likely that a neutral alternative like *chair* will take its place, for compounds in both *-man* and *-woman* are also stigmatized. And *person* may itself elude the stigma that has been attached to it. It is an old, established word, after all, and a productive one (*personality, persona, parson, personal,* and *impersonate* all derive from or relate to it). *Webster's Ninth New Collegiate Dictionary* (1983) defines *person* as "human being, individual—sometimes used in combination esp[ecially] by those who prefer to avoid *man* in compounds applicable to both sexes." The example given is *chairperson.*

Prestige terms are more likely to be candidates for neutralization in the standard language: there are no cries for the revision of *garbageman,* for example. The federal regulation of terminology will also have its effect on usage. But awkward or ostentatious coinages like *personslaughter* and *wo/manslaughter,* though valuable as consciousness raisers which draw attention to a particular linguistic imbalance, face a greater battle for acceptance and probably bear the seeds—or the eggs—of their own destruction.

The meaning and use of *man* and *woman* and their synonyms and derivatives are important and still unresolved issues. The history which we have traced may help us to see that questions remain unanswered because the roles of men and women in our society have always been complex and to some extent uncertain. Discourse is also

184

necessarily complex and uncertain: words, like people, have a variety of meanings and functions, both prestigious and taboo, and like people they resist being pinned down. *Man* sometimes does and sometimes does not include *woman,* and sometimes we simply cannot tell whether it does or not. The sex neutrality of *person* may have been compromised, but then so has the sex neutrality of *man.*

NEW WORDS AND WOMEN

The issue of sex reference is not limited to honorifics or to words describing educational or occupational accomplishments. Some word coiners have used their skills to emphasize, both positively and negatively, new ways of looking at women and men. In 1970 a list of new words associated with the woman's movement appeared on the woman's page of the *Long Island Press,* together with announcements of engagements and news of a chrysanthemum show, and it included the following words or phrases, some of which are still current: *sexitized,* "acceptance of the male-oriented society"; *sexist,* "a male who sees women only as sex objects"; *male chauvinism,* "excessive or blind belief in male superiority"; *sexegration,* "a separation of groups by sexes"; *feminist,* "one who advocates the removal of restrictions that lead to discrimination"; *girlcott,* "opposite of boycott"; and *herstory,* "a woman's view of history" (Pauley 1970, 8).

The explosion of gender-related neology since the 1960s occasionally obscures the earlier attempts of commentators on the English language to come to terms with what *phallocentric* historians might have called the *woman question.* New words are coined to support or oppose the rights of women; to neutralize sex-specific terminology; to make neutral words sex-specific; to describe the changing roles of women and men; and in general to fill *gender gaps* in the vocabulary of English. Some of the terms, like *herstory,* are serious attempts to highlight through word play the previously undervalued contributions of women to civilization. *Herstory,* which is not recognized by any standard dictionaries or collections of new words though it continues to appear in printed sources, is defined by one feminist pamphlet as "1. The past as seen through the eyes of women. 2. The removal of male self-glorification from history." In contrast, *history*—which is not a blend of *his* and *story*—is defined as "the past as distorted by men" (Todasco 1973, s.v.).

In some cases, supporters of women's rights have used one term, and opponents another, related one. We have mentioned the example of *suffragist/suffragette. Women's liberation* is clipped by its detractors to *women's lib,* while feminists are demeaned as *libbers* (Shapiro 1985 offers a valuable history of terms associated with the woman's movement). *Sexegration* is cited in the *Long Island Press* (Pauley 1970) as a term deriving from the equal rights struggle. In contrast, the verb *desexigrate* appears in a leaflet opposing the adoption of the Equal Rights Amendment: "All public schools, college dormitories, and hospital rooms [would be required to] desexigrate" (cited in the *New York Times,* 7 February 1975, sec. 1, p. 37).

Many gender-related coinages are facetious parodies ridiculing the desire of some men and women to be treated fairly by language. Writing in *Time* magazine in 1972, Stefan Kanfer opposes any attempt by social reformers to tamper with our established vocabulary. The tradition of lexical innovation that characterizes the writing found in *Time* has given rise to the adjective *Timese,* but Kanfer is reluctant to allow outsiders a license to coin new words. Claiming that the feminist "attack on words is only another social crime," Kanfer rejects the notion that remodeling words which denigrate women and men can have a positive effect. Comparing the new feminism unfavorably to the civil rights movement he notes, "The change from Negro to black has helped to remake a people's view of itself. But it is a lone example." Kanfer goes on to ridicule the idea of gender-related language reform with a parodic list of the verbal excesses of "sispeak": the sex-reversed *cook one's gander, put up one's duchesses, shedonism, womandarin,* and *countessdown;* the sex-neutral *otto-it* (for *ottoman*) and *onefully* (for *manfully*); and *msanthropic, msapprehension* and *msguided,* from *Ms.* The derision with which Kanfer greets the language of the woman's movement is a tacit acknowledgment of the force of such reforms.

Old Words and New

Neologism is nothing new for the supporters and opponents of women's rights. In 1834 the writer "C. P.," warning his readers that the women of his day were becoming too much like men, raises the fearful specter of *gynecocracy,* 'a government of women' (121). In contrast,

Thomas Wentworth Higginson ([1881] 1972), a supporter of the education and emancipation of women, speaks of *girlsterousness* (from *boisterous*), a reflection of the energy exhibited by America's more enlightened women and girls, who are in Higginson's opinion noisier—he means this in a positive sense despite the stereotyping—than men and boys (193–94).

The prefix *gyn-*, from the Greek *gyne*, 'woman,' popular in scientific words, was also employed in negative coinages: *gynecocracy* and its variants date from the seventeenth century, and generally, though not invariably, reflect a dim view of women in administrative roles, while *gynander*, labeled as "rare" by the *OED* though it is often included in books of synonyms, referred to women with male characteristics. Following a common pattern in which a pejorative term is forcibly turned into a positive one, a number of modern feminists have reactivated *gyn-*. In *Gyn/Ecology: The Metaethics of Radical Feminism* (1978), Mary Daly uses a number of *gyn-* coinages, including the title word itself, as well as *gynergy* ('female energy'), *gynergetic, gynography* (antonym for *pornography*, whose initial element derives from Greek *porne*, 'prostitute'), *gynocentric* ('woman-centered'), *gynaesthesia* ('women's synaesthesia'), and *gynocide* ('what patriarchic society does to women').

A large number of gender-related coinages are formed by distorting a standard word to give it a feminine or masculine significance, for example, *hufemity*, based on *humanity; shemale*, 'woman'; and *cinemama*, 'movie actress' (1935), based on *cinema*. Fashion terms are often gender-specific, and are changed as frequently as styles. In 1959, for example, the *New York Times* advertised *he-o-tards*, masculine garments derived both in appearance and etymology from *leotards*. Another practice is to alter the sex-specific element in a compound or phrase, for example, *chorus boy* (1943) from *chorus girl* (1894); *womanpower* (1942) from *manpower* (1862); *housefather* (1901) from *housemother* (1834); and the recent *househusband* (1970) from *housewife*.

Semantic gaps in the language often reveal cultural bias. Bobbye Sorrels (1983) maintains that the absence of feminine equivalents for *emasculation* and *castration* demonstrates that male sexuality is valued in our society while female sexuality is ignored or silenced (89). One example of gender-related coinage designed to fill a semantic gap in

187

English is *matriheritage,* created in 1886 by the anthropologist Sir G. Campbell as a parallel to *patrimony,* since the analogical form *matrimony* was already committed to another meaning (*OED,* s.v.). New words such as *herstory* are coined not only to fill gender gaps, but to politicize language, to draw attention to or revise linguistic and cultural assumptions as well. Some, like *wobody* and *huperson* (neutralizing the *man* in *woman* and *human*), are described by Miller and Swift as "ideas whose time has gone" (1980, 7). Una Stannard (1977) uses *womban* to emphasize the negative stereotype of woman as a baby-making machine (315). And Maija S. Blaubergs (1978) advocates emphasis on such feminines as *In Goddess We Trust* because women have been hidden by language and must be made more noticeable.

In *Gyn/Ecology,* Mary Daly explains that her aim in coining "woman-made" terms is to unmask deceptive words and provide alternative meanings for prefixes. Daly employs her methods liberally, both in *Gyn/Ecology* and in her more recent *Pure Lust: Elemental Feminist Philosophy* (1984), which contains a glossary of over four hundred new words. Daly rejects coinages like *herstory* as humiliating to women, preferring instead neologisms which target and humiliate men, for example, *man-ipulated* and *mister-ectomy* (*Gyn/Ecology* 24n; 239). She plays on meanings—*male-functioning* for *malfunctioning, birthwrong* for *birthright;* and she revives less known or obsolete meanings, for example, *glamour* (from *grammar*), 'a witch's spell or power.' Responding to the general tradition of negativity associated with women's words and to the long-established practice of defining women linguistically in terms of their physiology, Daly turns the tables with such terms as *androlatry, cockocracy, jockdom, jockocratic, phallicism, phallocracy,* and *phallogrammar.*

Unlike most feminist writers, Daly frequently avoids *woman,* employing instead the more visible synonym *crone,* a negative word made positive to indicate a rejection of the male standards that she feels are normally used in defining females. Other alternatives to *woman* include *spinster* (for Daly *spin* means 'think' and the ending revives the feminine sense of *-ster*), *sister, webster,* and *hag.* Compounds include *crone-ology* and *crone-ography,* 'the writing of women's history'; *hag-ography* and *hag-ology,* "the writings of the Great Hags"; *haggard,* redefined as 'intractable, willful, wanton, unchaste, independent of men.' Ancestors are *foresisters* or *forespinsters* rather than *forefathers*. One negative feminine term, *fem-*, is retained in its pejorative sense in *feminitude*, "the state of servitude of women in a phallocratic world," and *fembot*, a blend of *female* and *robot*.

Gender-related neologisms come in two forms: the gender-specific, offered by proponents and opponents of the woman's movement, as well as by others whose concern is not social or political; and the gender-neutral, often but not always intended to reverse what is perceived to be the masculine domination of the English vocabulary. Terms like *bat child* for *bat boy* and *youth scouts* for *boy* or *girl scouts,* as well as others like the job-related *waitron* or *salesperson,* are proposed in order to remove or prevent discrimination and to provide equal opportunity for the sexes to engage in particular activities or employment. Their success as words is secondary to the success of their social design. One gender-related word class, the pronoun, has been an object of concern both to grammar reformers and, somewhat later, to feminists. Over the centuries, the efforts to create a sex-neutral pronoun have concerned more language reformers and resulted in more solutions than any other question involving language and gender. These efforts merit a chapter of their own.

CHAPTER 10

The Word That Failed

It is a mistake to fixate on the third person singular.
Mary Daly

Because pronouns serve as the major linguistic expression of gender in Modern English, it is fitting that this study of grammar and gender should begin and end with a discussion of pronouns. Just as their obscure origins have excited the imaginations of etymologists, leading them into erroneous assumptions about human and grammatical gender, the complexities of pronoun use have fired the passions of reformers bent on the difficult task of making English simple, logical, regular, or fair to men and women. Among the many gender-related reforms proposed for the English language, the creation of a common-gender pronoun to replace the generic masculine *he* in a sentence like *Everyone loves his mother* stands out as the one most often advocated and attempted, and the one that has most often failed.

The increased interest in language and sex over the past two decades has produced quite a few epicene pronouns, but the lack of such a pronoun in English has been of concern to grammarians and word coiners for some two hundred years. The first epicene pronouns were coined not to redeem women from a condition of lexical obscurity but to restore linguistic efficiency and grammatical correctness to language. In all, more than eighty bisexual pronouns—little words such as *ne, ter, thon, heer, et,* and *ip*—have been proposed since the eighteenth century, and because many word coiners worked in isolation and received little publicity, some of the same forms were invented more than once, most notably versions of the blends *hesh, himer,* and *hiser.*

The absence of a third person singular common-gender pronoun was noted in the eighteenth century, when some language authorities, notably Joseph Priestley, Hugh Blair, and Lindley Murray, campaigned against irregularities in agreement between pronoun and antecedent. Murray's fifth rule of syntax, for example, states that a pronoun must agree with its antecedent in gender and in number ([1795] 1968, 148). There are no difficulties in gender agreement for the first and second person pronouns, and the third person plural, all of which are common gender, but with the third person singular, strict number and gender concord can sometimes be achieved only through the use of the coordinate *he or she*.

Of the following four alternatives, use of the plural in the first— what can be called for convenience the 'singular *they*'—is most often condemned by language authorities, although it is probably the most common, particularly in informal English. The pairing of the masculine and feminine in the second, though it alone follows the agreement rule to the letter, is rejected as ugly and cumbersome.

1. Everyone loves their mother.
2. Everyone loves his or her mother.
3. Everyone loves her mother.
4. Everyone loves his mother.

The generic *she* of the third sentence is seldom considered as a possibility. Only sentence four satisfies the demands both of number concord and style. The fact that it violates gender concord is either ignored or rationalized by alleging the inclusiveness of the masculine pronoun, and the generic masculine has become the approved construction.

SINGULAR *THEY*

Despite its status as a standard construction, many writers consider common-gender *he* to be a less than satisfactory solution to the problems caused by the lack of an epicene English pronoun. Some grammarians, strict constructionists of the laws of syntax, regard the generic masculine as a violation of the rules of pronoun concord, and both grammarians and feminists maintain that the generic masculine does not include women, but rejects them.

Most lexicographers, however, classify *he* as both a masculine and a common-gender pronoun. For example, Noah Webster (1828) re-

gards *he* as common gender when it stands for the generic sense of
man. Maurice Weseen (1928) takes the extreme view that the feminine is the only gender that actually expresses sex, and for Weseen,
sex is the mark of Eve: "[Common gender] is applied to the pronouns
he, his, and *him* when these are used to refer to antecedents in which
the idea of sex is not apparent or not important, in fact, in all cases in
which the antecedent is not clearly feminine."

Many writers have argued that such pronominal bias may be
avoided not by creating new words, but by the use of words already
present in the language. Elizabeth Cady Stanton used generic *she* in
her feminist revision of the Bible. Benjamin Spock, the twentieth-
century activist pediatrician, alternates generic *he* with generic *she* in
the fourth edition of *Baby and Child Care* (1976). As early as 1770,
Robert Baker recommended the construction *one . . . one's* rather than
one . . . his because the generic masculine is not balanced by a generic
feminine *one . . . hers* ([1770] 1968, 23–24), and in 1868 Richard
Grant White reminded his readers that a new common-gender pronoun was unnecessary because *one* had always served in that capacity.
Wolstan Dixey (1884) also favors an expanded use of *one* rather than
the adoption of a new pronoun, offering the example "Every man and
woman is the architect of one's own fortune." And a century later
Lillian E. Carlton (1979) recommends "As anybody can see for one's
self" and "Neither could take one's eyes from the other." But *one* has
never proved a popular pronoun in American English, perhaps because, as George L. Trager says, the user of English "intuitively per-
ceives its learned character, and inclines to ridicule it as pedantic"
(1931, 311).

There has been some support for the extension of *it* in place of the
generic masculine. *A Woman's New World Dictionary* (1973) defines
it as a "third person neuter pronoun now acceptable to use when sex
of referent is not known. Examples: The baby was happy with its
rattle; the applicant signed its name." Millicent Rutherford (1976)
supports *everyone . . . it.* And Herman Arthur (1980) offers "The
student entering college finds the first year most difficult. *It* discovers
that teachers no longer give daily assignments." Critics of *it,* in turn,
point to its impersonal nature as their main argument against its adoption.

She, one, and *it* seem unlikely to supplant common-gender *he.* Singular *they,* on the other hand, is widely used in speech and writing and, despite the stigma of ungrammaticality that has become attached to it since the eighteenth century, the construction shows no signs of dying out. The occurrence of the plural pronoun *they* in reference to indefinite nouns such as *person, someone,* or *everyone,* which are singular in form but often plural in meaning, is another example of semantic concord in English overriding grammatical concord. Singular *they* has a long history in Modern English, stretching back to the mid sixteenth century, and a distinguished one—it occurs in the works of Addison, Austen, Fielding, Chesterfield, Ruskin, and Scott, to cite only a few major English writers, and the *OED* notes that the absence of a singular common-gender pronoun renders "this violation of grammatical concord sometimes necessary." Furthermore, there is a strong precedent in English for the use of a plural pronoun in the singular: *we* used for *I,* a construction sometimes called the royal or the editorial *we,* occurs as early as Old English; and *you,* originally limited to the plural, supplanted the second person singular *thou* during the fourteenth century, and now serves as a pronoun of common number as well as common gender.

Some grammarians approve of the singular *they.* For example, Alexander Bain, in *A Higher English Grammar* (1879) defends its use:

> When both Genders are implied, it is allowable to use the Plural. . . . Grammarians frequently call this construction an error: not reflecting that it is equally an error to apply 'his' to feminine subjects. The best writers furnish examples of the use of the plural as a mode of getting out of the difficulty. [310]

In *A New English Grammar* ([1891] 1931), Henry Sweet finds two means of avoiding the "difficulty" of *he or she:* the generic masculine in more formal English and singular *they* in speech (2:72). But singular *they* is not always confined to speech. Citing many literary examples, Otto Jespersen (1922) concludes that the use of *they* is "not illogical" in reference to singular nouns like *everyone,* which imply plurality (138–40). In the syntax volume of his *Grammar* (1931), George Curme accepts the literary evidence of singular *they,* but he wrongly concludes that it is an obsolescent construction which survives only in "loose colloquial and popular speech" (3:557–58). In *A Grammar of Contemporary English* (1972), Randolph Quirk and his coauthors set forth a more tolerant version of this position. Singular *they* is labeled the informal construction, and generic *he* the formal, unmarked one, while coordinate *he or she* is rejected as "cumbersome" (370). However, in the section on universal pronouns (*everyone, each, each one*), there is no mention of formality constraints, and the reader is simply advised that such words may be construed either with the plural or the masculine (but not the feminine) singular (219).

Resistance to the singular *they* appears as early as the eighteenth century. Illustrating common violations of pronoun agreement both in gender and number, Lindley Murray corrects the sentence "Can any one, on their entrance into the world, be fully secure that they shall not be deceived?" to "Can any one, on *his* entrance into the world, be fully secure that *he* shall not be deceived?" ([1795] 1968, 148). And Goold Brown (1825) finds the sentence "No person should be censured for being careful of their reputation" incorrect "because the pronoun *their* is of the plural number, and does not correctly represent its antecedent noun *person,* which is of the third person, *singular,* masculine" (142).

By the second half of the nineteenth century, grammarians were more explicit about gender concord and the generic *he*. In his *Grammar of the English Language* (1863), Samuel S. Greene asserts that the absence of an epicene English pronoun is not sufficient justification for the grammatically irregular use of *they* in place of the generic masculine. Greene accepts a generic feminine only in reference to groups consisting entirely of females, and he finds the coordinate *him or her* awkward if not grammatically suspect (19).

The effect of such grammatical discussion is difficult to measure, but the persistence of singular *they* and its acceptance as correct if informal English by some modern grammars offers indirect evidence of the rejection of generic *he* by many writers and speakers. Sterling Leonard (1929) observes that the minute attention paid to pronoun agreement by the grammarians did not greatly influence nineteenth-century usage. In the matter of singular *they* he finds that "British usage is still equally unfettered," though "the greater conservatism of American writers, as usual, has led them to follow this rule more carefully" (225). In his 1932 survey of usage, Leonard reports that, while a large number of his two hundred usage judges approve the expression *everyone . . . their,* the majority opposes it, and the construction cannot yet be considered in good standing (105).

Some commentators express the hope that singular *they* may indeed provide an acceptable alternative to the problem of indefinite gender reference, although few usage critics are willing to sanction the construction. For example, Fowler (1926) prefers to fetter his own writing and British usage in general with the generic masculine. Acknowledging that *anybody can see for themselves* is the "popular" solution to the problem of reference, Fowler complains that "it sets the literary man's teeth on edge" (s.v. "number"). And Edward D. Johnson (1982) comments that singular *they* "annoys writers, who must forego the privileges the masculine pronoun has for millennia enjoyed in English and its root languages" (290).

Bergen and Cornelia Evans (1957) are among the few usage critics who prefer to liberate the grammar-bound Americans and redistribute the privileges of the pronouns. In the case of indefinites, they note, it is the plural rather than the masculine singular that enjoys the approval of the ages. Discussing *everybody* and *everyone,* the Evanses remind us that "these words are usually followed by a singular verb but they are usually referred to by the plural pronoun *they,* rather than the singular pronoun *he* . . . . This has been standard English for the word *everybody* for more than four hundred years, and for the word *everyone* for more than two hundred years" (164). Furthermore, the Evanses point out a limiting factor in the effectiveness of the generic masculine that its less thoughtful supporters usually ignore. While *his* may refer to *everyone* in the sentence *Everyone liked his dinner,* it cannot refer to *everyone* in a separate, coordinated clause. The sentence *Everyone liked the dinner, but he did not care for the dessert* is impossible in English; only the plural personal pronouns will do in such a case.

Some supporters of the generic masculine acknowledge that it is not the ideal solution to the problem of indefinite reference. In *The King's English* ([1906] 1924), H. W. Fowler and F. G. Fowler regret the absence of a common-gender English pronoun, though they also take exception to the practice of the nineteenth-century novelist Susan Ferrier, who rejected the generic masculine in favor of coordinate reference, for example, "Your friend must betake him or herself to some other crafts" (Ferrier 1898, 49). Ferrier also employed *their* in reference to indefinite singulars: "carrying one's head in their hand" (279); "a difference of opinion which . . . leaves each free to act according to their own feelings and opinions" (280). The Fowlers do not approve of *they* as a singular. Although they recognize that the generic masculine may be inherently unfair to women, they see no real alternative to its use. Unfortunately, the Fowlers regard Ferrier's "aversion" to the masculine pronoun as a matter which "may be referred to her sex," and they clearly regard the unfairness of the generic masculine as a minor problem, one of manners rather than sexual or political equality: "Ungallant as it may seem, we shall probably persist in refusing women their due here as stubbornly as Englishmen continue to offend the Scots by saying England instead of Britain" (67).

The Canadian humorist Stephen Leacock, also reluctant to give women their due, at least in language, trivializes the balancing of the masculine pronoun with the feminine as a matter of false politeness. In a serious moment Leacock objects to "the perpetual extension of the use of '*his* or *her*' where we used merely to use *his* when I was young." Writing in 1944, Leacock, like some of today's language critics, feels that the decline of the generic masculine is the direct result of the recent women's rights movement and feminist intimidation: "The women's vote has set up a sort of timid deference that is always afraid of omitting or insulting them" (39–40). Similarly, an unnamed but obviously male linguist participating in Sterling Leonard's survey of English usage expresses a preference for the generic *he* and belittles the coordinate *his or her* as just "a matter of pleasing the women" (1932, 103).

Singular *they* has held its own against the grammarians and the antifeminists, and there are some writers who remain optimistic that singular *they* will one day become acceptable. The lexicographer Alma Graham (1973) supports it, and Ann Bodine (1975) predicts that singular *they* will eventually be adopted as standard in response to social pressure. Contradicting Leonard's claim that the British rather than the Americans are more relaxed in their coordination of pronouns with indefinites, Casey Miller and Kate Swift (1977) see singular *they* as an indomitable reflex of the American spirit: "The use of *they* as a singular pronoun slips out in response to a healthy American instinct to include women when general references are made to people" (136).

Despite the current groundswell for singular *they*, neologism has its attractions, and word formers and reformers have not withheld their suggestions, serious or otherwise, for the third person, singular, common-gender pronoun: borrowings (French *on, le,* and *en,* as well as

Old Norse *hann*), blends (*thon, he'er, shem*), clippings (*e, per*), and root creations (*na, ip*). Revisions of the pronoun system in order to make English more responsive to the demands of sex and logic were actually proposed as early as the eighteenth century.

A NATIVE ENGLISH EPICENE PRONOUN

In 1789, William H. Marshall records the existence of a dialectal English epicene pronoun, singular *ou:* "'Ou will' expresses either *he* will, *she* will, or *it* will." Marshall traces *ou* to Middle English epicene *a*, used by the fourteenth-century English writer John of Trevisa, and both the *OED* and Wright's *English Dialect Dictionary* confirm the use of *a* for *he, she, it, they,* and even *I.*

The dialectal epicene pronoun *a* is a reduced form of the Old and Middle English masculine and feminine pronouns *he* and *heo.* By the twelfth and thirteenth centuries, the masculine and feminine pronouns had developed to a point where, according to the *OED,* they were "almost or wholly indistinguishable in pronunciation." The modern feminine pronoun *she,* which first appears in the mid twelfth century, seems to have been drafted at least partly to reduce the increasing ambiguity of the pronoun system. Julia Penelope Stanley and Susan W. Robbins (1978) argue that since the feminine rather than the masculine English pronoun was changed to maintain pronominal gender distinctions, the introduction of *she* in Middle English represents concrete evidence of the masculine domination of the language. But gender neutrality affected only parts of the pronoun paradigm: the oblique forms of the feminine pronoun remained distinct from the masculine and were not replaced.

Evidence from Modern English may prove instructive here. We find in British dialects both sex-neutral, unstressed forms like *a* and *un* and stressed sex-specific forms. In many instances, sex-neutral and sex-specific forms are used interchangeably: *she* may compete not only with *a* and *un,* but with *hoo,* or *u* as well, both reflexes of the OE feminine pronoun *heo,* which did not entirely disappear. In addition, the sex-specific forms may sometimes be applied without regard to referential sex distinctions. According to Wright's *English Dialect Grammar* ([1905] 1968), *her* is used in some dialects as the unemphatic or interrogative of *he, him* may refer to female animals, and so on. The form and function of the Middle English pronouns may have been equally flexible. This suggests that sex neutrality in the Middle English pronoun system may have served as an alternative to rather than a replacement for sex-specific pronouns, and that a dual system of epicene and gendered pronouns has continued—in some dialects—down to the present, though the epicene forms are generally perceived as nonstandard.

In any case, *she* was eventually included in the dialect that became Standard English. However, competing, potentially epicene nonstandard pronominal forms persisted, particularly in unemphatic positions, and not all male or female speakers adopted standard *she* to the exclusion of these neutral forms. It would not be difficult to see the Modern English singular *they*—which is used by speakers and writers of standard as well as nonstandard dialects—as part of this same dual system of gendered and sex-neutral pronouns. But whether or not the genius of the language favors the continued use of sex-neutral pronouns, it is clear from the number of artificial epicene pronouns which have been coined that many English speakers wish that the Middle English pronoun system had become entirely unisex.

THE FIRST ARTIFICIAL EPICENE PRONOUNS

Artificial common-gender pronouns first appear not in natural languages but in artificial ones constructed with regard to logical principles. John Wilkins's *Philosophical Language* (1668) may contain the earliest artificial epicene pronoun, although it is not clear that Wilkins himself intended this to be the case. Wilkins employs gender-specific particles to delimit his otherwise common-gender nouns as masculine or feminine. But Wilkins's pronouns do not exhibit these particles. The third person singular, for example, contains neither the masculine ', pronounced [ra], nor the feminine ', pronounced [ro]. One could conclude that such an unmarked pronoun is epicene, except for the fact that Wilkins translates its possessive form, pronounced [he], as *his*. Furthermore, the table of personal pronouns contains masculine and feminine forms, but no neuters (389). Wilkins apparently thinks of the third person singular as generically masculine rather than epicene. Although he translates *Father* in the *Pater Noster* as sex-neutral

198

Parent, Wilkins invariably renders the third person singular pronoun as *he,* even in reference to *Parent.*

Despite the mixed evidence in Wilkins's treatment of pronouns, the epicene pronoun did become an explicit feature of many artificial languages. In fact, the first artificial epicene pronoun whose certainty we can attest was coined not for English but for *Langue Nouvelle,* an artificial language which is briefly sketched by Diderot in his *Encyclopédie* (1751). Diderot rejects gender as both a grammatical and a referential category on the grounds of simplicity, and Langue Nouvelle contains only two personal pronouns, the singular, common-gender *lo,* and the plural *zo* (9:268–71). Recent artificial languages employ the epicene pronoun almost as a matter of course, though unlike Langue Nouvelle they include sex-specific pronouns as well. Epicene *gi* is a feature of Esperanto, and is used for all things, persons, and animals whose name does not reveal their sex. C. Cardenas (1923) builds the indefinites *oni* (sg.) and *esi* (pl.) into Hom-Idyomo; Jespersen (1929) notes that Ido has common-gender *lu,* and he includes epicene *le* (sg.) and *les* (pl.), as well as the sex-specific third person plural pronouns *los* (m.) and *las* (f.), in his own creation, Novial. Mondial contains epicene *on* (Heimer 1947), and Babm has *x* (sg.) and *xa* (pl.) (Okamoto 1962).

Calls for English Epicene Pronouns

William S. Cardell (1827) defends the existence of common-gender pronouns in languages often regarded as primitive by pointing to our own epicene plural: "It is no more philosophically improper that savages should say *he,* for one person, *male* or *female,* than that polite scholars should say *they,* for ten of either sex" (64). Other commentators actually do suggest that a third person singular epicene pronoun would be a useful addition to English. The conservative language critic Richard Meade Bache (1869) comments that "a personal pronoun which should be non-committal on the question of sex would be a great convenience" (78). In 1878 an anonymous correspondent to the *Atlantic Monthly* mentions an editorial in the *Christian Union* in 1876 or 1877 calling for the creation of a new pronoun; and the correspondent argues that such development is an essential part of linguistic evolution: "It should long since have grown on our speech, as the tails grew off the monkeys," and he or she laments, "My only comfort [is] the fact that I am not alone in my misery. How often do I see a fellow-mortal pause in the middle of a sentence, groping blindly for the missing word" (Contributors' Club, 639–40).

The epicene pronoun became a popular topic in 1884, when a number of concrete proposals were discussed in the literary journals. In a letter to *The Literary World,* William D. Armes of Oakland, California, calls for the creation of a new word to fill the English gender gap. Armes considers the use of the plural *their* where a singular is required "incorrect but expressive," and in criticizing the coordinate *his or her* as "cumbersome but inexact" he himself uses generic *he:* "If the speaker is one accustomed to speak by the card, he says, 'Every one is the architect of his or her own fortune.'"

Samuel Ramsey regards the development of a sex-neutral pronoun as one of our greatest needs: "The English language is not rich in pronouns, and there are few careful writers or speakers who have not felt the want of more" ([1892] 1968, 322–23). Gilbert M. Tucker agrees (1895, 10), as does H. L. Mencken (1934), who would like an alternative to clumsy *he or she* or singular *they* which, despite its honorable history, has been made infamous by "the schoolma'ams [who] are so hot against it." And Porter G. Perrin, in his often-reprinted *Index to English* (1939), says, "We need a pronoun to represent either-he-or-she" (s.v. "gender"). Although he is doubtful of the success of *thon* or any other epicene pronoun, Otto Jespersen remarks that the lack of a "both-sex pronoun" is often felt (1949, 204), and Sir Ernest Gowers, in his revision of Fowler's *Modern English Usage* (1965), sees the epicene pronoun as a necessary feature of an ideal language (s.v. "number").

THON

In 1884 Charles Crozat Converse, an American lawyer and hymn-writer, created *thon,* the most widely publicized of the epicene pronouns. Converse was motivated by a concern that since time is money, communication must be rapid as well as grammatically correct. He urges the adoption of the new sex-neutral pronoun, which he has designed so as to guarantee its successful adoption by the general public: it bears a natural rather than an arbitrary connection to its meaning. It is formed "from English word-elements and sounds already in common use." And it is a blend—Converse calls it an "abbreviation"—a type of word which he regards as highly desirable in the nineteenth-century world of fast-paced communication.

Converse searched for several years for a suitable pronoun, rejecting non-English words and clippings until finally, "by cutting off the last two letters of the English word _that_ and the last letter of the word _one,_ and uniting their remaining letters in their original sequence in these two words, I produced that word now proposed for the needed pronoun—to wit, THON; to the _th_ in which I would give the same sound as in _they_" (1884, 55).

He recommends _thon_ because of "its literal and euphonic resemblance to the other pronouns," as well as its supposed phonetic transparency: "Its final consonant has a neutral savor significant of its purport." According to Converse, _thon_ will reduce the need to recast sentences or to "plunge on defiantly through some common, yet hideous solecism" (presumably, singular _they_). As an example Converse offers, "If Mr. or Mrs. A. comes to the courthouse on Monday next I will be there to meet _thon._"

The announcement of _thon_ (together with possessive _thons_ and uninflected accusative _thon_) provoked a flurry of discussion and further word creation. _Thon_ was picked up by Funk and Wagnalls's _Standard Dictionary_ in 1898, and was listed there as recently as 1964. It was also included in _Webster's Second New International Dictionary,_ though it is absent from the first and third, and it still has supporters today (Morehead 1955; Titcomb 1955).

Three Earlier Pronouns

Expressing a strong disapproval of _thon,_ the editor of the _New York Commercial Advertiser_ (7 August 1884, 3) finds Converse "bitten with the old malady, a desire for a common pronoun singular." This is nothing new: "If Mr. Converse thinks he has done anything original . . . as he seems to do, he is ill informed as to the history of the craze for a new pronoun." Although no exact names, dates, or places are mentioned, two earlier failed pronouns are cited:

> Thirty years ago, or more, attempts were made to apply precisely the method of combination and abbreviation which [Converse] has adopted. The earliest result which we remember was 'ne, nis, nim' and a very serious effort indeed was made to introduce this bastard word form into

use. Later somebody suggested a combination of 'his' and 'her,' making 'hiser,' and one or two newspapers used the form for a time.

The writer is convinced that words like *thon, ne,* and *hiser* cannot survive because new linguistic forms must spring up naturally and spontaneously, as did *its,* the most recent addition to the pronoun system. And he or she approves of the traditional generic *he* as well as the singular *they,* which was once thoroughly acceptable usage but is now unjustly maligned: "The grammar mongers who bestride education in our day did not live to impose laws on speech when Addison and Steele wrote."

In his column "Words and Their Uses," Richard Grant White (1868) reports a suggestion received from two of his readers, writing independently, that *en,* "or some more euphonious substitute," be adopted as a new common-gender pronoun. Although his readers' suggestions are made on practical and stylistic rather than feminist grounds, White defends the generic masculine by trivializing the epicene pronoun in hyperbolic, antifeminist fashion: any objection to the *man . . . he* construction "is for the consideration of the next Women's Rights Convention, at which I hope it may be discussed with all the gravity beseeming its momentous significance." White reluctantly tempers his remarks by recalling that *one* has always served as a sex-neutral alternative:

> As a slight contribution to the amenities of the occasion, I venture to suggest that to free the language of the oppression of the sex and the outrage to its dignity, which have for centuries lurked in this use of *man,* it is not necessary to say, 'If a person wishes to sleep, *en* mustn't eat cheese for supper,' but merely, as the speakers of the best English now say and have said for generations, 'If one wishes to sleep, one mustn't, etc.'

Alternatives to *Thon*

Otto Jespersen (1894) believes that a common-gender pronoun can reduce sex bias in language: if *thon* were substituted for *he* in the sentence "It would be interesting if each of the leading poets would tell us what he considers his best work," then "ladies would be spared the disparaging implication that the leading poets were all men." But Jespersen sees no chance that *thon* will become popular. He finds *he or she* "cumbrous," *he* alone "inaccurate," and leans instead toward singular *they,* which he finds well represented in standard literary texts (27–29).

The editor of *Correct English,* Josephine Turck Baker, warns a reader seeking advice on *thon* to use this neologism advisedly, and to avoid singular *they,* which is always incorrect (1913, 156). Another language authority, the lexicographer James C. Fernald (1919), admits that "we long for a genderless singular of the pronoun of the third person to match the genderless plural," though he rejects *thon* as "unworkable." Fernald, who claims that English is basically a genderless language, finds that generic *he* is unexceptionable and advises his readers to steer around the awkward *he or she.* While Converse and the other early coiners of epicene pronouns did not have women's rights specifically in mind, Fernald, like White, is quick to damn the new words by raising the specter of the woman's movement: "The masculine has stood as the representative gender for a 'time whereof the memory of man runneth not to the contrary,' and that immemorial prescription still holds good, even in this period of militant feminism" (257).

Responding to Converse's proposal, Francis H. Williams (1884) faults *thon* because it bears no resemblance to *he* or *she,* because its nominative and accusative forms are identical, and because it might be confused in print with *thou.* This last fear proves justified: two typographical errors obscure a reference to Converse's pronoun in Jespersen's *Modern English Grammar:* "A preposed *thou* [i.e., proposed *thon*] has not been successful" (1949, 204). Williams is convinced that "sooner or later, a singular number and common gender pronoun must be invented," and he offers his own set, *hi, hes, hem* as candidates for adoption.

Edgar Alfred Stevens (August 1884) objects to *thon* for similar reasons, though he regards an epicene pronoun as "absolutely necessary to the perfection of our language," and he points to the early use of *it* in such a capacity—"Lose no friend without an effort to hold *it*"—as well as to the present-day use of *it* in personal references: "Is *it* a boy or girl?" But Stevens notes that *it* cannot serve in sentences such as "Let *it* who merits it bear the palm." Stevens is one of the first pronoun coiners to comment on the need to include women more sensibly in the language, though his suggestion for a common-gender pronoun is the French masculine article *le,* which he finds appropriate because it can be declined exactly like the English *he: le, lis, lim.*

Maria Butler replies to Stevens, recommending the use of the plural *they* to avoid the inelegance of a neologism. She calls for teachers and the press to lift the taboo on this usage, warning that the creation of new words will disturb the shade of Noah Webster. Stevens (November 1884) remarks in turn that history shows innovation to have improved the English language. We have already borrowed heavily from French, and Stevens offers to return some of those borrowings in exchange for *le*. He also furnishes an example of the use of his new paradigm: "If any boy or girl will diligently pursue the course I have marked out for *lim*, *le* will surely reach the goal of *lis* ambition."

Emma Carleton, also replying to Stevens's proposal, finds it shameful "that our language should so long have suffered for a simple pronoun, and no man [*sic*] have risen to supply the missing word." Consequently she offers the epicene pronoun *ip*:

> It is a word unlike any pronoun now in use, yet with a family likeness to the impersonal pronoun '*it*,' and susceptible of being declined similarly. It has a short, sharp, distinctive sound which will prevent its being confused with any other word now in the language; its individual characteristics being as clearly defined as those of *if*, *it*, or *in*, the only words for which it might possibly ever be mistaken. As it will come into our language a total stranger, albeit with strong suggestions in its face of several illustrious old Latin families, it is therefore not handicapped by a previous record of any kind, and there appears no obstacle to our readily and rapidly becoming familiar with its appearance and signification. [1884, 186]

Carleton concludes her proposal with an example that carefully avoids the generic masculine: "If any man or woman has aught to urge against the eligibility of this word to the vacant office in question, let *ip* now speak or forever after hold *ips* peace."

James Rogers (1889) disapproves of *thon* "because every one has to be told how to pronounce it" and because it is too long. Rogers prefers "the shortest and easiest" pronouns, exemplified by his own creations, *e*, *es*, and *em*. Rogers derives *e* from *he*, while *em* comes from *them*, as in "Let 'em' come." Working at about the same time as Converse, though outside the literary mainstream, the language reformer Elias Molee completely revised the English pronoun system in his *Plea for an American Language* (1888). Molee created three gender-specific third person plural pronouns, masculine *hem* (*he* + *them*), feminine *lem* (*lady* + *them*), and neuter *tem* (*it* + *them*), and he also devised a set of fully inflected singular and plural common-gender pronouns: *ir* (pronounced [ir]), *iro,* and *im* for the singular, and *thir, thiro,* and *thim* for the plural.

The following list presents a chronology of the epicene pronouns.

ca.1850   ne, nis, nim; hiser. *New York Commercial Advertiser,* 7 August 1884, 3

1868   en. Cited by Richard Grant White (1868, 241–44)

1884   thon, thons. Charles Crozat Converse (1884, 55)

hi, hes, hem. Francis H. Williams (1884, 79–80)

le, lis, lim (from the French); unus; talis. Edgar Alfred Stevens (1884, 294)

hiser, himer (hyser, hymer). Charles P. Sherman, *The Literary World,* 6 September 1884, 294

ip, ips. Emma Carleton (1884, 186)

1888   ir, iro, im (sg.); thir, thiro, thim (pl.). Elias Molee (1888, 200–01)

1889   ons (from *one*). C. R. B., *Writer* 3:231

1890   e (from *he*), es, em (from *them*). James Rogers (1890, 12-13)

1891   hizer. Forrest Morgan (1891, 260–62)

1912   he'er, him'er, his'er, his'er's. Ella Flagg Young, *Chicago Tribune,* 7 January, Sec. 1, p. 7

1927   ha, hez, hem; on. *The Forum* 77:265–68; attributed by Mencken (1937, 460*n*) to Lincoln King, of Primghar, Iowa

hesh (heesh), hizzer, himmer; on. Fred Newton Scott (Scott mentions earlier creation of *on*), *The Forum* 77:754; Mencken adds, "In 1934 James F. Morton, of the Paterson (N.J.) Museum, proposed to change *hesh* to *heesh* and to restore *hiser* and *himer*" (1948, 370).

ca.1930   thir. Sir John Adams, cited by Philip Howard (1977, 95)

1934   she, shis, shim; gender-specific parallel to *he, his, him.* Cited by Philip Ballard (1934, 7–8)

1935   himorher; hes (pron. [hɛs]), hir (pron. [hir]), hem; his'n, her'n. "The Post Impressionist," *Washington Post,* 20 August, 6

1938	se, sim, sis. Gregory Hynes, "See?" _Liverpool Echo,_ 21 September; cited by Mencken (1948, 370)
ca.1940	heesh. A. A. Milne; cited by Maxwell Nurnberg (1942, 88–90)
1945	hse. Buwei Yang Chao (1972, xxiv)
1970	she (contains _he_), heris, herim. Dana Densmore, "Speech is the Form of Thought," _No More Fun and Games: A Journal of Female Liberation_ (April); cited in _Media Report to Women_ 3.1 (January 1975): 12.
	co (from IE *_ko_), cos. Mary Orovan ([1972] 1978)
	ve, vis, ver. Varda (Murrell) One, _Everywoman,_ 8 May 1970, 2
1971	ta, ta-men (pl.); a borrowing from Mandarin Chinese. Leslie E. Blumenson, _New York Times,_ 30 December
1972	tey, term, tem; him/herself. Casey Miller and Kate Swift, "What about New Human Pronouns?" _Current_ 138:43-45
	fm. Paul Kay, April _Newsletter of the American Anthropological Association_ 13:3
	it; z. Abigail Cringle rejects epicene _it,_ preferring z. _Washington Post,_ 2 May 1972, Sec. A, 19
	shis, shim, shims, shimself. Robert B. Kaplan, June _Newsletter of the American Anthropological Association_ 13:4
	ze (from Ger. _sie_), zim, zees, zeeself; per (from _person_), pers. Steven Polgar proposes the _ze_ paradigm; John Clark offers _per._ September _Newsletter of the American Anthropological Association_ 13:17–18
1973	na, nan, naself. June Arnold, _The Cook and the Carpenter_ (Plainfield, Vt.: Daughters, Inc.)
	it; s/he. "A Woman's New World Dictionary," 3–4
	s/he; him/er; his-or-her. Cited and rejected by Gordon Wood, "The Forewho—Neither a He, a She, nor an It," _American Speech_ 48:158–59
	shem; herm. Quidnunc, "_Thon_—That's the Forewho," _American Speech_ 48:300–02
	se (pron. [ši]), ser (pron. [šir]), sim (pron. [šım]), simself. William Cowan, Department of Linguistics, Carleton University (Ottawa); _Times Two,_ 24 May 1973
	j/e, m/a, m/e, m/es, m/oi; jee, jeue. Monique Wittig (1975)

employs the slashed pronouns as feminines, and cites the latter two which employ the more traditional feminine *e*.

1974 ne, nis, ner. Mildred Fenner (1974, 110) attributes this to Fred Wilhelms.

she (includes *he*). Gena Corea, "Frankly Feminist," reprinted as "How to Eliminate the Clumsy 'He,'" in *Media Report to Women* 3.1 (January 1975): 12

en, es, ar. David H. Stern, *Los Angeles Times,* 19 January 1974, Sec. 2, p. 4

hisorher; herorhis; ve, vis, vim. Cited by Amanda Smith, (1974, 29), who prefers singular *they.*

shem, hem, hes. Paul L. Silverman, *Washington Post,* 17 December 1974, Sec. A, 17

1975 hir, herim (facetious). Milton Mayer, "On the Siblinghood of Persons," *The Progressive* 39:20–21

hesh, himer, hiser, hermself. Jan Verley Archer, "Use New Pronouns," *Media Report to Women* 3.1 (January 1975): 12

se (pron. [si]). H. R. Lee, *Forbes,* 15 August 1975, 86

ey, eir, em; uh. Christine M. Elverson, *Chicago Tribune,* 23 August 1975, Sec. 1, p. 12

h'orsh'it (facetious blend of *he, she, or it*). Joel Weiss, *Forbes,* 15 September 1975, 12

1976 ho, hom, hos, homself (from Lat. *homo,* 'man,' and prefix *homo-,* 'the same, equal, like'). Donald K. Darnell, in Donald K. Darnell and Wayne Brockriede, *Persons Communicating* (Englewood Cliffs, N.J.: Prentice-Hall), 148

he or she; to be written as (s)he. Elizabeth Lane Beardsley, "Referential Genderization," in Carol C. Gould and Marx W. Wartofsky, eds., *Women and Philosophy* (New York: G.P. Putnam's Sons), 285–93

she, herm; hs (facetious; pron. "zzz"). Paul B. Horton (1976, 159–60)

it. Millicent Rutherford (1976, 11)

ca.1977 po, xe, jhe. Cited as recent and ephemeral by Miller and Swift (1977, 130). Paul Dickson (1982, 113) attributes *jhe,* pronounced "gee," to Professor Milton A. Stern of the University of Michigan.

E, E's, Em; one. *E* was created by psychologist Donald G.

MacKay (1983) of the University of California at Los Angeles.

1977   e, ris, rim. Werner Low, *Washington Post*, 20 February, Sec. C, 6

sheme, shis, shem; heshe, hisher, himmer. Thomas H. Middleton, "Pondering the Personal Pronoun Problem," *Saturday Review*, 9 March 1977, 59. *Sheme*, etc. proposed by Thomas S. Jackson of Washington, D.C.; Middleton also cites proposals for *heshe, hisher, himmer*.

em, ems. Jeffrey J. Smith (using the pseudonym TINTAJL jefry), *Em Institute Newsletter* (June 1977)

1978   ae. Cited by Cheris Kramer, Barrie Thorne, and Nancy Henley, "Perspectives on Language and Communication," *Signs* 3:638–51, as occurring in fiction, especially science fiction

hir. Ray A. Killian, *Managers Must Lead!* (AMACOM) press release; cited in "The Epicene Pronoun Yet Again," *American Speech* 54:157–58

hesh, hizer, hirm; sheehy; sap (from *Homo sapiens*). Tom Wicker, "More About He/She and Thon," *New York Times*, 14 May 1978, Sec. 4, 19. *Hesh*, etc., proposed by Professor Robert Longwell of the University of Northern Colorado; *sheehy* by David Kraus of Bell Harbor, N.Y.; *sap* (facetiously) by Dr. Lawrence S. Ross of Huntington, N.Y.; Wicker adds that several readers offered blends of *he, she,* and *it*.

heesh, hiser(s), herm, hermself. Leonora Timm (1978, 555–65)

1979   one. Lillian Carlton (1979, 156–57)

et, ets, etself. Aline Hoffman of Sarnia, Ontario; cited by William Sherk (1979)

hir, hires, hirem, hirself. Jerome Ch'en, Professor of History at York University, 6 January 1979, *New York Times*, 18

shey, sheir, sheirs; hey, heir, heirs. Paul Encimer favors the first over the second paradigm. *The Peacemaker* 32:2–3

1980   it. Herman Arthur (1980, 30–32)

1981   heshe, hes, hem. Ronald C. Corbyn, "Getting Around Sexist Pronouns," *Anthropology Newsletter* 22:10–11

1982   shey, shem, sheir. Mauritz Johnson; cited by William Safire
        (1982, 30)

        E, Ir. Subject and possessive forms, created by the Broward
        County, Florida, public schools; cited by Paul Dickson
        (1982, 113)

1984   hiser. McClain B. Smith, 20 January, *Ann Arbor News,* Sec.
        A, 6

        hes. Ernie Permentier, *Ms.,* May 1984, 22

        hann. Steven Schaufele takes this from Old Norse, already
        the source of some English pronouns; it is analogous to
        Finnish *han. Colorless Green Newsflashes* 4 (November
        1984): 3

1985   herm. Jenny Cheshire traces this to the magazine *Lysis-
        trata.* "A Question of Masculine Bias," *Today's English*
        1:26

PATTERNS OF NEOLOGY

There is often little or no information available to help us analyze the
process whereby epicene pronouns come into being. For example,
June Arnold uses *na* and *nan,* without comment, for all the third
person pronouns in her novel *The Cook and the Carpenter* (1973),
whereas in *Sister Gin* (1975) she silently reverts to conventional pronoun usage. Sometimes, however, the devisers of sex-neutral pronouns describe the process involved in the formation of their neologisms. This is the case with *thon.* It is also the case for the set *he'er,
him'er, his'er* which was coined by Ella Flagg Young in 1912 and
which, like *thon,* is included in the Funk and Wagnalls *Standard Dictionary.*

Under the headline "Mrs. Ella Young Invents Pronoun," the *Chicago Tribune* of January 7, 1912, reports that Young, superintendent
of the Chicago schools, addressed a meeting of school principals as
follows:

> A principal should so conduct his'er school that all pupils are engaged
> in something that is profitable to him'er and where the pupil is required
> to use knowledge in school in accomplishing his'er task. . . . I don't see
> how one can map out the work for the fifth or sixth grade when he'er
> has always done the work in the grades above or below. [sec.1, p.7]

Young, a student of John Dewey and a prominent American educator in her own right—she was elected head of the National Education Association in 1910—explained her pronoun remodeling: "The problem has bothered me frequently and the solution of it occurred to me as I was on my way to this meeting. Most of the pronouns of the feminine gender end in 'er, and so all you have to do to make the common pronoun is to take the masculine form and add 'er." The principals enthusiastically resolved to implement the suggestion made by their superior in their own work. According to Mencken, Young also tried to induce the NEA to adopt her invention, but despite the optimism of Young and her supporters, her epicene pronoun survived only in the dictionary.

Although we do not learn whether Young's coinage was motivated by feminist or grammatical concerns, or perhaps by both, her remarks indicate that she expected her audience to be familiar with the notion of the "common pronoun." Like other wordsmiths, Young is aware of the absence of an epicene pronoun, but ignorant of previous creations: her word is independent of the earlier *hiser* coined circa 1850 and once again in 1884. Her explanation also shows that the influence of the generic masculine is difficult to overcome: although the epicene pronoun is supposed to be sex-neutral, neologists often base their new pronouns on the masculine *he* rather than the neuter *it*. As Young herself admits, her pronouns—like words in *-ess*—consist of feminine endings tacked onto masculine stems.

He/She Blends

Most of the creators of sex-neutral pronouns form their new words from blends of the various inflections of the masculine and feminine singular pronouns, *he, his, him, she,* and *her.* Not every neologist offers a complete paradigm, and the possessive *hiser* and its variants are coined most often: *hiser* appears circa 1850 and again in 1884 (as *hyser*), 1891 (*hizer*), 1912 (*his'er*), 1927 (*hizzer*), 1975, 1977 (*hisher*), 1978 (as *hiser* and *hizer*), and 1984 (see the list above).

While in most blends the masculine element precedes the feminine, this pattern is occasionally reversed. Thus alongside *hiser* we find *shis* (1934, 1972, 1977), *sis* (1938), *heris* (1970), *hires* (1979), and *sheir* (1979, 1982), the last actually a blend of *she* and *their*. A third pattern consists of variations on _his: hez_ (1927), _hs_ (1976), _hos_ (1976), and _hes_ (1981, 1984).

Object pronoun forms follow similar patterns, with _himer_, first used in 1884, being one of the most common: _him'er_ (1912), _himorher_ (1935), _himer_ (1975), and _himmer_ (1977). The feminine precedes in _shim_ (1934, 1972), _sim_ (1938), _shem_ (suggesting a blend with _them_ rather than _him_, 1973, 1974, 1977, 1982), _herim_ (1970, 1975), _herm_ (1973, 1976, 1978, 1985), and _hirem_ (1979). There are also variations on _him: hem_ (1927, 1935, 1974) and _hom_ (from Latin _homo_, 'man,' and _homo-_, 'the same,' 1976).

Subject pronoun forms blending _he_ and _she_ are not coined as often as object or possessive forms. Though _hiser_ appears around 1850, the earliest subject blend, _he'er_, is created in 1912. _Hesh_ (1927, 1975, 1978, 1982) and its variants _heesh_ (1927, ca. 1940, 1978), _hes_ (1935, 1974), and _heshe_ (1981) are the most common. As with the possessive and object forms, the feminine pronoun precedes in only a few coinages. Sometimes it is simply _she_ (1934, 1970, 1976). In these cases it may be considered to embrace _he_, and it forms the basis of an independent epicene paradigm, for example _she, heris, herim_ (1970). In one instance, _she, shis, shim_ (1934), we are dealing not with an epicene pronoun but with a reform of the feminine paradigm which supplies distinct possessive and objective pronouns to match the masculines. We also find subjective _hir_ (1979), _sheme_ (1977), and _sheehy_ (1978). The anomalous, truly neutral blend _hse_ (1945), created by Buwei Yang Chao for her Chinese cookbook, is defined as "my usual way of pronouncing _he_ and _she_ without distinction when I speak English" (xxiv). Subject forms based on _he_ include _ha_ (1927), _ho_ (1976), and _hey_ (1979).

Even when the paradigm is apparently based on feminine precedence, it may be declined according to the masculine pattern, with a neutral, uninflected subject form analogous to _he_ (and sometimes _she_ as well), a possessive in -_s_, like _his_, and an object form in -_m_ corresponding to _him_. Thus _se_ (1938), which may be viewed as a blend of _she_ and _he_, though it may also derive from the Latinate _se_, 'self,' is declined _se, sis, sim_. The phonetically related _ze, zees, zim_, coined in 1972, is modeled on the German pronoun, _sie_, though it is supplied with English masculine endings. Another popular paradigm, based on the subject form *e,* suggestive of the unaspirated pronunciation of *he,* also follows the masculine declension: *e, es, em* (1890); *E, E's, Em* (1977); and *e, ris, rim* (1977), which contains the *r* of the feminine pronoun but is inflected like the masculine. *E, Ir* (1982), however, does not follow the masculine declension. Both *le, lis, lim* (1884) and *ne, nis, nim* (ca. 1850) are masculine in inflection, though *ne, nis, ner* (1974) and *ve, vis, ver* (1970) are balanced in morphology, employing a masculine possessive and a feminine objective form.

Three neologists stress fairness to both sexes in explaining the formation of their new pronouns. Fred Wilhelms chooses the initial letter for his paradigm *ne, nis, ner* by going through the alphabet "roughly halfway" from the *h* in *he* to the *s* in *she* (cited in Fenner 1974). David H. Stern creates *en, es, ar* (1974) because the *n* reminds him of the indefinites *someone* or *no one,* while the *s* suggests *his* and the *r, hers,* "so that orientation to the sexes is preserved without favoring one or the other." Of the oblique forms in his paradigm *e, ris, rim* (1977) Werner Low remarks, "It's a trade-off: the lady gets the first letter, the gentleman the other two. Nothing could be more equitable."

Other epicene patterns invented more than once include *en* (invented twice, independently, in 1868, 1974), *em* (1977); *ons* (1889), *on* (1927); *ir,* (1888, 1982); *ne* (ca. 1850, 1974), *na* (1973); *it* (1972, 1973, 1976, and 1980), *et* (1979). Coinages based on the third person plural include *thir* (ca. 1930), *tey, ter, tem* (1972), *ey, eir, em* (1975), *shey, sheir, sheirs* (1979), *hey, heir, heirs* (1979), and *shey, shem, shir* (1982). In addition to *thon* and *ip,* unique coinages include *co* (1970), *fm* (1972), *po, xe, jhe* (1977), *ae* (1978), and *per* (1972).

Although Donald MacKay (1983) claims that he can measure the efficiency of epicene pronouns, none of the neologisms has enjoyed widespread use. Miller and Swift (1977, 118) report that the student newspaper of the University of Tennessee, *The Daily Beacon,* tried the *ter* paradigm but dropped it after three months because of ridicule and misunderstanding, and there are other reports of the experimental use of *co, hesh* and *per* (as well as *thon*).

THE WORD THAT FAILED

A variety of hopeful but often contradictory arguments have been used to recommend the various epicene pronouns. These new words are proclaimed as advantageous because they are like, or in some cases unlike, the pronouns we already use. The etymology of many of the new pronouns is felt to be transparent, but even if they are confessed to be opaque, the pronouns are touted as natural, unambiguous, instantly recognizable, easy to learn, and easy to use. Epicene pronouns will improve English, it is said, because they are more grammatical than generic *he,* which is not really generic, or singular *they,* which is, after all, a plural, and because they are stylistically preferable to the coordinate but cumbersome *he or she.* Common-gender pronouns also eliminate the sexism of the generic masculine, an advantage stressed by neologists writing since 1970, although a feminist rationale is attributed to the restructured feminine paradigm *she, shis, shim* (1934). Ultimately the new pronouns are advertised as convenient; some proponents go so far as to claim that they fill "a crying need." According to Maxwell Nurnberg (1942), A. A. Milne alleged, in defense of *heesh* (ca. 1940), that "if the English language had been properly organized by a businessman or a Member of Parliament, then there would be a word which meant both 'he' and 'she.'"

Opponents of pronoun reform maintain that generic *he* does not exclude women, or if it does, the exclusion is not serious. Roy Copperud rejects the notion that generic *he* renders women invisible: "It is doubtful that readers, apart from feminists searching for suggestions of discrimination, think in masculine terms in reading [generic masculine] statements" (1980, 146). In contrast, psychologists Donald MacKay (1983), Wendy Martyna (1978), and a number of their colleagues report experiments indicating that men, women, and children respond to male words, generic or not, by thinking of male images.

The opponents argue further that epicene pronouns are not transparent, unambiguous, or easy to use; that they are phonetically and visually awkward; and that they are the creations of a feminist conspiracy. They are also categorized as unnatural and unnecessary: if English needed a common-gender pronoun, language reformer Richard Grant White remarks, it would have developed one on its own. Still other language critics, who favor the idea of sex neutrality but oppose the introduction of new words, prefer to adopt singular *they* as a standard form. In 1974 Amanda J. Smith proposed just such a measure at the Southern Regional Conference of the National Organization for Women. In the same year, Nancy Faires Conklin encouraged *anybody . . . they,* which she identified as the form most widely used "outside of academic or hypercorrect upper middle-class circles" (60–61). Sharon Blands (1980), a San Francisco writer, urged that, like ethnic slurs, *he* should not "continue to be with us when other forms, like 'you' and 'they,' are just as useful." While some supporters of sex-neutral language point to the widespread use of singular *they* and predict that it will eventually supplant generic *he,* many feminists and grammarians oppose singular *they* as incorrect or hopelessly stigmatized. And the second person pronoun can only replace the masculine in a limited number of cases: *Everyone liked his dinner* cannot be rewritten *Everyone liked your dinner.*

The feminist word coiner Mary Daly warns, "It is a mistake to fixate on the third person singular" (1978, 18), and Mary-Claire van Leunen (1978), announcing her decision to retain the traditional generic masculine pronoun, rejects a variety of alternatives: generic *she* because it draws too much attention to itself; *tey* because it is too bold; *one* because it is neither vivid nor particular; and *its* because it is too harsh a joke. Van Leunen offers a consolation to her readers: "We feminists might adopt the position of pitying men for being forced to share their pronouns around" (5).

The critics of epicene pronouns do not need to put up much of a fight, for the words seem to fail even when they are unopposed. It is difficult for new pronouns which arise naturally, like *its,* to make their way into the paradigm. It is more difficult still for an artificial pronoun to succeed. Despite the popularity of *he–she* blends with word coiners, their acceptance by the general public is further hampered by the fact that *hesh, himmer* and *himher* are American slang terms for 'effeminate male' (Berrey and Van den Bark 1942, 372). Yet the repeated failure of epicene pronouns does not discourage new attempts at word coining. Even those few brave souls who know both the history of the word and the odds against success are still willing to gamble.

Most coiners of new pronouns have no specific plan in mind to ensure the adoption of their creations, other than the basic attraction of the new words themselves. One neologist, Jeffrey J. Smith (writing as TINTAJL jefry) formed the Em Institute and issued the *Em Institute Newsletter* to publicize *em* (1977), which functions not only as an epicene pronoun but an honorific title, an adjective meaning 'human,' and a replacement for generic *man.* Smith believes the existence of *'em* as a colloquial variant of *them* will give his own creation an advantage.

The approach of Smith and his colleagues to language reform has obviously not worked well. Realizing this, the psychologist Donald MacKay, advocate of *per* (1972) and *E* (1977), has recently outlined what he regards as a sure fire program of pronoun renovation. MacKay (1983) recommends that the mechanism of prescriptive grammar be invoked to enforce the adoption of a new common-gender pronoun, which will be determined scientifically: using existing neologisms, the ideal characteristics of new words will be distilled. New forms displaying these ideal characteristics will be invented, and the new forms will be tested against the old ones to determine which offer "the greatest benefit and the least cost, where benefits facilitate communication (including learning, comprehension, and use of the language over very long periods of time) and costs make communication more difficult (relative to all other means of expressing the same concept)." The resulting prescription will be "written into prescriptive grammars, taught in our schools, and followed in our publishing systems so as to bring about a permanent change in the language" (50-52).

MacKay's optimism reflects an oversimplified view of the workings of English. We cannot legislate new words into existence, and no unified mechanism of prescriptive grammar exists to enforce a rule, should we manage to agree on one. Furthermore, it is not likely that a new pronoun with ideal characteristics can be devised in the same way we create wonder drugs or market pet food. The history of the epicene pronoun suggests that while it may be perceived by some as a needed word, it remains for the language in general an unnecessary one.

Whatever one's stand on feminism, usage, neologism, or language change, we can learn two things from the history of the unhappy epicene pronoun. The repeated coining of gender-neutral pronominal paradigms suggests, like the avoidance of generic *man* in favor of synonymous words, that opposition to the generic masculine in English has gone on for some time and will persist for some time to come. In his article "The Origin of Grammatical Gender" (1899), Benjamin Wheeler notes a reluctance on the part of English speakers to specify gender in dealing with indefinites:

Epicene pronouns like *everybody* . . . are often forced to a betrayal of sex by the personal pronoun; thus in *Somebody left his* [*her*] *umbrella*. The inclination to evade the pressure is felt in the temptation to say, *Somebody left their umbrella*. [536]

Despite the desire to avoid sex reference, the repeated failure of common-gender pronouns should indicate that in order to be effective, the challenge to the generic masculine will probably come from a different direction, most likely from a set of alternatives already present in the language rather than an innovation which people must be coaxed or forced to use. Perhaps that set will be the one even now employed by many writers and speakers who wish to be both inclusive and inoffensive, while remaining stylistically unobtrusive: singular *they,* in combination with an occasional *he or she* and, when these choices are stylistically inappropriate, the rephrasing of sentences to eliminate the need for a sex-indefinite pronoun.

CHAPTER 11

Conclusion

Whatsoever [men] cannot sufficiently twattle with Their tongues,
they cannot contain themselves there,
but they must publish it with their Pennes.
The Womens Sharpe Revenge

Despite the failure of the epicene pronoun, attempts to make the English language fairer to women and men persist, and now and then a victory is claimed. Citing the prevalence of *Ms.* and a tendency to avoid generic *he,* the lexicographer Sol Steinmetz (1982) sees the movement to desex English as the first successful language reform since the eighteenth-century grammarians and usage critics began to make us self-conscious about the double negative and the split infinitive. Other language commentators are less sanguine about the efforts of today's gender reformers. Philip Howard, for example, finds the attempt to neutralize English misguided. Howard does not oppose women's rights; rather, he objects to meddling with our vocabulary and syntax. Insisting that "injustice exists in real life, not in dictionaries," Howard concludes that if we end the real forms of sex discrimination, the English language will look after itself, and he warns that the use of sex-neutral words and pronouns corrupts language and harms the cause of equality for women (1977, 95).

Maija Blaubergs (1980) has enumerated and countered the arguments put forth against tampering with the expression of gender in English. The opponents of language reform maintain, for example, that there is no necessary connection between the treatment of gender in language and the degree of sexism in a given society. They argue that feminists ought to focus their concern not on language, but on more significant expressions of sexism like discrimination in employment. Linguistic prejudice, it is further claimed, is in the ear of the beholder: *man* may function successfully as a true generic, while many users of allegedly gender-neutral forms such as singular *they* are perfectly willing to exclude women from their scope of reference. We are also warned that innovation will destroy our literary and linguistic heritage. If that is not sufficient, there is always the appeal to freedom of speech: no one has the right to tell people how to modify their language habits. Finally there is the appeal to linguistic history, which asserts that deliberate language change is difficult if not impossible to effect, and therefore should not be attempted.

Some of these arguments are valid. Languages without gender may be found in cultures that are demonstrably more sexist than ours, and deliberate change in English is difficult if not impossible to bring about, as the history of the epicene pronoun has shown. But that cannot stop efforts to eradicate what sexism there is in our society. It is true that when social structures change, language follows, but it has always been clear that words are valuable, even essential tools in motivating change. We do have freedom of speech (though freedom of grammar is another matter altogether), but that argument can be used by language reformers as well as their opponents. It is evident from the historical record of English, and from a look at current language controversies, that language reformers and critics have always felt obliged to meddle with our language habits in the name of logic, reason, linguistic purity, tradition, perfection, common sense, science, religion, and politics. And it is also evident that we ignore language authorities as much as we adhere to their judgments. Furthermore, the English language has been changing for centuries without invalidating our literary heritage: if anything, the awareness of language change reminds us of the need to preserve the treasures of our past.

Though language change is difficult to legislate, the question of sexism in language differs from many of the standard language controversies—whether broad issues like spelling reform or particular items like *data* as a singular or plural noun—because it involves not just questions of pronunciation, grammar, and usage, but our linguistic sensitivities as well. In the past, language that has been insulting to particular groups of English speakers has been proscribed from Standard American English: though they have always had to fight for linguistic recognition, we tend to honor—by consensus more often than prescription—the wishes of minorities with respect to language use. For example, in the 1870s both Webster's and Worcester's dictionaries responded to complaints over their inclusion of the verb *jew,* 'to cheat, defraud, or swindle,' despite its clear marking as nonstandard and defamatory, and the word was quietly withdrawn from these lexicons, though it persists in actual usage. More recently, a suit to force the *Oxford English Dictionary* to revise its definition of *Jew* was dismissed for lack of merit. In the 1930s, a movement to capitalize the initial letter in *negro* drew fierce resistance from Northern newspaper editors, who objected on etymological and grammatical grounds, though the spelling *Negro* is now standard. In the 1960s *Negro* was replaced by *black,* and currently an editorial controversy exists over the capitalization of the word in such phrases as *Black English.*

It is to be expected, then, that if enough people become sensitized to sex-related language questions, such forms as generic *he* and *man* will give way no matter what arguments are advanced in their defense. While quantitative evidence suggests that speakers may still prefer *lady* over *woman,* at least in certain contexts, we might safely guess that *woman* remains the term of choice in carefully edited prose, and that its range is expanding. One also suspects that *girl* is rapidly disappearing in reference to adult women, even in colloquial speech, because the informal rules of politeness have marked such usage as disparaging.

There is no doubt that injustice exists in real life, but as we have seen in the chapters above, it apparently exists in dictionaries and other works about language as well. Those who have written about the English language over the years have contributed, wittingly or not, to the mistaken notion that Eve's language is not Adam's, and is therefore not as good as Adam's. These pages represent only an incomplete history of attitudes toward women, men, and the English language. Yet they are a start, an attempt to place the present debate over language and sex within the broader context of our linguistic history, to raise our consciousness about the linguistic treatment of grammar and gender in the same way that the woman's movement has raised our consciousness about language use in present-day English.

Much of today's research in sociolinguistics suggests that, at least for English, most gender differences are the result of complex sociological or situational, not just biological factors, and that the stereotypes of men's and women's language are based not so much on human nature and the differences between the sexes, but on the accidents of

social class, education, income, occupation, and a variety of other social and personal variables (Smith 1985). In many cases gender
stereotypes prove to have no connection at all with actual language
use. Close analysis suggests that men use "women's" language and
women use "men's," that there may be very few real sex differences in
the English language, that we need to refine our techniques of analysis
to isolate the differences that do exist.

Nonetheless, the stereotypes persist. They may be illusions, but
they are powerful and persistent ones. In this historical treatment of
images of sex in works about the English language, we have attempted
to illuminate both the deep antifeminist tradition that underlies our
ideas about language and the tradition of language reform that seeks
to combat inaccuracy and imperfection in our native tongue. There is
nothing inherently sexist about the English language. Rather, attitudes toward men, women, and language—opinions usually formed
by men, but often formed and shared by women as well—created the
biases against women's language, and many of these biases have become encoded in our words. Some radical feminists have displayed an
equally subjective bias against what is perceived as men's language.
Examining the history of this linguistic prejudice will not necessarily
teach us how to combat it: language reform, at least for English, is a
difficult and uncertain process. But language does change, as do attitudes; and social factors clearly can contribute to such change. While
Grammar and Gender advocates no specific reform, it does demonstrate the need for more realistic attitudes toward language use and
toward the description of English. Although we may not be able to
control the future of our language very well, we can hope that an
increased awareness of our linguistic history will prevent the English
language from repeating at least some of the mistakes of its past. More
specifically, we can hope that works about the language—dictionaries,
thesauruses, grammars, usage guides, and theoretical commentaries—will acknowledge woman's position as a visible and independent
linguistic partner in the creation and perpetuation of English, and that
Eve's language will become for men and women not the muted words
of servitude but a voice of authority.

Ackerman, Louise. 1962. *Lady* as a synonym for *woman*. *American Speech* 37:284–85.

Addison, Joseph. 1713. *The guardian*. Ed. J. C. Stephens. Lexington: University of Kentucky Press.

Agopoff, Noubar. 1967. *Unilingua: Langue universelle auxiliare*. Paris: Klincksieck.

Alford, Henry. 1864. *The queen's English*. London.

Algeo, John. 1977. Grammatical usage: Modern shibboleths. In *James B. McMillan: Essays in linguistics by his friends and colleagues*, ed. James C. Raymond and I. Willis Russell, 53–71. University: University of Alabama Press.

American Heritage dictionary of the English language. 1969. Ed. William Morris. Boston: Houghton Mifflin.

Anderson, Chester R. 1951. *American Business Writing Association Bulletin* (October): 8.

Anderson, James. 1792. Grammatical disquisitions. *The Bee* 11:120–30; 193–204; 240–50.

Antrim, Benajah J. 1843. *Pantography*. Philadelphia.

Archer, Verley. 1975. Use new pronouns. *Media Report to Women* 3.1:12.

Armes, William D. 1884. Wanted—a new pronoun. *The Literary World* (Boston), 14 June, 199.

Arnauld, Antoine, and Claude Lancelot. [1660] 1969. *Grammaire générale et raisonnée*. Reprint. Paris: Paulet.

Arthur, Herman. 1980. To err is huperson; to forgive, divine. *American Educator* 4.4:30–32.

Ash, John. [1761] 1967. *Grammatical institutes*. Reprint. Leeds: Scolar.

Ayres, Alfred [T. E. Osmun]. 1882. *The verbalist*. New York: Appleton.

Bache, Richard Meade. 1869. *Vulgarisms and other errors of speech*. Philadelphia.

Bailey, Nathan. 1736. *Dictionarium Britannicum.* 2d ed. London.

Bain, Alexander. 1879. *Higher English grammar.* New York: Holt.

Baker, Josephine Turck. 1899. Editorial note. *Correct English* 1:20.

―――. 1913. Editorial note. *Correct English* 14:156.

Baker, Robert. [1770] 1968. *Reflections on the English language.* London. Reprint. Menston: Scolar.

Baker, Russell. 1973. Nopersonclature. *New York Times,* 4 March, sec. 4, p. 13.

Ballard, Philip B. 1934. *Thought and language.* London: University of London Press.

Barber, Charles. 1964. *Linguistic change in present-day English.* University: University of Alabama Press.

Barnhart, Clarence, Sol Steinmetz, and Robert K. Barnhart. 1973. *Barnhart dictionary of new English since 1963.* New York: Barnhart/Harper and Row.

―――. 1980. *The second Barnhart dictionary of new English.* New York: Barnhart/Harper and Row.

Baron, Dennis E. 1981. The epicene pronoun: The word that failed. *American Speech* 56:83–97.

―――. 1982a. *Going native: The regeneration of Saxon English.* Publication of the American Dialect Society, no. 69. University: University of Alabama Press.

―――. 1982b. *Grammar and good taste: Reforming the American language.* New Haven: Yale University Press.

―――. 1984. Is it [mɪs] or [mɪz]? *Verbatim* 11 (Autumn): 10.

Baron, Naomi. 1971. A reanalysis of English grammatical gender. *Lingua* 27:113–40.

Barzun, Jacques. 1974. A few words on a few words. *Columbia Forum* (Summer): 17–19.

Bayle, Pierre. [1697] 1720. *Dictionaire historique et critique.* 3d ed. Paris.

Beard, Mary R. 1946. *Woman as force in history: A study in traditions and realities.* New York: Macmillan.

Beattie, James. [1788] 1968. *Theory of language.* Reprint. Menston: Scolar.

Bebout, Linda. 1984. Asymmetries in male-female word pairs. *American Speech* 59:13–30.

Benveniste, Emile. [1969] 1973. *Indo-European language and society.* Trans. Elizabeth Palmer. Coral Gables: University of Miami Press.

Berger, Thomas. 1983. *The feud.* New York: Delacorte.

Berrey, Lester V., and Melvin Van den Bark. 1942. *The American thesaurus of slang.* New York: Crowell.

Bierce, Ambrose. [1911] 1943. *The Devil's dictionary.* Reprint. Cleveland: World.

Bingham, Caleb. 1785. *The young ladies accidence*. Boston.

Blair, Hugh. 1783. *Lectures on rhetoric and belles lettres*. London.

Blands, Sharon. 1980. Other voices. *San Francisco Examiner*, 11 February, 37.

Blaubergs, Maija S. 1978. Changing the sexist language: The theory behind the practice. *Psychology of Women Quarterly* 2:244–61.

———. 1980. An analysis of classic arguments against changing sexist language. In *The voices and words of women and men*, ed. Cheris Kramarae, 135–47. Oxford: Pergamon.

Bloomfield, Leonard. [1933] 1965. *Language*. Reprint. New York: Holt, Rinehart and Winston.

Blount, Thomas. 1656. *Glossographia*. London.

Bodine, Ann. 1975. Androcentrism in prescriptive grammar. *Language and Society* 4:129–46.

Bolinger, Dwight L. 1942. Among the new words. *American Speech* 17:269.

———. 1968. *Aspects of language*. New York: Harcourt, Brace and World.

Bollack, Leon. 1899. *La langue bleue: Langue internationale pratique*. Paris.

Bornstein, Diane. 1978. As meek as a maid: A historical perspective on language for women in courtesy books from the middle ages to *Seventeen* magazine. In *Women's language and style*, ed. Douglas Butturff and Edmund L. Epstein, 132–38. Akron: L. and S. Books.

Bosworth, Joseph. 1898. *An Anglo-Saxon dictionary*. Ed. T. Northcote Toller. Oxford: Oxford University Press.

Bower, Laurie. 1983. *English word-formation*. Cambridge: Cambridge University Press.

Bradley, Henry. 1911. *The making of English*. New York: Macmillan.

Brewer, E. Cobham. [1894] 1898. *Dictionary of phrase and fable*. Reprint. Philadelphia.

Brightland, John. 1711. *A grammar of the English tongue*. London.

Brown, Goold. 1825. *Institutes of English grammar*. New York.

———. [1851] 1880. *Grammar of English grammars*. 10th ed. New York.

Brown, Stanley M., and Lillian Doris. 1954. *Business executive's handbook*. 4th ed. New York: Prentice-Hall.

Brugmann, Karl. 1897. *The nature and origin of the noun genders in the Indo-European languages*. Trans. Edmund Y. Robbins. New York: Scribners.

Buchanan, James. [1762] 1968. *The British grammar*. London. Reprint. Menston: Scolar.

Bullions, Peter. 1841. *Principles of English grammar*. Albany.

———. 1868. *Practical grammar of the English language*. New York.

Burgess, Anthony. 1976. Dirty words. *New York Times Magazine*, 8 August, 6.

Burgess, Gelett. 1906. *Are you a bromide? or, the sulphitic theory.* New York: B. W. Huebsch.

Burnet, James (Lord Monboddo). [1773] 1967. *Of the origin and progress of language.* Reprint. Menston: Scolar.

Butler, Maria. 1884. The missing word. *The Current,* 25 October, 260–61.

Buwei, Yang Chao. [1945] 1972. *How to cook and eat in Chinese.* Reprint of 3d ed. New York: Random House.

Calmet, Augustin. 1729. *Dictionarium historicum, criticum, chronologicum, geographicum, et literale sacrae scripturae.* Translated as *Calmet's great dictionary of the Holy Bible.* Charlestown, Mass., 1812.

Camden, William. [1605] 1614. *Remaines, concerning Britaine.* Reprint. London.

Campbell, George. 1776. *The philosophy of rhetoric.* London.

Cardell, William S. 1825. *Essay on language.* New York.

———. 1827. *Philosophic grammar of the English language.* Philadelphia.

Cardenas, C. 1923. *Hom-Idyomo: Outline of an auxiliary international language.* Leipzig: Sperling.

Carleton, Emma. 1884. The missing word. *The Current,* 20 September, 186.

Carlton, Lillian E. 1979. An epicene suggestion. *American Speech* 54:156-57.

Casaubon, Meric. 1650. *De quatuor linguis commentationis.* London.

Cawdry, Robert. 1604. *A table alphabeticall.* London.

Century Dictionary. 1889. 6 vols. New York: The Century Co.

Chamberlain, Alexander. 1912. Women's languages. *American Anthropologist* 14:579-81.

Chesterfield, Lord (Philip Dormer Stanhope). 1754. *The World* 101 (December): 605–10.

Cleland, John. 1766. *The way to things by words, and to words by things.* London.

———. 1768. *Specimen of an etymological vocabulary.* London.

Cockeram, Henry. 1623. *The English dictionarie.* London.

Colby, Frank. [1944] 1947. *The practical handbook of better English.* Rev. ed. New York: Grosset and Dunlap.

Conklin, Nancy Faires. 1974. Toward a feminist analysis of linguistic behavior. *University of Michigan Papers in Women's Studies* (February): 60–61.

Connoisseur. 1754. No. 44, 221–26.

Contributors' Club. 1878. *Atlantic Monthly* 42:637-50.

Converse, Charles Crozat. 1884. A new pronoun. *The Critic,* 2 August, 55.

Cook, Daniel. 1959. A point of lexicographical method. *American Speech* 34:20.

Cooper, James Fenimore. 1828. *Notions of the Americans: Picked up by a travelling bachelor.* 2 vols. Philadelphia.

————. [1838] 1956. *The American democrat.* Reprint. New York: Vintage.

Copperud, Roy. 1980. *American usage and style: The consensus.* New York: Van Nostrand Reinhold.

Crabb, George. 1816. *English synonymes.* London.

Crombie, Alexander. [1802] 1830. *The etymology and syntax of the English language explained and illustrated.* 3d ed. London.

Curme, George O. 1931. *Syntax.* Boston: D. C. Heath.

Dalgarno, George. [1661] 1968. *Ars signorum.* Reprint. Menston: Scolar.

Daly, Mary. 1978. *Gyn/Ecology: The metaethics of radical feminism.* Boston: Beacon Press.

————. 1984. *Pure lust: Elemental feminist philosophy.* Boston: Beacon Press.

Davies, Hugh Sykes. 1964. Grammar and style. In *Modern essays on writing and style,* ed. Paul C. Wermuth, 17–24. New York: Holt, Rinehart and Winston.

Depauw, Linda Grant. 1982. *Seafaring women.* Boston: Houghton Mifflin.

De Quincey, Thomas. [1840–41] 1897. Style. In *Collected writings,* vol. 10, ed. David Masson, 134–245. London.

Devis, Ellin. 1801. *The accidence; or first rudiments of English grammar, designed for the use of young ladies.* 10th ed. London.

Dickson, Paul. 1982. *Words.* New York: Delacorte Press.

Diderot, Denis. 1751. *Encyclopédie, ou dictionnaire raisonné* 9:268–71. Neufchâtel.

Dike, Edwin B. 1933. Obsolete words. *Philological Quarterly* 12:207–19.

————. 1937. The suffix -ess. *Journal of English and Germanic Philology* 36:29–34.

Dixey, Wolstan. 1884. Wanted—a new pronoun? *The Literary World,* 28 June, 213.

Donatus. 1926. *The ars minor of Donatus.* Ed. and trans. Wayland Johnson Chase. University of Wisconsin Studies in the Social Sciences, no. 11. Madison.

Dubois, Betty Lou, and Isabel M. Crouch. 1979. Man and its compounds in recent prefeminist American-English. *Papers in Linguistics* 12:261–69.

Duncan, Daniel. [1731] 1967. *A new English grammar.* Reprint. Menston: Scolar.

Durand, Marguerite. 1936. *Le genre grammatical en français parlé à Paris et dans la région parisienne.* Paris: Bibliothèque du français moderne.

Dutch, Robert A., ed. 1965. *The St. Martin's Roget's thesaurus of English words and phrases.* New York: St. Martin's Press.

Eble, Connie C. 1976. Etiquette books as linguistic authority. In *The second LACUS forum, 1975,* ed. Peter A. Reich, 468–75. Columbia, S.C.: Hornbeam.

Elgin, Suzette. 1980. *The gentle art of verbal self-defense.* Englewood Cliffs, N.J.: Prentice-Hall.

Ellis, Havelock. [1894] 1929. *Man and woman.* 2d ed. Boston: Houghton Mifflin.

Elstob, Elizabeth. 1715. *The rudiments of grammar for the English-Saxon tongue.* London.

Erades, Paul A. 1956. Contributions to modern English syntax, a note on gender. *Moderna Sprak* 50:2–11.

Esquire's guide to modern etiquette. 1969. Philadelphia: J. B. Lippincott.

Evans, Bergen. 1959. *Comfortable words.* New York: Random House.

Evans, Bergen, and Cornelia Evans. 1957. *Dictionary of contemporary American usage.* New York: Random House.

Fearn, John. 1824–27. *Anti-Tooke.* London.

Fell, John. [1784] 1967. *An essay toward an English grammar.* Reprint. Menston: Scolar.

Fenner, Mildred S. 1974. After all. *Today's Education* 63:110.

Fernald, James C. 1919. *Expressive English.* New York: Funk and Wagnalls.

Ferrier, Susan. 1898. *Memoir and correspondence of Susan Ferrier.* Ed. John A. Doyle. London.

Flexner, Stuart Berg. 1975. Preface to the *Dictionary of American slang,* ed. Harold Wentworth and S. B. Flexner. 2d ed. New York: Crowell.

———. 1976. *I hear America talking.* New York: Simon and Schuster.

———. 1982. *Listening to America.* New York: Simon and Schuster.

Fodor, Istvan. 1959. The origin of grammatical gender. *Lingua* 8:1–41, 186–214.

Follett, Wilson. 1966. *Modern American usage.* New York: Hill and Wang.

Forbes, Harry B. 1947. Letter. *New York Times,* 19 July, 12.

Fowler, H. W. 1926. *Modern English usage.* Oxford: Clarendon Press.

———. 1965. *Modern English usage.* 2d ed., ed. and rev. Sir Ernest Gowers. Oxford: Oxford University Press.

Fowler, H. W., and F. G. Fowler. [1906] 1924. *The king's English.* 2d ed. Oxford: Clarendon Press.

Fowler, William Chauncey. 1868. *English grammar.* New York: Harper.

Frailey, Lester E. 1948. *Handbook of business letters.* New York: Prentice-Hall.

Frailey, Lester E., and Edith Schnell. 1952. *Practical business writing.* New York: Prentice-Hall.

Francis, W. Nelson, and Henry Kučera. 1982. *Frequency analysis of English usage.* Boston: Houghton Mifflin.

Frazer, James G. 1900. A suggestion as to the origin of gender in language. *Fortnightly Review* 73 (January): 79–90.

Funk, Isaac K., ed. 1893. *Standard dictionary of the English language.* New York: Funk and Wagnalls.

Funk, Wilfred. 1950. *Word origins and their romantic stories*. New York: Funk and Wagnalls.

Gill, Alexander. [1619] 1972. *Logonomia anglica*. Reprint. Stockholm: Almqvist and Wiksell.

Gilman, D. C. 1885. The use and abuse of titles. *North American Review* 140:258–68.

Ginzberg, Louis. 1909. *The legends of the Jews*. 7 vols. Trans. Henrietta Szold. Philadelphia: Jewish Publication Society.

Gould, Edward S. 1867. *Good English*. New York.

Graham, Alma. 1973. The making of a nonsexist dictionary. *Ms.*, December, 12–16.

Greene, Samuel S. 1863. *Grammar of the English language*. New York.

Greenough, James B., and George Lyman Kittredge. [1901] 1920. *Words and their ways in English speech*. Reprint. New York: Macmillan.

Greenwood, James. 1722. *An essay toward a practical English grammar*. 2d ed. London.

Hale, Sarah J. 1865. Diminutions of the English language. *Godey's Lady's Book* 70:464.

Hall, Edward T. [1959] 1968. *The silent language*. Reprint. New York: Fawcett.

Hall, Fitzedward. 1872. *Recent exemplifications of false philology*. New York: Scribner, Armstrong.

———. 1873. *Modern English*. New York: Scribner, Armstrong.

Hall, J. Lesslie. 1917. *English usage*. Chicago: Scott, Foresman.

Hancock, Cicely Raysor. 1963. "Lady" and "woman." *American Speech* 38:234–35.

Hanna, J. Marshall, Estelle Pophan, and Esther Kihn Beamer. 1968. *Secretarial procedures and administration*. 5th ed. Cincinatti: South-western Publishing.

Harder, Kelsie B. 1964. The suffix '-ee.' *American Speech* 39:294–96.

Harmer, L. C. 1954. *The French language today*. London: Hutchinson's University Library.

Harper dictionary of contemporary usage. 1975. Ed. William and Mary Morris. New York: Harper and Row.

Harris, James. [1751] 1765. *Hermes, or a philosophical inqviry concerning vniversal grammar*. 2d ed. London.

Hecht, Marie B., Joan D. Berbach, Sally A. Healy, and Clare M. Cooper. 1973. *The women, yes!* New York: Holt, Rinehart and Winston.

Heimer, Helge. 1947. *Mondial: An international language*. Lund: AB Gleerupska.

Hench, Atcheson L. 1941. Miscellany. *American Speech* 16:229–30.

Henshall, Samuel. 1798. *The Saxon and English languages reciprocally illustrative of each other*. London.

Herder, Johann Gottfried. [1772] 1966. *On the origin of language*. Trans. Alexander Gode. New York: Ungar.

Hickes, George. 1689. *Institutiones grammaticae Anglo-Saxonicae, et Moeso-Gothicae*. Oxford.

Higginson, Thomas Wentworth. [1881] 1972. *Women and the alphabet*. Reprint. New York: Arno.

Hofland, Knut, and Stig Johansson. 1982. *Word frequencies in British and American English*. Bergen, Norway: NAVF, the Norwegian Computing Centre for the Humanities.

Horne Tooke, John. [1786] 1806. *The diversions of Purley*. 2 vols. Philadelphia.

Horton, Paul B. 1976. A sexless vocabulary for a sexist society. *Intellect* 105 (December): 159–60.

House, Homer C., and Susan E. Harmon. 1926. *Handbook of correct English*. New York: Longmans, Green.

Howard, Philip. 1977. *New words for old*. New York: Oxford University Press.

Howells, William Dean. 1906. Our daily speech. *Harper's Bazar* 40:930–34.

Hutchinson, Lois Irene. 1956. *Standard handbook for secretaries*. 7th ed. New York: McGraw-Hill.

Ihre, Johann. 1769. *Glossarium suiogothicum*. Upsala.

James, Henry. 1905. *The question of our speech*. Boston: Houghton Mifflin.

———. 1906–07. The speech of American women. *Harper's Bazar* 40:979–82, 1103–06; 41:17–21, 113–17.

Jamieson, John. 1840–41. *An etymological dictionary of the Scottish language*. Edinburgh: W. Tait.

Jefferson, Bernard L., Harry H. Peckham, and Hiram R. Wilson. 1931. *Freshman rhetoric and practice book*. Garden City, N.Y.: Doubleday.

Jespersen, Otto. 1894. *Progress in language*. Copenhagen.

———. [1905] 1923. *Growth and structure of the English language*. 4th ed. New York: D. Appleton.

———. 1922. *A modern English grammar on historical principles*. Part 2. Heidelberg: Carl Winter.

———. 1924a. *Language: Its nature, development and origin*. New York: Henry Holt.

———. 1924b. *The philosophy of grammar*. New York: Henry Holt.

———. 1927. The ending '-ster.' *Modern Language Review* 22:129–36.

———. 1929. *An international language*. New York: W.W. Norton.

———. 1949. *A Modern English Grammar*. Vol. 7. Copenhagen: Munksgaard.

Johnson, Edward. 1982. *The Washington Square Press handbook of good English*. New York: Washington Square Press.

Johnson, Richard. [1706] 1969. *Grammatical commentaries*. Reprint. Menston: Scolar.

Johnson, Samuel. 1755. *A dictionary of the English language*. London.

Joly, André. 1975. Toward a theory of gender in modern English. In *Studies in English grammar*, ed. André Joly and Thomas Fraser, 227–87. Paris: Editions universitaires.

Jones, Leslie. 1972. *Eurolengo: The language for Europe*. Newcastle upon Tyne: Oriel Press.

Jones, Rowland. [1764] 1972. *The origin of language and nations*. Reprint. Menston: Scolar.

———. [1768] 1972. *Hieroglyfic*. Reprint. Menston: Scolar.

———. 1769. *The philosophy of words*. London.

———. [1771] 1970. *The circles of Gomer*. Reprint. Menston: Scolar.

Junius, Francis (the younger). 1743. *Etymologicum anglicanum*. Oxford.

Kanfer, Stefan. 1972. Sispeak: A Msguided attempt to change herstory. *Time,* 23 October, 79.

Kay, Mairé Weir, ed. 1976. *Webster's collegiate thesaurus*. Springfield, Mass.: G. and C. Merriam.

Kerl, Simon. 1861. *A comprehensive grammar of the English language*. New York.

[Kersey, John]. 1702. *New English dictionary*. London.

Key, Mary Ritchie. 1975. *Male/female language*. Metuchen, N.J.: Scarecrow Press.

Kington-Oliphant, T. L. 1873. *The sources of standard English*. London: Macmillan.

Klein, Ernest. [1966] 1971. *Klein's comprehensive etymological dictionary of the English language*. Reprint. Amsterdam: Elsevier.

Kneevers, Charyl. 1984. Seminar paper, University of Illinois, Urbana.

Knowlson, James. 1981. *Universal language schemes in England and France 1600–1800*. Toronto: University of Toronto Press.

Knutson, Artur. 1905. *The gender of words denoting living beings in English*. Lund.

Kramarae, Cheris. 1975. Excessive loquacity: Women's speech as represented in American etiquette books. Paper presented at the Speech Communication Association Conference, July, Austin, Texas.

———. 1981. *Women and men speaking*. Rowley, Mass.: Newbury House.

Krapp, George Philip. 1927a. *A comprehensive guide to good English*. Chicago: Rand McNally.

———. 1927b. *The knowledge of English*. New York: Henry Holt.

Laird, Charlton. 1971. *Webster's new world thesaurus*. Cleveland: William Collins.

Lakoff, Robin. 1975. *Language and woman's place*. New York: Harper and Row.

Landor, Walter Savage. [1824–26] 1927. Imaginary conversations. In *The complete works of Walter Savage Landor,* vol. 5, ed. T. Earle Welby, 1–101. London: Chapman-Hall.

Langenfelt, Gösta. 1951. *She* and *her* instead of *it* and *its*. *Anglia* 70:90–101.

Leacock, Stephen. 1944. My particular aversions. *American Bookman* (Winter): 39–40.

Leonard, Sterling A. 1929. *The doctrine of correctness in English usage 1700–1800*. University of Wisconsin Studies in Language and Literature, no. 25. Madison.

————. 1932. *Current English usage*. Chicago: National Council of Teachers of English.

Lepsius, Karl Richard. 1880. *Nübische grammatik*. Berlin: Hertz.

Lewis, Charlton T., and Charles Short, eds. [1879] 1966. *A Latin dictionary*. Reprint. Oxford: Clarendon Press.

Lily, William. [1567] 1945. *A shorte introduction of grammar*. Reprint. New York: Scholars' Facsimiles and Reprints.

Lloyd, Susan M., ed. 1982. *Roget's thesaurus of English words and phrases*. Harlow: Longman.

Lodowyck, Francis. [1646] 1969. *A common writing*. Reprint. Menston: Scolar.

Lowth, Robert. 1762. *A short introduction to English grammar*. London.

Lurie, Charles N. 1927. *How to say it: Helpful hints on English*. New York: G. P. Putnam's Sons.

Lye, Edward. 1772. *Dictionarium saxonico et gothico-latinum*. London.

MacKay, Donald G. 1983. Prescriptive grammar and the pronoun problem. In *Language, gender and society*, ed. Barrie Thorne, Cheris Kramarae, and Nancy Henley, 38–53. Rowley, Mass.: Newbury House.

Maetzner, Eduard. 1874. *An English grammar*. 2 vols. Trans. C. J. Grece. London: John Murray.

Mager, Nathan H., and Sylvia K. 1974. *Encyclopedic dictionary of English usage*. Englewood Cliffs, N.J.: Prentice-Hall.

Maittaire, Michael. 1712. *The English grammar*. London.

Marchand, Hans. 1969. *The categories and types of present-day English word formation*. 2d ed. Munich: Beck.

Marcoux, Dell R. 1973. Deviation in English gender. *American Speech* 48:98–107.

Maréchal, Sylvain. 1801. *Projet d'une loi portant défense d'apprendre à lire aux femmes*. Paris.

Marshall, W. [1789] 1873–74. *Rural economy of Glocestershire*. Reprinted as *Provincialisms of the vale of Gloucester*. Publication of the English Dialect Society, no. 2, 55–60. London: Truebner.

Martin of Dacia. 1961. *Martini de Dacia oper.* Ed. Henry Roos. Copenhagen: GAD.

Martin, Benjamin. 1748. *Institutions of language.* London.

Martyna, Wendy. 1978. What does 'he' mean? *Journal of Communication* 28:131–38.

———. 1980. Beyond the he/man approach. *Signs* 5:482–93.

Maurer, David. [1939] 1981. Prostitutes and criminal argots. In David Maurer, *Language of the underworld,* pp. 111–18. Lexington: University Press of Kentucky.

Mawson, C. O. Sylvester. 1911. *Roget's international thesaurus of English words and phrases.* New York: Crowell.

McGill, Alexander T. 1858. An address before the literary societies of Oxford Female College, at their anniversary, June 24, 1858. Oxford, Ohio.

McKnight, George H. 1923. *English words and their background.* New York: D. Appleton-Century.

———. 1928. *Modern English in the making.* New York: D. Appleton-Century.

Meillet, Antoine. 1948. *Linguistique historique et linguistique générale.* Paris: Champion.

Mencken, H. L. 1919. *The American language.* New York: Knopf. 2d ed. 1921; 3d ed. 1926; 4th ed. 1937.

———. 1934. Needed words. *Chicago Herald Examiner,* 10 September, 8, 10.

———. 1945. *The American language: Supplement 1.* New York: Knopf.

———. 1948. *The American language: Supplement 2.* New York: Knopf.

Meredith, Mamie. 1930. Doctresses, authoresses and others. *American Speech* 5:476–81.

———. 1952a. 'Amanda the administratress' and other women workers. *American Speech* 27:224–25.

———. 1952b. Be a cabette. *American Speech* 27:74–76.

———. 1955. 'Mimeo Minnie,' 'Sadie the office secretary,' and other women office workers in America. *American Speech* 30:299–301.

Merriam, Eve. 1964. *After Nora slammed the door: American women in the 1960s, the unfinished revolution.* Cleveland: World.

Michael, Ian. 1970. *English grammatical categories and the tradition to 1800.* Cambridge: Cambridge University Press.

Miller, Casey, and Kate Swift. 1977. *Words and women: New language in new times.* Reprint. New York: Anchor Press.

———. 1980. *The handbook of nonsexist writing.* New York: Lippincott and Crowell.

Minshew, John. 1625. *The guide into tongues.* 2d ed. London.

Mitchell, James. 1908. *Significant etymology.* Edinburgh: Blackwood.

Moe, Albert F. 1963. "Lady" and "woman." *American Speech* 38:295.

Molee, Elias. 1888. *Plea for an American language.* Chicago.

Monboddo, Lord. *See* Burnet, James.

Morehead, Albert H. 1955. English at a loss for words. *New York Times Magazine.* 11 September, 27.

Morgan, Forrest. 1891. An indeterminate pronoun. *Writer* 5:260–62.

Mulcaster, Richard. [1562] 1925. *Elementarie.* Ed. E. T. Campagnac. Oxford: Clarendon Press.

Müller, Max. [1860] 1866. *Lectures on the science of language.* First series. 5th ed. London: Longmans, Green.

———. 1864. *Lectures on the science of language.* Second series. London: Longmans, Green.

Murray, Alexander. 1823. *History of the European languages.* Ed. David Scot. Edinburgh.

Murray, Lindley. [1795] 1968. *English grammar.* Reprint. Menston: Scolar.

———. 1797. *English grammar.* 3d ed. York.

Nelme, L. D. [1772] 1972. *An essay towards an investigation of the origin and elements of language and letters.* Reprint. Menston: Scolar.

Nicholson, George A. 1916. *English words with native roots.* Chicago: University of Chicago Press.

Nurnberg, Maxwell. 1942. *What's the good word? A new way to better English.* New York: Simon and Schuster.

Ohmann, Carol. 1971. Emily Brontë in the hands of male critics. *College English* 32:906–13.

Okamoto, Fuishiki. 1962. *Babm: Universal auxiliary language.* Tokyo: the author.

Onions, C. T. 1966. *Oxford dictionary of English etymology.* Oxford: Clarendon Press.

Orovan, Mary. [1972] 1978. *Humanizing English.* New York: the author.

[P., C.] 1834. Man-assimilation (something not to be read by the ladies). *Knickerbocker* 4:117–22.

Palmer, A. Smythe. [1883] 1969. *Folk-etymology.* Reprint. New York: Greenwood.

Parsons, Elsie Clews. 1913. *The old-fashioned woman: Primitive fancies about the sex.* New York: G. P. Putnam's Sons.

Partridge, Eric. [1947] 1974. *Usage and abusage.* Reprint. Harmondsworth: Penguin Books.

———. 1959. *Origins: A short etymological dictionary of modern English.* 2d ed. London: Routledge and Kegan Paul.

Pauley, Gay. 1970. Women's lib lingo replaces girl talk. *Long Island Press,* 21 November, 8.

Peabody, Andrew P. 1867. *Conversation: Its faults and graces.* Boston.

Peck, Harry T. 1899. *What is good English?* New York: Dodd, Mead and Co.

[Pegge, Samuel]. [1809] 1818. *Anonymia; or, ten centuries of observations on various authors and subjects.* 2d ed. London.

Pei, Mario. 1949. *The story of language.* Philadelphia: J. B. Lippincott.

————. 1969. *Words in sheep's clothing.* New York: Hawthorn.

Perrin, Porter G. 1939. *An index to English.* Chicago: Scott, Foresman and Co.

Peyton, V. J. [1771] 1970. *The history of the English language.* Reprint. Menston: Scolar.

Phillipps, K. C. 1984. *Language and class in Victorian England.* Oxford: Blackwell.

Piozzi, Hester Lynch Thrale. [1794] 1968. *British synonymy.* Reprint. Menston: Scolar.

A plea for a word. 1795. *Atlantic Monthly* 76:431–32.

Pokorny, Julius. 1959. *Indogermanisches etymologisches wörterbuch.* vol. 1. Bern: A. Francke.

Port Royal, the gentlemen of. 1696. *The art of speaking.* London.

Poston, Lawrence, III. 1965. Oh I smell false Latine. *American Speech* 40:78.

Pound, Louise. 1928. Chorine. *American Speech* 3:368.

————. 1942. Foreword to the *American thesaurus of slang,* by Lester V. Berrey and Melvin Van den Bark. New York: Crowell.

Prentice-Hall complete secretarial letter book. 1978. Englewood Cliffs, N.J.: Prentice-Hall.

Priestley, Joseph. 1761. *The rudiments of English grammar.* London.

————. 1777. *A course of lectures on oratory and criticism.* London.

Priscian. 1855. *Institutionum grammaticarum.* Ed. Martin Hertz. Vol. 2 of *Grammatici Latini,* ed. G. T. H. Keil. Leipzig: Tuebner.

Quinn, Michelle. 1982. *Katharine Gibbs handbook of business English.* New York: Free Press.

Quirk, Randolph, Sidney Greenbaum, Geoffrey Leech, and Jan Svartvik. 1972. *A grammar of contemporary English.* London: Longman.

Ramsey, Samuel. [1892] 1968. *The English language and English grammar.* Reprint. New York: Haskell House.

Ramus, Peter. 1612. *Grammatica.* Hanover.

Read, Allen Walker. 1934. Noah Webster as euphemist. *Dialect Notes* 6:385-91.

Reed, Samuel Rockwell. 1888. *Offthoughts about women and other things.* Chicago.

Restorator. 1801. The Columbian language, no. 15. *New England Palladium* 18 (2 October): 1.

Richardson, Charles. 1836. *A new dictionary of the English language.* London.

Riehl, Wilhelm H. [1882] 1904. *Die Familie.* 12th ed. Stuttgart.

Robins, R. H. [1951] 1971. *Ancient and mediaeval grammatical theory in Europe*. Reprint. Port Washington, N.Y.: Kennikat.

Rodale, J. I. 1961. *The synonym finder*. Emmaus, Pa.: Rodale Books.

Rogers, James. 1890. Letter. *Writer* 4:12–13.

Roget, Peter Mark. [1852] 1858. 7th ed. *Thesaurus of English words and phrases*. London: Longman.

Roget's II: The new thesaurus. 1980. Boston: Houghton Mifflin.

Ruskin, John. [1866] 1905. The ethics of the dust. In *The complete works of John Ruskin,* vol. 18, ed. E. T. Cooke and Alexander Wedderbun, 189–368. London: George Allen.

Rutherford, Millicent. 1976. One man in two is a woman. *English Journal* (December): 11.

S. S. S. 1875. Pronouns. *The American Bibliopolist* 7:163–65.

Safire, William. 1982. *What's the good word?* New York: Times Books.

Samuels, M. L. 1972. *Linguistic evolution, with special reference to English.* Cambridge: Cambridge University Press.

Saunders, Alta Gwinn. 1949. *Effective business English*. 3d ed. New York: Macmillan.

Sayers, Dorothy. 1969. The human not-quite human. In *Masculine/Feminine,* ed. Betty and Theodore Roszak, 116–22. New York: Harper and Row.

Schulz, Muriel. 1973. How sexist is Webster's Third? *Vis à Vis* 2.4:7–15.

———. 1975. The semantic derogation of women. In *Language and sex: Difference and dominance,* ed. Barrie Thorne and Nancy Henley, 64–75. Rowley, Mass.: Newbury House.

Sexton, Patricia. 1970. How the American boy is feminized. *Psychology Today,* January, 23–29, 66–67.

Shapiro, Fred R. 1985. Historical notes on the vocabulary of the women's movement. *American Speech* 60:3–16.

Shaw, Harry. 1975. *Dictionary of problem words and expressions*. New York: McGraw-Hill.

Sherk, William. 1979. *Brave new words*. Toronto: Doubleday.

Shipley, Joseph T. 1945. *Dictionary of word origins*. New York: Philosophical Library.

Shirley, James. [1651] 1969. *Grammatica Anglo-Latina*. Reprint. Menston: Scolar.

Siger de Courtrai. 1913. *Summa modorum significandi*. Ed. G. Wallerand. Louvain.

Silveira, Jeanette. 1980. Generic masculine words and thinking. *Women's Studies International Quarterly* 3:165–78.

Skeat, Walter W. 1910. *An etymological dictionary of the English language.* 4th ed. Oxford: Clarendon Press.

Skinner, Stephen. 1671. *Etymologicon linguae anglicanae*. London.

————. 1689. *Gazophylacium anglicanum: Containing the derivation of English words, proper and common.* London.

Sklar, Elizabeth S. 1983. Sexist grammar revisited. *College English* 45:348-58.

Smith, Amanda J. 1974. Revising the language. *Washington Post,* 11 April, sec. A, 29.

Smith, Philip M. 1985. *Language, the sexes and society.* Oxford: Blackwell.

Smith, Thomas. 1568. *De recta et emendata linguae Anglicanae scriptione dialogus.* Paris.

Somner, William. 1659. *Dictionarium Saxonico-Latino-Anglicanum.* Oxford.

Sorrels, Bobbye D. 1983. *The nonsexist communicator: Solving the problems of gender and awkwardness in modern English.* Englewood Cliffs, N.J.: Prentice-Hall.

Southey, Robert. 1847. *The doctor.* London.

Spender, Dale. 1980. *Man made language.* London: Routledge and Kegan Paul.

Stanley, Julia Penelope. 1977a. Gender-marking in American English: Usage and reference. In *Sexism and language,* ed. Aileen P. Nilsen, Haig Bosmajian, H. Lee Gershuny, and Julia P. Stanley, 43–74. Urbana, Ill.: National Council of Teachers of English.

————. 1977b. Paradigmatic women: The prostitute. In *Papers in language variation,* ed. David L. Shores and Carol P. Hines, 303–21. University: University of Alabama Press.

————. 1978. Sexist grammar. *College English* 39:800–11.

Stanley, Julia Penelope, and Susan W. Robbins. 1978. Going through the changes: The pronoun *she* in Middle English. *Papers in Linguistics* 11:71-88.

Stanley, Julia Penelope, and Cynthia McGowan. 1979. Woman and wife: Social and semantic shifts in English. *Papers in Linguistics* 12:491–502.

Stannard, Una. 1977. *Mrs. Man.* San Francisco: Germainbooks.

Stanton, Elizabeth Cady. 1895. *The woman's Bible.* Reprinted as *The original feminist attack on the Bible.* New York: Arno, 1974.

Steadman, J. M. 1935. A study of verbal taboos. *American Speech* 10:93-103.

————. 1938. Affected and effeminate words. *American Speech* 13:13–18.

Steinmetz, Sol. 1982. On language: The desexing of English. *New York Times Magazine,* 1 August, 6.

Stevens, Edgar Alfred. 1884. The missing word. *The Current,* 30 August, 294; 8 November, 294.

Stopes, Charlotte C. 1908. *The sphere of "man": In relation to that of "woman" in the Constitution.* London: T. Fisher Unwin.

Success with words. 1983. Pleasantville, N.Y.: Reader's Digest.

Svartengren, T. Hilding. 1927. Feminine gender in Anglo-American. *American Speech* 3:83–113.

———. 1928. The use of the personal gender for inanimate things. *Dialect Notes* 6:7–56.

———. 1954. The use of feminine gender for inanimate things in American colloquial speech. *Moderna Sprak* 48:261–92.

Sweet, Henry. [1891] 1931. *A new English grammar; logical and historical.* 2 vols. Reprint. Oxford: Clarendon Press.

Swift, Jonathan. [1712] 1957. A proposal for correcting, improving and ascertaining the English tongue. In *Prose works of Jonathan Swift,* vol. 4, ed. Herbert Davis, 3–21. Oxford: Blackwell.

Taylor, J. M., and E. H. Haight. 1915. *Vassar.* New York: Oxford University Press.

Taylor, Thomas, trans. 1793. *Cratylus,* by Plato. London.

Thomas of Erfurt. [ca. 1300] 1972. *Grammatica speculativa.* Ed. and trans. G. L. Bursill-Hall. London: Longman.

Thornton, Richard H. [1912] 1962. *An American glossary.* 3 vols. Reprint. New York: Ungar.

Thurot, F. Ch. [1869] 1964. *Extraits de divers manuscrits latins pour servir à l'histoire des doctrines grammaticales au moyen âge.* Reprint. Frankfurt am Main: Minerva.

Tilley, Morris P., ed. 1950. *A dictionary of the proverbs in England in the sixteenth and seventeenth centuries.* Ann Arbor: University of Michigan Press.

Timm, Leonora A. 1978. Not mere tongue in cheek: The case for a common gender pronoun in English. *International Journal of Women's Studies* 1:555–65.

Titcomb, Caldwell. 1955. He, she, and 'thon.' *New York Times Magazine,* 2 October, 6.

Todasco, Ruth, Gail Lockman, Agnes Meyer, and Jessie Sheridan. 1973. *An intelligent woman's guide to dirty words.* Chicago: The Feminist English Dictionary.

Toller, T. Northcote. 1921. *An Anglo-Saxon dictionary: Supplement.* Oxford: Oxford University Press.

Trager, George L. 1931. French *on*—English *one. Romanic Review* 22:311-17.

Trench, Richard Chenevix. 1855. *English past and present.* London.

Trible, Phyllis. 1973. Depatriarchalizing in biblical interpretation. *Journal of the American Academy of Religion* 41:30–48.

Tucker, Gilbert M. 1895. *Our common speech.* New York: Dodd, Mead and Co.

Tucker, Susie I. 1967. *Protean shape: A study in eighteenth-century vocabulary and usage.* London: University of London, the Athlone Press.

Turner, Rosa Shand. 1977. The increasingly visible female and the need for generic terms. *Christian Century* 94:248–52.

United States Department of Labor. 1975. *Job title revisions to eliminate sex- and age-referent language from the dictionary of occupational titles, third edition.* Washington, D.C.: Government Printing Office.

Urquhart, Thomas. [1656] 1970. *Logopandecteision.* Reprint. Menston: Scolar.

Van Leunen, Mary-Claire. 1978. *A handbook for scholars.* New York: Knopf.

Verstegan, Richard. 1605. *A restitution of decayed intelligence: in antiquities. Concerning the most noble and renowned English nation.* Antwerp.

Vives, Juan Luis. 1523. *De institutione christianae feminae.* Translated by Richard Hyrd as *A very frutefull and pleasant boke called the instruction of a Cristen woman.* London, 1531.

Vizetelly, Frank H. 1929. *A desk-book of twenty-five thousand words frequently mispronounced.* 4th ed. New York: Grosset and Dunlap.

Wachter, Johann Georg. 1737. *Glossarium germanicum.* Leipzig.

Watts, Isaac. 1725. *Logick.* London.

Webster, John. 1654. *Academiciarum examen.* London.

Webster, Noah. 1828. *An American dictionary of the English language.* New York: S. Converse.

Wedgewood, Hensleigh. 1872. *A dictionary of English etymology.* 2d ed. New York: Macmillan.

Weekley, Ernest. 1921. *An etymological dictionary of modern English.* London: J. Murray.

Wescott, Roger W. [1974] 1978. Women, wife-men, and sexist bias. In *Verbatim: Volumes I and II,* 15–16. Essex, Ct.: Verbatim.

Weseen, Maurice H. 1928. *Crowell's dictionary of English grammar and handbook of American usage.* New York: Crowell.

Wheeler, Benjamin Ide. 1899. The origin of grammatical gender. *Journal of English and Germanic Philology* 2:528–43.

Wheelock, Phyllis. 1947. Letter. *New York Times,* 4 August, 16.

White, Richard Grant. 1868. Words and their uses. *The Galaxy* 6:235–44.

———. [1870] 1891. *Words and their uses.* 19th ed. Boston: Houghton Mifflin.

———. 1881. *Every-day English.* Boston: Houghton Mifflin.

Whitford, Robert C., and James R. Foster. 1955. *Concise dictionary of American grammar and usage.* New York: Philosophical Library.

Wilkins, John. 1668. *An essay towards a real character, and a philosophical language.* London.

Williams, Francis H. 1884. Letter. *The Critic,* 16 August, 79–80.

Wilson, Thomas. [1553] 1962. *Arte of rhetorique.* Reprint. Gainesville, Fla.: Scholars' Facsimiles and Reprints.

Wilson, Thomas. 1724. *The many advantages of a good language to any nation.* London.

Winograd, Terry. 1984. Computer software for working with language. *Scientific American* 251 (August): 130–45.

Withington, Robert. 1937. 'Lady,' 'woman,' and 'person.' *American Speech* 12:117–21.

Wittig, Monique. 1973. *Le corps lesbien.* Paris: Editions de minuit. Translated by David LeVay as *The Lesbian body.* London: Peter Owen, 1975.

Wolfe, Susan J., and Julia Penelope Stanley. 1981. Linguistic problems with patriarchal reconstructions of Indo-European culture: A little more than kin, a little less than kind. In *The voices and words of women and men,* ed. Cheris Kramarae, 227–37. Oxford: Pergamon.

A woman's new world dictionary. 1973. Ed. Norma Wilson. *51%: A Paper of Joyful Noise for the Majority Sex,* 3 and 4.

Worcester, Joseph Emerson. 1860. *A dictionary of the English language.* Boston.

Wright, Joseph. 1898–1905. *English dialect dictionary.* 6 vols. London: Frowde.

———. [1905] 1968. *The English dialect grammar.* Reprint. Oxford: Clarendon Press.

Wyld, H. C. [1920] 1936. *A history of modern colloquial English.* 3d ed. Oxford: Blackwell.

To find terms listed in the text but not individually cited in this index, the reader should consult the entry "Lists."

Junius, Francis: etymologies, 35, 40,
41, 43, 44, 48, 49
juve femme, 114

Kanfer, Stefan, 186
Kay, Mairé Weir, 145
Kempe, Anders, 58
Kerl, Simon, 103, 127–28
Kersey, John, 71
Key, Mary Ritchie, 10
Kittredge, George Lyman, 159
knave: in gender compounds, 113
knave-gerlys, 113
knight: in gender compounds, 113
knight-child, 113
Kramarae, Cheris, 9, 10, 62, 87
Krapp, George Philip, 178

lad, 6, 39, 144
ladies and gentlemen, 3
lady: contrasted to *lord,* 32; in gender
compounds, 113, 114; 'prostitute,'
154; alternative to *woman,* 155,
156, 158, 159, 160, 219; 'wife,'
157; vocative, 163
lady-actor, 114
lady doctor, 5, 111, 113, 114
lady lawyer, 8
lady patroness, 115
lady typewriter, 114
La Follette, Fola, 166
Lakoff, Robin, 9
Landor, Walter Savage, 127
Lane, Harriet, 57
Langenfelt, Gösta, 105
language acquisition, 2, 59, 88
Langue Nouvelle (artificial language),
199
lapis, 93–94
lass, 39, 144
Latin: as masculine language, 66–67
laundress, 127, 128
laughter, 63
lawn, 77
Leacock, Stephen, 196
Leonard, Sterling A., 194, 196
Lepsius, Karl R., 92
libbers, 186
Lily, William, 98
lioness, 29

lists: etymologies, *lad/lass, boy/girl,*
39–40; words for prostitute, 42–
45; *bride,* 48; supposed women's
words, 83–84; words in *-ess,* 121;
words in *-ette,* 124–25; alternatives
to *Mr., Miss, Mrs.,* 167; alternatives
to *man,* 149; epicene pronouns,
205–09
Lloyd, Susan M., 145
Lodowyck, Francis, 24
loquacity: women's supposed, 31, 57,
62, 72, 78
lord, 32
lords and ladies, 3
Lowth, Robert, 98, 109

McGowan, Cynthia, 9–10
MacKay, Donald, 212, 213, 215
McKnight, George H., 69
Maetzner, Eduard, 104
maid: etymology, 29, 41, 45, 51; in
gender compounds, 113; in academic degrees, 7, 129, 174; synonym for *woman,* 144; alternatives
to, 182
maidechild, 113
mail carrier, 7
mailman, 7
Maittaire, Michael, 21, 71–72, 110
majorette, 124
male, 4, 29, 114, 144
male aunt, 114
male bawd, 114
male chauvinism, 185
male-functioning, 188
male hustler, 114
male model, 112
male nurse, 7, 113
male prostitute, 111
male whore, 114
male widowhood, 114
mama, 40, 50
man: in gender compounds, 8; source
of *woman,* 11, 25; as masculine, 11,
137–38, 185; derivation, 17–18,
37–38, 45; as common gender, 110,
137, 139–40, 185, 217; in Old English, 138–39; in Middle English,
139; definitions, 141–43, 153; synonyms, 143–46, 149